Taking Steps Toward God

Exploring Spiritual Formation

Clancy P. Hayes

CONTENTS

ACKNOWLEDGMENTS

I wish to express gratitude to Vic Ostrom, who whet my appetite for the study of Spiritual Formation, when I was a seminary student. I am thankful to Dr. Paul Brooks and Dr. LeRoy Bartel for allowing me the opportunity to teach at Southwestern Assemblies of God University (SAGU). I also owe a debt of gratitude to Dr. Kermit Bridges, the President of SAGU who requested that a Spiritual Formation course be added to the required curriculum of our university. I will forever appreciate the confidence that Dr. Bartel placed in me, when he requested that I develop the new Spiritual Formation course, which we called "Authentic Christianity." My thanks goes to Dr. Mike Clarensau, the current dean of the Bible and Church Ministries Department at SAGU, who has continued to support me in my role as the primary instructor of our spiritual formation course, and has permitted me to write this new textbook for the course.

This book would never have come to fruition, if it were not for the encouragement of Dr. Bruce Rosdahl, chair of the Bible and Theology department at SAGU. He asked me to consider writing a textbook for use in our Spiritual Formation course. Dr. Rosdahl is one of my greatest cheerleaders and I will forever give thanks to God for putting him and his wife June into my wife's and my life.

I want to reserve my greatest gratitude for Rachel Hayes, my wife of over four decades. She has sacrificed a great deal to allow me to pursue my dream to teach at the university level. Any spouse, who has journeyed through the academic process, leading to a doctorate, knows the challenges she overcame. In addition, she has spent many hours laboring over this manuscript, identifying grammatical errors I missed and advocating for readers, as she requested clarification of concepts and sentence structure. This book is much better because of her. But, of even more importance, I am a better person because of her love and strength. Rachel I love you!

Finally, I want to express thanks to Jesus who has been patient with me in my own spiritual journey. He graciously sent the Holy Spirit to guide me into all truth and doesn't give up on me when I fail to make progress, as quickly as perhaps I should. It is my desire to continue to take steps toward God, throughout my life, as I deepen my love for Him and share the fruit of that love with others.

INTRODUCTION

There are many books on the market that cover the topic of spiritual formation. It is fair to ask why another book needs to be added to the collection. This book is specifically written to meet the needs of a freshman level university course that is taught at Southwestern Assemblies of God University (S.A.G.U). It is written to be used over a semester as a starting point for discussions, and to motivate young adults to take steps toward God. You will notice that each chapter ends with study guide questions. These can be used by the reader to reflect on the chapter. If used as a textbook, these questions can serve as a basis for quizzes and examinations.

Although this book is written for a particular purpose, it also has many other applications. Individuals could use this book in their devotional time as they take steps toward God. This book could be used to serve as the curriculum for a Sunday school class or a small group. I envision some pastors and youth pastors using the content in this book as sermon starters.

This book is broken into four units of study. The first unit lays out the case for the importance of spiritual formation, the process of spiritual growth, and key concepts that form a foundation for the spiritual growth process. The second unit focuses on spiritual disciplines a person can use to enhance their personal relationship with God. The third unit addresses spiritual disciplines that increase a person's capacity to fulfill the command to "love others" through healthy relationships. And the fourth unit examines how one's worldview, shaped by one's spiritual formation, affects key areas of a Christian's life.

This book assumes the reader has taken the first step of salvation. It also assumes readers will be at different places in their spiritual journey. The author's intent is that everyone on a spiritual journey will find information to help them take a few steps toward God, as a result of reading this book.

Spiritual formation does not occur overnight. This book encourages individuals to take steps toward God. It is my prayer that those who read this book will not become discouraged by how far they are from God, but they will become encouraged to discover that spiritual maturity is attainable, one step at a time.

UNIT ONE

EXPLORING THE IMPORTANCE OF SPIRITUAL FORMATION

ONE

WHAT IS SPIRITUAL FORMATION?

The term "spiritual formation" gained popularity in the last few decades in the Western world, but the concept spans the history of Christianity. Spiritual formation is defined as an intentional process of spiritual growth that leads a person to accurately reflect Christ through his or her life.

Jesus declared the importance of spiritual formation in the Great Commission (Matthew 28:19-20). The Early Church fleshed out Jesus' command, in its earliest days, by the priority given to fellowship, prayer, and the study of Scripture (Acts 2:43-47). Additional examples of the priority of spiritual formation in the Early Church include Barnabas' mentoring of Paul and John Mark (Acts 9:27-30; 15:39), Paul's oversight of Timothy and Titus (1 Timothy 1:2; Titus 1:4), as well as various admonitions given by the apostles in their writings to the fledgling church fellowships of the first century to be strong and grow in the Lord. (See 1 Corinthians 1:10; Galatians 5:16; Ephesus 5:1-2; Philippians 1:27; and 1 Thessalonians 4:1.) Spiritual formation must continue as a priority for the follower of Jesus.

A Description of Spiritual Formation

There are various ways to define the purpose and importance of spiritual formation. One method is to focus on the outward expression of one's spirituality that reflects the inner transaction that has taken place in the person's life. This view argues the biblical postulate "By this all people will know that you are my disciples, if you have love one for another" (John 13:35). This view argues that spiritual formation must involve both the inner person, as well as the outward actions of the believer. It is not enough to worship God without loving others. In like manner, it is not enough to serve others without serving God. Both elements must be present, if true spiritual formation is taking place.

Others argue that not only is heart (worship of God) and hand (service to others) involved in spiritual formation, but spiritual formation must also include a transformation of the attitude of the person. When the apostle Paul spoke to the Philippian Christians, he emphasized the importance of having the correct attitude toward one another. He told them to be of one mind, to do nothing out of selfishness, and to be people of humility (Philippians 2:1-5).

Another element which must be considered when dealing with spiritual formation is the intellectual dimension. The apostle Paul, speaking to the Romans, argued the intellectual component of spiritual development was foundational. He states,

> How then will they call on him in whom they have not believed? And how are they to believe in him of whom they have not heard? And how are they to hear without someone preaching? And how are they to preach unless they are sent? As it is written, 'How beautiful are the feet of those who preach the good news!' But they have not all obeyed the gospel. For Isaiah says, 'Lord, who has believed what he has heard from us?' So faith comes from hearing, and hearing through the word of Christ" (Romans 10:14-17).

Spiritual formation must come full circle because knowledge without application leads to empty religion. A great illustration of spiritual formation gone awry are the Pharisees of the first century. They knew all there was to know about religion. They practiced religious activities flawlessly. But, they failed to complete the circle, which was evidenced through their pride. For spiritual formation to take place, there must be a transformation of the mind, the soul (which is reflected in our behavior), and the spirit.

Spiritual formation is a holistic process activated through the accumulation of biblical knowledge, interaction within the community of believers, and a relationship with Jesus that leads believers to be better able to reflect God's image to the world through service to God and humanity.

A Brief History of Spiritual Formation

The discipline leading to spiritual growth can present a daunting challenge to the believer. It would be easier if spiritual growth just happened, but it does not. The Early Church saw the need to develop an intentional approach to spiritual development.

By the end of the first century, and the early part of the second century, numerous heresies emerged within the Church. Some of the heresy centered on the nature of Christ (Docetism and Cerintheians), the authenticity of the Scriptures (Marcionites), and the means to salvation (Gnosticism). However, syncretism poised the greatest danger to the Early Church. Gentiles brought their various mystery religions, cultic rituals, and imperial worship with them into their newly formed relationship with Jesus. Unfortunately, in many cases, belief in Jesus became an add-on to the spiritual house they had been living in previously. Biblical Christianity called for more. True belief in the claims of Christ required that a total transformation take place mandating a renunciation of all other spiritual allegiances. This would not happen without intentionality.

The second century Church developed systems that would assist in "sanctifying" new believers. The Church began to institutionalize practices that had previously been organic in nature. Practices such as water baptism were preceded with times of instruction. The Lord's Supper, which had previously been practiced from home to home, now became the centerpiece of the church experience as people were taught the meaning of it and were provided a context for its practice. The church began to be the place where people anticipated prayer would take place and proclamation would provide a clear understanding of the truth, of the gospel. The church began to be the custodian of truth. This did not begin as a control factor, but it was necessitated to keep the gospel pure. The church established liturgy which was designed to provide a systematic and repetitive expression of the key elements of the Christian faith, so all believers would have a common understanding and a strong faith based in truth.

Soon after the second century, Church leaders began to teach, or at least indicate, that the individual could not grow without the structures made available to them through the Church. The role of the priest increased as the role of sacraments began increasingly to be seen as the vehicle of grace in a person's life. During the Dark Ages, the people became totally dependent on the clergy for their spiritual care. The priests taught the congregants what they felt was important, at times in conflict with the teachings of Scripture. This resulted in vulnerable congregants who were more loyal to the teachings of the Church than they were to the teachings of Jesus.

Martin Luther, and the Reformers who followed, moved the focus back onto the Bible. Luther taught that the Bible alone provided necessary guidance for spiritual growth. With the advent of the printing press and increased literacy rates, individuals were encouraged to study the Bible on their own in a quest to shape their own spiritual journey with the guidance of the Holy Spirit. The local church provided assistance in this process by teaching people how to study the Bible properly, and through the proclamation of the Word.

In the nineteenth century, spiritual formation was focused primarily on education. In the twentieth century, those who lead discipleship programs began to see the need to move beyond the mind to the conduct of the believer. The Sunday school became a key element in the spiritual formation of believers. It began primarily as an educational vehicle for the poor children in the community, but soon became a vehicle for sharing the Bible with not only children, but also with teens and adults. The Sunday school primarily focused on communicating biblical truth in a cognitive fashion, however in the more effective Sunday schools, students took what they learned and put it into practice in their daily lives.

In recent years, the importance of the local church in the spiritual formation of individuals has come under fire. These individuals believe that spiritual formation is not done best through sitting in a chair and listening to someone preach or teach the Bible. These individuals believe, at best, people who rely on spiritual formation through proclamation embrace a faith that will save their souls but does very little to help them live out their lives in a world screaming for their attention. These individuals criticize the local church and the problems that reside there. They point to people who seem to not be able to get along with each other as evidenced by the conflict seen in many congregations. They point to the number of spiritual leaders, who have been formed by listening to preaching and teaching, who have fallen into the temptations they warn those that they teach to avoid. These observations lead many to conclude the church has been ineffective in the spiritual formation process.

Although many feel the church, in its present form, has not produced a great yield from its spiritual formation efforts, it would be fool hearted to argue that the church has wasted its' efforts. It is true that many in the church have accepted a religious experience over a relationship with Christ. One cannot make a blanket statement that no one grew through the efforts the local church has made through its preaching and teaching. Over the last two centuries, millions of individuals have come to know Jesus Christ as their Savior as a result of preaching and teaching ministries in the local church. Over that same period of time, millions have grown in their faith, been baptized in water, and have perpetuated the faith through their lives. Just as discipleship transitioned from one system to another throughout the centuries, it may be time for us to transition again. But in our hope to be more effective in the future, we must not denigrate the past efforts of sincere Christians. We must also not take the local church out of the equation, as it is the key to Christ's design for meeting the needs of a broken world.

The current trend in spiritual formation is a personal journey embarked on by individual Christians. Some would argue this journey can be done as a solo event, without assistance from a community of believers. Although I see the value in an individual approach, and I will be spending a great deal of time in this book describing methods by which an individual can grow in Christ, I must be clear the biblical model of spiritual formation is done in a collective group who have the opportunity to nurture, encourage, discipline, and hold one another accountable. The church must not own the spiritual formation process, but they must participate in it.

With the tension between the "church approach" to discipleship and the "individual approach" in focus, and understanding the need for both, the direction of the rest of this chapter will deal with plans to help individuals implement a personal spiritual growth process.

A Strategy for Effective Spiritual Formation

Spiritual growth requires a strategy. Some will choose a strategy to remain spiritual infants. Others will choose a strategy to grow strong in their faith. You may say you have not consciously decided on a strategy for yourself, but you have. If you have not intentionally designed a plan to grow in Christ, you have intentionally chosen not to grow in Him. In this section of the chapter, I want to help you get started developing a strategy that will put you on a road to spiritual growth, or move you along a path that you are already on. If you'll combine the principles found in this chapter with information you find throughout the rest of this book, I believe that you will see yourself more closely reflecting the priorities of Christ, in all aspects of your life.

Finding a Partner

The first decision, in developing a spiritual growth strategy, is to determine if you will use a spiritual director/coach or if you will embark on the journey alone. Experts in the arena of spiritual formation encourage the use of some type of spiritual director. Many believe for healthy spiritual formation to take place, you need someone who is a spiritual authority over you who will keep you accountable and who will give you direction and guidance. In addition, they believe you need to have someone who is at a horizontal relationship with you who you can talk to and have common experiences with. Finally, they believe, you should have a person in your life who is not as spiritually mature as you are, so you can assist them as a part of your personal development, as well as theirs. This type of network will provide you with the accountability you need, as well as an avenue to put into practice the key components of your spiritual development.

Spiritual Directors have been a part of the Church throughout the years. A Spiritual Director (some people would rather call them a mentor or coach) is a sounding board for the individual who is attempting to grow in Christ. This individual helps the person who wants to develop spiritually to recognize the voice of God, as the person attempts to discern the direction of the Holy Spirit. The ultimate Spiritual Director must be the Holy Spirit, but sometimes we need help in order to determine what He desires from us.

Selecting a Spiritual Director is a key component to your success, as you grow in Christ. You must select somebody you trust and a person who has demonstrated spiritual maturity in their own life. Many people avoid selecting a Spiritual Director because they fear the person will stand in judgment over them. In most cases, if the person you select is spiritually mature and loves you, they will do everything in their power to encourage you. They will share the struggles they have gone through to reach the level of spiritual maturity they have attained. They will become a model for you to replicate when it is time for you to mentor someone else.

Great danger awaits those who choose to go it alone. When the person seeking to grow spiritually gets weary, backing away from the commitment will become much easier for the solo spiritual traveler. Lacking an accountability partner/mentor/spiritual director has proven the demise of many who start the spiritual journey.

A realistic view of self and sin helps disciples avoid personal defeats. The Bible indicates spiritual development is progressive. It is not unusual for Christians to take three steps forward in their spiritual development and then one step back. (See Romans 7.) The Holy Spirit is in continual contact with the believer to make the believer aware of regression in one's spiritual development and to encourage them to get back on track. These setbacks do not disqualify an individual as a follower of Jesus. Realizing spiritual growth does not continually move toward God allows individuals to make mistakes and grow through them, without undue levels of guilt and shame.

Selecting a Tool

Contemporary leaders in the field of spiritual formation point to "spiritual disciplines" as key tools in helping people grow in their relationship with Jesus. Varying authors offer lists of tools to use in the development of one's spiritual life. In this book, I will focus on a set of spiritual tools that I have found to be meaningful for my own spiritual development, as well as those that I have seen work well in the development of others. The list of tools that I will be providing throughout the various chapters are not exhaustive. In like manner, it is not necessary for a believer to use all of the tools which will be presented. It will be important for you to try out some of the tools and find out how they work in your own spiritual development. There are some tools, such as Bible study and prayer, which will be essential for all believers. Without knowing what God says through His Word and through active communication with Him, it is very difficult for spiritual growth to take place. But some of the other tools that will be presented, such as fasting and extended times of solitude, may be activities that you occasionally use, or perhaps do not use at all in your spiritual development.

Spiritual disciplines are not an end in themselves. Spiritual disciplines have no inherent spiritual value. They only become valuable as they lead to a deeper relationship with Jesus and bring about a more Christ-like lifestyle. Therefore, the motivation behind engaging in spiritual disciplines determines their value in the Christian's life.

Once a person has selected a spiritual director and selected tools for spiritual growth, a conscious refocusing of the believer's life can take place.

Conclusion

Spiritual formation is non-negotiable in the Christian's life. The local church has the responsibility to encourage spiritual formation and even to offer programs that help in the process. But ultimately the person desiring to grow in Christ must assert his or her will to make it happen. Spiritual formation best occurs in a relationship with a spiritual mentor who encourages, provides resources, and holds the devotee responsible for his or her actions. Successful spiritual formation will result in a changed heart, changed priorities, and changed behavior, as the believer takes steps toward God.

Study Guide Questions

1. What is the definition of the term "spiritual formation"?

2. What three areas of a person's life must be transformed for effective spiritual formation to take place?

3. What heresies arose in the late first and early second century's that began to negatively influence Christianity?

4. What was the primary vehicle for spiritual formation in the 19th and 20th century?

5. What is the current trend in spiritual formation?

6. What three relationships should every Christian have in their spiritual formation journey?

7. How can having a spiritual director/coach/mentor help you move toward spiritual maturity?

8. Explain the progressive nature of spiritual formation.

9. Which two spiritual disciplines are essential for all believers to engage?

10. What determines the effectiveness of a spiritual discipline?

TWO

EXPLORING SPIRITUAL GROWTH

Spiritual growth is a process. Many people want to grow in their experience with Christ in a rapid fashion. Nothing that is healthy grows quickly. One of the few things that metastasize rapidly is forms of cancer cells which destroy the body. Well-formed muscles are only cultivated over a period of weeks and months through hard work. In much the same way, spiritual growth takes time, effort, and sometimes even pain. But the result of this process is a healthy relationship with God. In this chapter, we will look at the purpose of spiritual growth, the stages of spiritual growth, and finally, the process of spiritual growth.

The Purpose of Spiritual Growth

When I ask the question, "What do you think is the purpose of spiritual growth?" I get various responses. Some people argue the purpose to seek spiritual growth is to not stagnate in their current spiritual condition. Others respond that spiritual growth allows them to avoid yielding to the lies of Satan. Yet, others argue the purpose of spiritual growth is to deepen their intimacy with God. Each of these answers has validity, but Jesus gave us His reasoning for spiritual growth which supersedes all others. He stated the reason we should want to grow spiritually is so we can bring glory to the Father (John 15:8).

When a person grows in Christ, they begin to look more and more like Christ. The apostle Paul instructed the people in the Corinthian church to imitate him as he imitated Jesus (1 Corinthians 11:1). This statement presupposes that Paul's life was worth emulating. Paul felt confident, that when people saw him, they would see Jesus. Not all Christians have risen to the place where they can have that level of confidence. But it should be the goal of every Christian to live in such a way that when people see us, we will be a positive representation of Jesus. It should be our goal that when we walk into a supermarket, people will see our attitude, our actions, and even our purchases, and think positive thoughts, rather than wishing they were not in the store with us. Those who mature in Christ will demonstrate it through their patience, their kindness, and their unselfish acts towards others. Paul explains, "But the fruit of the Spirit is love, joy, peace, patience, kindness, goodness, faithfulness, gentleness, self-control; against such things there is no law (Galatians 5:22-23.)

Followers of Christ must understand we are the only face of God people will ever see. The majority of nonbelievers will never make their way into a church to hear a sermon or sing worship songs in a congregation. Since those who do not follow Jesus will not hear a gospel message preached from behind the pulpit, it is our responsibility to take the gospel to them. Often the message will not be communicated through our words, but reflected in our deeds.

God was so concerned about the maturation process of the Christian, He placed specific people in the church to help others grow in their spiritual lives (Ephesians 4:11-14). Sometimes we make the mistake of thinking these spiritual gifts of leadership are put in place to run an organization and to serve the needs of people. Paul helps us to understand there is a larger role for spiritual leaders to play than to visit hospitals, perform weddings, and minister at funerals. There is nothing wrong with leaders doing any of these activities, but spiritual leadership should reserve most of their time and effort for equipping individuals in the church to do ministry to fellow Christians and to reach the lost.

So what is the purpose of spiritual growth? The answer to this question is to help individuals learn to love God more, so that they can serve people better. In doing so, they will be a more effective representatives of Christ to the world. This will bring glory to God.

The Stages of Spiritual Growth

The stages of spiritual growth can best be explained by examining the physical growth process. The Bible is accustomed to using natural life to illustrate spiritual life. When Jesus tried to explain the salvation process to Nicodemus, He told him that salvation was like a person being born again. Jesus was so convincing in His argument that Nicodemus asked if he would have to reenter his mother's womb in order to take part in the kingdom of God (John 3:1-8). The Bible clearly identifies stages in spiritual development; spiritual infants (1 Corinthians 3:1), those who are leaving the elementary stage (Hebrews 6:1-2), and those achieving spiritual maturity (Ephesians 4:13, Hebrews 5:14). Let's take a look at each one of these stages.

Every Christian began their spiritual journey as a spiritual baby. Sometimes the more mature Christians will look at those who are in the spiritual infant stage with disdain. This level of arrogance is reserved for those who have forgotten what it was like when they first accepted Christ.

When I was a young father, I came home one day from work and my 6 month-old daughter was playing on the living room floor. I went over to pick her up to play with her, when I smelled a horrible odor arise from her diaper. I was not surprised because that's what babies do. So I picked her up, carried her into her bedroom where we had the changing table situated, and laid her on the table. I lifted her shirt and tickled her belly while I took the pins out of her cloth diapers. I lifted her legs and wiped away the cause of the stench. After disposing of the diaper into the diaper pail, I placed a clean diaper under her after having washed her bottom. I then put butt cream on her, sprinkled baby powder on her, and then fastened the diaper. I finally slipped on her plastic pants, pulled up her outer clothing, and blew on her belly just to watch her laugh. I took her back to the living room and set her on the floor. She was as good as new. It was as if she had never messed her diaper. I did this fully knowing that in just a little while she was going to mess her diaper again, and she would have to be cleaned up again. But neither I, nor her mother, minded changing our daughter's diapers on a regular basis. We understood this was the stage of life she was in, and we loved her. We knew she would grow out of this stage.

Baby Christians are going to mess up, as well. It is totally acceptable for a baby Christian to commit a sin, and when they are at church, they feel convicted by the Holy Spirit. In recognition of their sin, they go to the altar and ask God to clean them up. God lovingly takes off their spiritual diaper, and wipes away the mess they have created. He then applies spiritual butt cream to their spiritual bottoms, sprinkles some spiritual baby powder on them, re-diapers them and perhaps He even blows on their belly because He loves seeing the joy on their face when their heavenly Father cleans them up. And like my wife and I with our daughter, God is not surprised when these baby Christians mess up again. He is faithful to point out their sin. They will be back at the altar again, asking God for forgiveness and a fresh diaper. God does not mind cleaning up the messes of the baby Christian because that is the spiritual stage they are in, and He loves them.

Now my daughter is much older and has children of her own. If I go to her house today, and I smell toxic waste coming from her pants, there are only two reasons why this would be the case. One reason would be if she were handicapped in some fashion which prevented her from making it to the bathroom on her own. The other reason she might be hanging around her house with soiled pants is if she was just too lazy to get up and go to the bathroom.

There are some Christians who have followed Jesus for many years who are still running to the altar regularly to ask God to clean up their messes. I would suggest the same two reasons that result in a human adult not being able to go to the restroom, on their own are the reasons Christians continue to mess up spiritually. They may have had something traumatic in their lives which handicapped their spiritual development that prevents them from moving forward. If this is the case, the person has the responsibility to seek help in removing the hindrance, so they can move beyond the spiritual infant stage. This may be an addiction acquired early in life, an area of unforgiveness towards somebody who has hurt them deeply, or it could be a misunderstanding of what it means to be free in Christ. If there is no spiritual disability standing in the way of a person's spiritual development, the reason the person remains in a state of spiritual infancy is just plain laziness.

Babies are self-centered. Babies love being cared for by others. They seldom want to take on the responsibility of caring for themselves, let alone others. There comes a day when babies who refuse to grow up are no longer cute. A person who insists on remaining a baby Christian hinders their own health and the advancement of the kingdom of God.

The second stage of spiritual growth requires Christians to take more responsibility for their actions and attitudes. Christians are not fully mature at this point, but there is a distinct difference between people in this stage and people who are still in spiritual infancy. In a human realm, I like to think of it like the day that parents send their child off to school. The child still has many needs that must be taken care of by his or her parent, but the level of independence and responsibility has begun to grow on the part of child.

The writer of Hebrews states it this way, "Therefore let us leave the elementary doctrine of Christ and go on to maturity, not laying again a foundation of repentance from dead works and of faith toward God, and of instruction about washings, the laying on of hands, the resurrection of the dead, and eternal judgment" (Hebrews 6:1-2).

We must not stay in a stage where we're always worried about our personal salvation. There must come a time when we are secure enough in our salvation that we are the ones God uses to help clean up others. This is not to say we will never mess up again. When that occurs, God will be faithful to forgive us of our sins and to set us back on the right path, but this should not be an ongoing concern for the individual who has transitioned out of the infant stage and into a higher level of maturity.

The writer of Hebrews argues we should also not be in a state of confusion in regard to our liberty in Christ, and the basic doctrines of Christianity. There comes a time when we move beyond simply learning about Christ to the stage of being ministers for Christ. In this passage, the writer is concerned some of the people in the church were still debating the truth of the gospel. There comes a point in the Christian's life when he or she declares, with confidence, the gospel is true. They determine they are not going to turn back when situations become difficult. Christians, who have reached this spiritual stage, walk confidently in their faith, yet they are still in the process of learning all that it means to be mature in Christ.

A third stage in our spiritual development is what I like to call the "meat and potatoes" stage. The writer of Hebrews describes this level of maturity as a person who can eat solid food. "But solid food is for the mature, for those who have their powers of discernment trained by constant practice to distinguish good from evil" (Hebrew 5:14).

Spiritually mature people do not need somebody to tell them how to live. They have learned, over time, the difference between good and evil. They know when it is appropriate to turn off the television, or walk out of a movie theater, when the material becomes offensive. They know when it is appropriate to go into an establishment based on the reputation of the establishment, and what occurs in that location. They don't need somebody to tell them if a joke they are going to tell is inappropriate. They know what pleases God and what does not please Him. A spiritually mature individual knows how to live in liberty, without falling into libertinism. They are not going to exercise personal freedoms at the detriment of others.

The apostle Paul helps us understand what spiritual maturity looks like when he writes to the Corinthian church. He states, "Now concerning food offered to idols: we know that 'all of us possess knowledge.' This 'knowledge' puffs up, but love builds up. If anyone imagines that he knows something, he does not yet know as he ought to know. But if anyone loves God, he is known by God" (1 Corinthians 8:1-3).

Paul draws a distinction between selfish behavior and mature behavior. Spiritual immaturity results in prideful thinking, whereas spiritual maturity results in selfless behavior. The spiritually mature person knows how to say "No" to themselves, if it will benefit someone else. Paul concludes his explanation, regarding the importance of spiritual maturity, by making himself an example. He states, in regard to the issue of eating meat sacrificed to idols, which was a nonissue to some, but a big issue to others, "Therefore, if food makes my brother stumble, I will never eat meat, lest I make my brother stumble" (1 Corinthians 8:13).

The irony of spiritual maturity is that the more mature you are the less free you seem to be to those who observe you from the outside. This is not the same as living a legalist life. Rather, we live introspective lives. Just as mature adults make sacrifices for their children, and sometimes will even choose to not do something to set a good example for them, the spiritually mature adult finds sacrificial living, not only acceptable, but desirable as they watch the spiritually immature grow.

As mentioned earlier, spiritual growth is a process, and it takes time. Do not be discouraged if you are not as mature as you would like to be. Give yourself time and find somebody to help you through the process of growth. The result will be an ever-increasing maturity in Christ. Remember, a little forward progress is better than spiritual stagnation, and much superior to regressing in your faith. Be encouraged and keep taking steps toward God.

The Process of Spiritual Growth

There are conditions that encourage growth. The right mixture of sun, water, and fertilizer will encourage growth in a plant. Having the right attitude and applying the right amount of effort, in combination with faith, will help the believer grow spiritually. Let's look at the spiritual fertilizer Christians can apply that will give their spiritual growth a boost. The list of stimulants suggested here are by no means exhaustive.

Self-sacrifice is necessary for spiritual growth. Jesus was speaking to His disciples one day explaining to them the cost of discipleship. He said they had a choice to pursue the benefits of the world, or the eternal benefits that came from following Him. But in His explanation, He shared with them it was not going be an easy task. He said they would have to be determined to say "No" to themselves and to say "Yes" to the kingdom of God. In one of His more famous quotations, Jesus said, "If anyone would come after me, let him deny himself and take up his cross and follow me" (Matthew 16:24).

Few of us who live in Western society will have to face what the disciples faced in order to function within the kingdom of God. I wonder sometimes if we could have survived the persecution the early Christians faced. Today we face a different kind of struggle. Instead of Roman emperors chasing us or facing persecution from religious leaders, we face the persecution of being overworked, over materialized, and over sensitized. We live in a world that demands our attention, so much, we find it difficult to set aside time to spend in spiritual development. It's easier to put on a headset and listen to music, watch Netflix, or obtain another job so we can buy more stuff, than it is to take time to practice the spiritual discipline necessary to grow in Christ. Jesus' statement that His followers must be willing to take up a cross may look a little different today than it did in the first century, but the determination to follow Christ in the face of opposition is really no less difficult.

There must be intentional effort on our part to put into practice spiritual disciplines. Peter told those he wrote to that they needed to make every effort to develop the root system necessary to produce the fruit of the Spirit.

For this very reason, make every effort to supplement your faith with virtue, and virtue with knowledge, and knowledge with self-control, and self-control with steadfastness, and steadfastness with godliness, and godliness with brotherly affection, and brotherly affection with love. For if these qualities are yours and are increasing, they keep you from being ineffective or unfruitful in the knowledge of our Lord Jesus Christ (2 Peter 1:5-8).

There is no room for laziness in the kingdom of God. A healthy baby's attempt to turn over, to crawl, and eventually to walk is laborious. There is no excuse for baby Christians to not work diligently to gain spiritual muscles to move on to the next stage in their spiritual development. Please remember, working does not produce your salvation. But, if you are saved, you will work to develop your spiritual walk, as a natural byproduct of your life in Christ.

The next element which will help you in the development of your spiritual life is to study the word of God. There is a direct correlation between how much we know about God and how much we will believe in Him. (See 1 Timothy 4:6, 13). If we want to grow in Christ, we must make it a priority to read and study Scripture every day and live according to what it has to say.

There were some Jews who had accepted the truth of the gospel. Jesus shared these words to help them develop in their faith. He said, "If you abide in my word, you are truly my disciples, and you will know the truth, and the truth will set you free" (John 8:31-32).

The words that Jesus shared with the Jews are no less true today than they were then. One of the most beneficial things I ever did when I first dedicated my life to Jesus was to begin to read the Bible. I was so consumed with my love for Jesus, I couldn't put the Bible down. Instead of reading my textbooks for college, I would read my New Testament. Now I don't suggest that for every college student. Perhaps I should've been a little more balanced. But I could not help myself! In less than two months, I read the New Testament, cover to cover, feeding my soul on words and concepts that I found to be life-changing. Those two months served as a foundation to move me from the earliest stages of spiritual infancy toward spiritual independence. I believe the more you find yourself reading Scripture, the greater chance you will have to advance in your spiritual journey.

It's never enough to simply read and understand, or even desire to grow, but we must put into practice the principles that God teaches us. Christians must not minister to others to earn spiritual merit or to show people how mature they are like the Pharisees did in Bible times, but they must minister out of a motivation of genuine love for Jesus.

One of the ways the apostle Paul identified a mature individual was their ability to speak the truth in love (Ephesians 4:15). This is a harder task than it seems on the surface. Paul is saying a spiritually mature person doesn't mince words, but when they communicate the truth, people receive it because they understand there is no malice intended. They can accept correction because they know the person desires to build them up. When we are mature, all of our actions which are motivated by the spirit of God will result in the edification of others.

Another essential element in the spiritual growth process is on-going preparation. As budding actors look for an acting coach to show them skills they need to learn in order to get better at their craft, Christians need individuals to help them see spiritual blind spots and suggest ways to address them. The type of person the Christian should engage will be different at each stage of one's spiritual development.

When Christians are in the baby stage, they will need spiritual mothers who have the gift of unconditional love, the ability to protect them from themselves, and the desire to nurture them. But at the second stage, Christians are going to need a coach, who will help set boundaries, show them how to train and develop, and encourage them to live a self-regulating Christian life. When Christians move into the mature stage, they still need somebody to come alongside them and help fine tune their Christian walk. These people are often referred to as peers. They will become accountability partners. When Christians are in the mature stage, they should seek somebody with whom they can develop a relationship, with whom they can be honest, and who will challenge them to become all that God created them to be.

And finally we must have a sensitivity to the Holy Spirit. If we want to grow in Christ, we must learn to hear the Holy Spirit and walk in accordance with His direction. We will talk much more about this in a later chapter, but suffice it to say at this point that if we learn to set our minds on the Holy Spirit, we will live in fullness of Christ and will experience the peace that we all desire. (See Romans 8:5-6.)

There will be times it will be easier to give up than it will be to keep going. If you will continue making a little progress each day, before long you will see tremendous growth which will be obvious to others. "Practice these things, immerse yourself in them, so that all may see your progress" (2 Timothy 4:15).

Conclusion

Spiritual growth is non-negotiable for Christians. If we remain spiritual babies, we will demonstrate a level of selfishness that is not reflective of the selfless nature of Jesus. If the Church is to ever bring glory to God, the members of the Church must make it a priority to move into maturity so that their lives will reflect the love of God. It is only when the love of God is manifested in the world that the kingdom of God will ever expand as God desires. It is God's will that none should perish and that all should enter the kingdom of God (2 Peter 3:9). As believers we have a responsibility to live in such a way to make that possibility a reality.

Study Guide Questions

1. What did Jesus say was the purpose of spiritual growth?

2. How will Christians know if they are growing spiritually?

3. What gifts did Jesus give us to help us grow spiritually?

4. What three steps of spiritual growth are provided in this chapter?

5. How should mature Christians view those who are less mature?

6. List six elements that can jumpstart a person's spiritual development.

7. Why is spiritual maturity non-negotiable for Christians?

THREE

THE ROLE OF THE HOLY SPIRIT IN SPIRITUAL FORMATION

A key to taking steps toward God is to learn how to walk in the Spirit. Paul commands Christians to walk in the Spirit (Galatians 5:16-17, 25). It's important for us to discover what these two instructions mean and how they can be carried out in the Christian's life. This combination of being saturated by the Holy Spirit, as we dwell in Him and He dwells in us, and the obedient steps we take in response to the directions the Spirit gives to us will help us to develop into mature Christians.

The Indwelling Holy Spirit

Indwelled at Salvation

When we accept the authority of Jesus in our lives at salvation, the Holy Spirit indwells us. The Bible is clear, if we do not have the Holy Spirit living in us, then we are not truly followers of Jesus. Paul declares, "You, however, are not in the flesh but in the Spirit, if in fact the Spirit of God dwells in you. Anyone who does not have the Spirit of Christ does not belong to him" (Romans 8:9).

When we accept Jesus, the Bible tells us we are given the Holy Spirit to help us live righteously. Jesus states,

> I tell you the truth: it is to your advantage that I go away, for if I do not go away, the Helper will not come to you. But if I go, I will send him to you. And when he comes, he will convict the world concerning sin and righteousness and judgment: concerning sin, because they do not believe in me; concerning righteousness, because I go to the

Father, and you will see me no longer; concerning judgment, because the ruler of this world is judged (John 16:7-11).

The Baptism in the Holy Spirit

In the New Testament, there is a distinct experience believers encountered after their salvation. This experience was considered normal for all believers. We see the expectation of this second experience when the apostles Peter and John ask believers if they had received the Holy Spirit (Acts 8:14-17). The primary purpose of this Spirit baptism is to provide the believer with power to share the message of salvation. Jesus told His followers who had already placed their trust in Him, "But you will receive power when the Holy Spirit has come upon you, and you will be my witnesses in Jerusalem and in all Judea and Samaria, and to the end of the earth" (Acts 1:8).

Some groups today argue the baptism in the Holy Spirit and salvation are one in the same. Others argue the baptism in the Holy Spirit is no longer a part of the Christian experience. Pentecostals, who derive their name from the Day of Pentecost, argue the baptism of the Holy Spirit is a subsequent experience to salvation and continues to occur today. A key argument for the baptism in the Holy Spirit as a subsequent experience is found in Luke 24. Luke states that the disciples' minds were open to the truth of the resurrection of Jesus and the path to salvation. He explains that the disciples embraced the truth and began to live in that truth. It is not until the Day of Pentecost that the disciples were baptized in the Holy Spirit.

The list of people "filled with the Spirit" in the Early Church is impressive. The deacons who served the widows were full of the Spirit (Acts 6:3). Peter was full of the Spirit (Acts 4:8). Stephen was full of the Spirit (Acts 7:55). Paul was full of the Spirit (Acts 13:9). The New Testament lists other individuals who were full of the Spirit, before the death and resurrection of Jesus made salvation possible, such as Elisabeth (Luke 1:41), Zacharias (Luke 1:67), and even John the Baptist while he was still in the womb (Luke 1:15). These individuals were anointed for special service under the limited access which was available to people prior to the Cross. After the resurrection, all believers had access to the Holy Spirit as a constant companion (Acts 2:17).

How Can You Know You Have Been Baptized in the Holy Spirit?

As has been stated already, you receive the Holy Spirit when you are saved. But if you desire a complete New Testament experience, you'll also want to be baptized in the Holy Spirit. You receive the baptism of the Holy Spirit in the same way that you receive your salvation. You ask God to baptize you, believing He has the ability to do so, and then you receive.

There has been increased debate in recent years concerning the initial physical evidence that proves that a person has actually been baptized in the Holy Spirit. I'm not going to take time here to debate this issue. Rather, I am simply going to unpack the experience as recorded by the New Testament writers.

There are five events where there is a recorded outpouring of the Holy Spirit on a group of believers in the New Testament. You'll find these events recorded in the following passages; Acts 2; 4; 8; 10; and 19. Let's look at each one of these individually and identify what occurred in each event that gave evidence to a group of believers that they had been baptized in the Holy Spirit.

The first example of an outpouring of the Holy Spirit is found in Acts 2. Jesus told His followers to wait before they started their task of spreading the gospel to all nations (Acts 1:4). We can read in Acts 2 the following account:

When the day of Pentecost arrived, they were all together in one place. And suddenly there came from heaven a sound like a mighty rushing wind, and it filled the entire house where they were sitting. And divided tongues as of fire appeared to them and rested on each one of them. And they were all filled with the Holy Spirit and began to speak in other tongues as the Spirit gave them utterance (Acts 2:1-4).

Luke identifies three physical signs that initially appeared when Christians in the Upper Room were baptized in the Holy Spirit on the Day of Pentecost. There was a sound like a mighty rushing wind, divided tongues as of fire appeared, and each individual spoke in an unknown language.

The second example of an infilling of the Holy Spirit is found in Acts 4. The disciples were under great persecution at this time. It was a moment when they needed special strength in their life. The same group, which were baptized in the Holy Spirit in Acts 2, were refilled during this time of need. We see this event through the eyes of Luke when he writes, "And when they had prayed, the place in which they were gathered together was shaken, and they were all filled with the Holy Spirit and continued to speak the word of God with boldness" (Acts 4:31).

The third occurrence of the baptism in the Holy Spirit is recorded in Acts 8:9-25. This account is instructive, on a number of levels. It is here we see a clear distinction between salvation and the baptism in the Holy Spirit. But for our purposes, I want to concentrate on what people saw or heard when the people were baptized in the Holy Spirit. Unfortunately, Luke does not provide what the evidence was, but it is very clear something occurred that precipitated Simon the sorcerer's response to the event. Listen to his words, "Now when Simon saw that the Spirit was given through the laying on of the apostles' hands, he offered them money, saying, 'Give me this power also, so that anyone on whom I lay my hands may receive the Holy Spirit'" (Acts 8:18-19).

Simon the sorcerer had seen it all. People who encountered him believed he possessed all spiritual power. But he saw something that was outside of his normal toolbox of spiritual trickery. Something occurred, which so impressed Simon that he wanted to add it to his repertoire. The Bible doesn't make it clear what Simon saw or heard, so we cannot use this example, in a definitive manner, in determining the normal expectation on the part of the believer when individuals were baptized in the Holy Spirit.

The fourth account of a group being baptized in the Holy Spirit occurs in Acts 10. Peter was addressing a group of Gentile believers. This was "out-of-the-box" for Peter because of his bias against Gentiles. But as he spoke to them, he became convinced they were Christians because God had chosen to baptize them in the Holy Spirit, in the same way he had been baptized in the Holy Spirit. And here is Luke's description of the events that occurred. "While Peter was still saying these things, the Holy Spirit fell on all who heard the word. And the believers from among the circumcised who had come with Peter were amazed, because the gift of the Holy Spirit was poured out even on the Gentiles. For they were hearing them speaking in tongues and extolling God" (Acts 10:44-46).

In this account, there are two things that are identified as evidence individuals were baptized in the Holy Spirit. They gave praise to God, and they spoke in tongues. Peter was probably impressed with both of these responses, but the one which would have stood out to him was the Gentiles were speaking in languages which they did not know. Peter could identify with them because this was a shared experience. He, too, had spoken in other languages when he was baptized in the Holy Spirit on the Day of Pentecost.

Let's look at the final example of a group being baptized in the Holy Spirit. This account is found in Acts 19. Let's view Luke's retelling of the events.

And he said to them, "Did you receive the Holy Spirit when you believed?" And they said, "No, we have not even heard that there is a Holy Spirit." And he said, "Into what then were you baptized?" They said, "Into John's baptism." And Paul said, "John baptized with the baptism of repentance, telling the people to believe in the one who was to come after him, that is, Jesus." On hearing this, they were baptized in the name of the Lord Jesus. And when Paul had laid his hands on them, the Holy Spirit came on them, and they began speaking in tongues and prophesying. (Acts 19:2-6).

Once again, Luke makes a distinction between repentance, which was evidenced through the baptism of John, and the baptism in the Holy Spirit. But the thing I want you to see in this passage is when the baptism in the Holy Spirit occurred, two evidences were on display. The people prophesied, and the people spoke in tongues.

If you examine these five accounts in the book of Acts, the only physical evidence that occurs, in all of the events, where a physical evidence is recorded, is speaking in tongues. Luke isn't attempting to defend a particular theology of the baptism in the Holy Spirit. He simply recorded what he saw. People today can debate what the initial physical evidence of the baptism in the Holy Spirit is, but there is no debate concerning what New Testament believers expected to see and hear when a person was baptized in the Holy Spirit.

Three things I want to be extremely clear about. I am not saying a person who has not been baptized in the Holy Spirit is not saved. I clearly believe the Bible teaches when you are saved, you receive the Holy Spirit. The baptism in the Holy Spirit is an additional opportunity to receive power to reach others with the message of salvation. The second thing I want to be clear about is a believer should not seek the initial physical evidence of speaking in tongues. Believers should seek Christ, and ask Him to baptize them in the Holy Spirit. Tongues will come naturally, as a result of the baptism. The third thing I want to be clear about is a person who is baptized in the Holy Spirit is not spiritually superior to the believer who has not been baptized in the Holy Spirit.

The purpose of the baptism in the Holy Spirit is to provide power to evangelize, especially when believers face persecution. This may explain why some missionaries associated with organizations which limit the baptism in the Holy Spirit to the New Testament era have been known to seek the baptism in the Holy Spirit when they are ministering in difficult countries. The baptism in the Holy Spirit also provides the believer with a prayer language that aids in achieving the will of God even when we do not know how to pray. (See Romans 8:26.)

Walking in the Holy Spirit

Once we have the Holy Spirit living in us, we need to learn to walk in the Spirit. As with any element of our spiritual formation, learning to walk in the Spirit is a process. I think about my children as they were learning to walk. At first, they would pull themselves up on the couch. They would then take a step or two with the support of the furniture. Eventually, they would venture away from the couch, and take an uncertain, unassisted step. It was not unusual for them to fall. They would give up for a little while, but then they would try again. Over time, their confidence grew as one step led to another. As their father, I would hold out my hands encouraging them to make their way to me. Because they trusted me, they would take the risk and venture toward me. Eventually, they were running around the house with no thought of tripping or falling.

In a similar way, new Christians have to learn how to walk in the Spirit confidently. There will be times when they will fall in their effort to walk successfully. But over time, as they learn to trust God more, and to hear his voice, they will be able to walk in the Spirit. In a coming chapter, we will discover various ways to hear God's voice which will enable you to walk in confidence.

When we learn to walk in the Spirit, He will give us guidance. The New Testament records examples of people who walked in the Spirit. Philip, a deacon in the church, was given direction by the Holy Spirit to go to the chariot of the eunuch. When he arrived, the Holy Spirit made an opportunity for Philip to share the gospel (Acts 8:29-35). Peter was told by the Holy Spirit to go to the house of Cornelius (Acts 10:19, 20; 11:12). This was a major turning point in the expansion of the Church. The Church expanded beyond Jewish believers because Peter was willing to listen to the Holy Spirit, and then to walk in the Spirit. Paul was also willing to listen to the Holy Spirit and walk according to the Spirit's direction. The Holy Spirit told Paul not to go to some of the places he intended to go (Acts 16:7-8). We really don't know what Paul avoided as a result of listening to God and walking in the Spirit, but it is likely Paul would have encountered something that would hinder the kingdom work God had designed for him if he had disobeyed.

Walking in the Spirit will result in God leading you to assist others to connect with Christ or to help a person further their spiritual development. If we will keep our ears tuned to the Holy Spirit, He will guide us to those who are receptive to the gospel or to those who need specific encouragement. When we walk according to our own spirit, we tend to do those things which benefit us. When we walk in the Spirit, we will do things which benefit the kingdom of God.

If you have never practiced walking in the Holy Spirit, I encourage you to take a risk. Throughout your day, seek to hear His voice, and when you do, obey it. You may fail a time or two as you begin taking steps, but it won't be long before you are walking with confidence. The more you walk; the more confident you will grow.

Abiding in the Spirit

As we saw earlier, Jesus told His followers to abide in Him (John 15:4). The term "abide" means to live in. Another way to say this is "be saturated with the Spirit." In order to be saturated with the Spirit, we must be cognizant of Him in our lives. We do not have to wait until we are in a worship service to encounter the Holy Spirit. As we will see in a later chapter, worship should help us to recognize the presence of God that already exists within us and to bring honor to Him through obedience.

If we will abide in the Holy Spirit, there are many great results that await us. Let's look at a few of the things we can expect, if we abide in the Holy Spirit.

Abiding in the Holy Spirit will result in a person living in measured freedom. Paul states, "But you are not controlled by your sinful nature. You are controlled by the Spirit if you have the Spirit of God living in you" (Romans 8:9, NTL). We are free in Christ, but that does not mean we can run over someone else to get what we want. We are free from the power of sin, but we are still being controlled. God places controls on our lives to protect us and to protect the kingdom of God.

I have had the privilege of taking a few trips to countries less developed than the United States. One of the common features of these nations, which differentiate them from the United States, is the driving practices of the people. I remember being in the Dominican Republic. There was one place specifically I remember where traffic came to a total halt because cars were converging from different directions. It seemed everyone thought traffic lights were decorations, or suggestions at best. In Mongolia, streets were built for two lanes of traffic, but seldom did I see less than three, and sometimes four cars, attempting to go down these two lanes. It was not extremely safe to be on the sidewalks. And in Cambodia, the cars seem to stay in their lanes, but the motorbikes zoom in and out without consideration for others on the highway. I can give many other examples, but the chaotic nature of the traffic, in many of the countries that I visit, make me appreciate the traffic laws which are enforced in the United States.

Much like the traffic in these other countries, our spiritual communities will be chaotic if everyone simply gets to do what they desire. There has to be community standards, if the community wants to thrive. The standards for the Church are established by God and enforced by the Holy Spirit. If everyone would abide in the Spirit, and walk in the Spirit, the Church would thrive, and the kingdom of God would be expanded as it was in the first century.

Walking in the Spirit will also make us sensitive to the Holy Spirit. The more we focus on the Holy Spirit, the more aware we will be of what the Spirit wants to do within us and through us. God speaks through Ezekiel saying these words, "And I will put my Spirit within you, and cause you to walk in my statutes and be careful to obey my rules" (Ezekiel 36:27).

The more you are in a relationship with a person, the more you will learn about the person and you will be better able to fulfill the desires of the individual. A man who is attempting to impress a woman will listen to her intently. He will discover what food she likes, what type of music she appreciates, and the type movies she enjoys. Once he has discovered these things, he will invite her to an intimate dinner making sure the music in the background is to her liking. He will follow the dinner with just the right movie which he knows she will appreciate. He will impress her, not because of what he does, but because she will recognize he cared enough to listen and attempted to please her.

As we abide in the Spirit, we will learn to listen intently to what He says to us and do those things we know bring Him pleasure. We will discover that the Holy Spirit desires for us to love Christ more and to serve our fellow brothers and sisters. Taking time to learn the preferences of the Holy Spirit will deepen our appreciation for Him and help us to take steps toward God. Jesus tells us we can know the Holy Spirit in a personal way. He states, "And I will ask the Father, and he will give you another Helper, to be with you forever, even the Spirit of truth, whom the world cannot receive, because it neither sees him nor knows him. You know him, for he dwells with you and will be in you" (John 14:16-17).

Abiding in the Holy Spirit will also provide us with confidence. Jesus said, "But the Helper, the Holy Spirit, whom the Father will send in my name, he will teach you all things and bring to your remembrance all that I have said to you" (John 14:26).

There will be times in our Christian walk where we will feel discouraged and perhaps even defeated. It is at those times, we need to remember what Jesus has said about us, and draw confidence from His words, even when the circumstances of our lives look impossible. If we abide in the Holy Spirit, we can draw strength from Him. Too often when hard times come, our attention becomes focused on our problems. Instead of focusing on our problems, we can focus on the Holy Spirit who is in us, and allow Him to speak the truth to us which will give us confidence.

There are many other benefits that come from abiding in the Holy Spirit, but suffice it to say, focusing our minds on Him will direct our minds to the priorities of God. The Holy Spirit is given to us to help us focus our attention on Christ and His kingdom.

Conclusion

Let me conclude this short chapter on the role of the Holy Spirit in the believer's life by simply reminding you that the Holy Spirit has been given to you to help you develop in your spiritual walk with God. Each of us who have accepted Jesus as our Savior have the Holy Spirit living in us. The Bible says we need to be continually filled with the Holy Spirit. I do not believe this means we need more of the Spirit in us. Rather, we need to recognize His presence more fully. When we do, we will seek all that is available to us through the Spirit. Those who have the Holy Spirit living in them will walk differently than those who walk in the flesh. It is my challenge to you to take a step toward God as you make it a practice to walk in the Spirit.

Study Guide

1. When does the Holy Spirit first indwell a person?

2. What is the purpose of the baptism in the Holy Spirit?

3. Based on the material found in the book of Acts, what is the initial physical evidence of the baptism in the Holy Spirit?

4. What should a Christian do if they desire to be baptized in the Holy Spirit?

5. What must a person do in order to successfully walk in the Holy Spirit?

6. Where does the Holy Spirit live?

7. What can a believer do to be saturated in the Holy Spirit?

8. What are three results of abiding in the Holy Spirit listed in this chapter?

FOUR

UNDERSTANDING BIBLICAL FAITH

In some church traditions, faith simply refers to one's belief in Jesus Christ. Other traditions, such as the Pentecostal movement, tend to see faith as an activating source which brings about movement on the part of God. Faith is clearly a component of a believer's life. Some people's faith was very strong, as in the case of the Roman soldier (Matthew 8:13), while others seemed to have less faith, such as the father who asked Jesus for a miracle (Mark 9:24).

What is Faith?

So, what is the difference between strong faith and weak faith? Is faith something we accumulate over time? Do more spiritual people have greater faith, and less spiritual people have less faith? And how does one obtain faith?

If you have been around the church very long, you probably have heard somebody say, "If you just had enough faith, God would have answered your prayer." This statement may have made you feel spiritually inferior, and perhaps somewhat guilty. When somebody makes a statement such as this, it places the responsibility of a person's miracle on the shoulder of the person who needs the miracle, or on the person who is praying for the miracle. This kind of teaching leads to unnecessary condemnation, and has led some to leave the church.

I witnessed the damage which can be done as a result of this type of teaching a few years back when I returned to my home church in the state of Maine. I had just completed preaching, and after a short time of prayer, the pastor dismissed the service. I went into the congregation to greet my old friends. As I was shaking hands and hugging necks, I saw a woman patiently standing waiting for me to greet her. The pastor, who was a good friend of mine, was greeting people near me when I approached this woman. She looked extremely serious. She pointed her finger directly at me and then she moved her finger in the direction of the pastor. She nearly shouted, "You lied to me!"

I quickly reviewed what I had said in the sermon that morning and realized I had not said anything directly to her, nor had I lied. I asked her how I had lied to her. She quickly began to tell me her story.

This woman was a mother of a friend I had grown up with. I had heard that her son had been sick, but she laid out the details very clearly for me. Her son was an elder in the church, loved Jesus dearly, was a great father, and was a testimony to everybody he interacted with. He had unexpectedly been diagnosed with brain cancer. The doctor said it was inoperable and, if not for a miracle, he would die shortly. This mother told me she, her son, and his family began to pray desperately for his healing. She went on to tell me that preachers had assured her if she just had enough faith, her son would be healed. So, she believed, as hard as she could believe. She read her Bible consistently. She gave in the offering, above and beyond what she had ever done before, to demonstrate her faith to God. She had heard that if she took her son to healing evangelists, this would demonstrate faith. She encouraged her son to go with her to church services to be prayed for any time there was a healing evangelists in the area.

This mother passionately believed God was going to heal her son. She was not afraid to tell anyone who would listen that her son was going to be healed. To her dismay, God did not heal her son. At least He didn't heal him on this side of death. Because of poor teaching, this mother was left to decide if God was a liar or were the people who represent Him liars?

Fortunately for this mother, she chose to identify God's messengers as the liars (or at least mistaken), rather than God. She could have immediately walked away from her faith because of this poor theology, but she was still hanging onto her faith in Jesus Christ. She was to be commended. I tried to explain that I had not lied to her and I would never have told her what she thought these preachers had taught her about faith. I tried to explain true biblical faith, but at this moment she was so distraught, she did not want to hear any more from a preacher. She walked away frustrated. I couldn't blame her.

Many people have been hurt by a misrepresentation of the truth about faith. This is the reason I want to take this opportunity to unpack what I believe the Bible teaches about faith and to help you practice your faith in a biblical fashion and help you assist others who have been spiritually harmed by poor teaching.

How Do We Gain Faith?

So, "How does one gain more faith?" A better question may be, "How much faith is enough faith?" And finally, "How do I know when I have enough faith to satisfy God?"

When some people talk about having enough faith, it almost sounds as if there is a predetermined quantity of faith that will move the hand of God, but He restricts us from knowing what that quantity is. Kind of like a carrot on a stick which keeps a horse moving forward in a quest to capture the prize, these people imply that God keeps the correct amount of faith dangling in front of our desperate noses, so we will exert more energy to obtain what we desire.

When we want something from God, it can seem like we must jump into our spiritual truck, backup to a faith pile, shovel faith into the back of our truck, and return to God to find out if we have accumulated enough faith. When we don't get the answer that we desire, we back our spiritual truck to the faith pile again, shovel on a bit more faith, return to God and ask Him if this amount of faith meets His requirement. And if we still do not get our desired result, we must keep going back to the faith heap repeatedly until we fulfill the demands of God. It's not that we don't want to do everything necessary to appease God, it's just that we do not know how much it will really take to get Him to move on our behalf.

The Bible is very clear that God is not a malevolent figure sitting in heaven laughing at us as He toys with our emotions. God loves us and desires to bless us. There really is not "enough faith." The Bible states faith as small as a mustard seed is all that is necessary to make a mountain move (Matthew 17:20-21). The mustard seed was the smallest seed known to humans at the time that Jesus lived on earth. And a mountain would have been the largest object a person would encounter during that time. Jesus was teaching that the smallest amount of faith, when associated with God's will, is greater and more powerful than the greatest item on earth. Faith is anchored in God. He is the source of faith. The mountain is a part of the temporal world. Most of our problems are tied to the temporal world. Jesus was saying that all temporal problems will have to submit to eternal power, if God chooses to act.

The Bible does tell us, however, there is a way for us to increase our faith. We must understand, however, we are not increasing our faith in faith. In other words, increased faith does not mean we must believe more deeply that something is going to happen, but increased faith means I must trust Christ more. The Bible says faith comes by hearing the word of Christ (Romans 10:17). The more we know about Jesus, the more we will trust Him. The more we trust Him, the more confidence we will have that what He does on our behalf is sufficient. This was the message I was trying to communicate to the distraught mother on the Sunday morning, in the story I just told. It was natural for her to hurt due to the loss of her son. And it was also appropriate for her to point out the teaching she had received had damaged her. But the true question she had to answer was if she could trust Jesus with the decision He made concerning her son. Faith in Jesus does not always mean we will understand why He chooses to do what He chooses to do in a particular situation. It means I will trust Him, regardless of the circumstances in my life.

Whenever there is a student in my class confined to a wheelchair, I ask the other students in the class who they think has more faith; a person sitting in a wheelchair or a person who is able-bodied? This always proves to be a bit awkward because it puts the person in wheelchair in the spotlight. No one in the class wants to imply that the person is confined to his or her wheelchair because the individual does not have enough faith to get up and walk. But some able-bodied students are thinking this is the situation. To ensure no additional discomfort occurs, I usually don't let anybody respond to the question. I quickly share my opinion. I explain that I believe the Christian confined to a wheelchair has greater faith than most able-bodied people. I tell them, it is easy to believe in God when life is going well for us. It is tougher to believe in a God, who loves us and blesses us, when He doesn't seem to be working on our behalf and life is difficult. For the individual in the wheelchair to continue to believe God is good and He is faithful requires a great deal more faith than the individual who is able-bodied.

Faith is not tested in the good times, but is tested in the darkest moments, when we face the most difficult challenges. It is in these turbulent times that I have to ask myself if God can truly be trusted. When we do not seem to receive what we think we deserve from God, we must focus on God's character through researching Scripture, and reflecting on His history of faithfulness.

How Does the Bible Define Faith?

Faith is the persuasion of the mind a certain statement is true. Its primary idea is trust. If a thing is true, it is therefore worthy of trust. Jesus said, "I am the way, the truth, and the life! Jesus answered. 'Without me, no one can go to the Father'" (John 14:6). If we do not believe firmly, in our mind, Jesus is the son of God, and He is the only way to the Father, then we do not have faith in Jesus. The apostle Paul taught, "If we follow our own desires, we cannot please God" (Romans 8:8). If we do not trust Jesus alone is the means to reaching the Father, then all the claims of Christianity are meaningless (1 Corinthians 15:14).

But if we do believe Jesus is the son of God, then it is essential to stand firm in our faith no matter the circumstances of life. Philippians 1:27 states, "Only let your manner of life be worthy of the gospel of Christ, so that whether I come to see you or am absent, I may hear of you that you are standing firm in one spirit, with one mind striving side-by-side for the faith of the gospel." Our faith also helps us to remember we have eternal life because we have placed our trust in the power of the death and resurrection of Jesus Christ. The apostle Paul tells the Thessalonian church, "But we ought always to give thanks to God for you, brothers beloved by the Lord, because God chose you as the first fruits to be saved, through sanctification by the spirit and belief in the truth" (2 Thessalonians 2:13).

Knowledge is an essential element in all faith. It is sometimes spoken of in Scripture as being equivalent to faith. In John 10:38, Jesus states, "But if I do His works, believe in the evidence of the miraculous works I have done, even if you don't believe Me. Then you'll know and understand that the Father is in Me and I am in the Father." Jesus did not expect blind faith from His followers, based on wishful thinking, or simply believing what some religious teacher had told them. He encouraged those who witnessed His ministry to examine what He was doing and to determine for themselves if He was worthy of their faith. If He was found worthy of a person's trust, the logical conclusion was the person would live in obedience to Him.

But knowledge and faith, even though sometimes used interchangeably in the Scripture, are distinct. People can believe something intellectually without it ever impacting their lives. True faith demands an assent to that belief through actions of the will which go beyond mere comprehension. John says it like this, "And by this we know that we have come to know Him, if we keep His commandments" (1 John 2:3).

If we fail to act upon our beliefs, we do not truly have faith. It is equally dangerous to act on beliefs which are not founded on truth. I can proclaim that God will provide me with a brand-new Corvette, based on a belief that God possesses the resources to give me the car and obviously would want me to have it. I can name it. I can claim it. I can put all my faith behind receiving this car, but if God has not told me He is going to provide the car, I am placing my hope in something that is not reality. Too often we find ourselves putting our faith in faith and believing that whatever we want will be what we get. Instead we must put our faith in God, and trust Him to provide those things He determines we need.

I do not have to understand all the nuances of something for me to put my trust in it. When I first boarded an airplane, at the age of 18-years-old, I took my seat knowing very little about the aerodynamics which governed the flight of an airplane. I definitely did not know how to pilot the plane, nor did I know how much fuel the airplane would require for us to arrive at our destination. I was very nervous that day as I got on the plane, but I trusted somebody smarter than me who knew how to operate the aircraft and the engineers who built it to withstand the demands of flying nearly 300 people across country in a multi-ton tube of metal. I demonstrated my faith in the pilot and engineers by taking my seat and listening carefully to the attendant's instructions.

There is no way a human is going to understand all the ways of God. But like the day that I sat on the aircraft and put my trust in those who knew more than I knew, oftentimes I must sit back, relax, and trust God even when life seems out-of-control.

Faith is an active principle. Believers must embrace the absolute truthfulness of every statement which comes from God. We place our faith in what God has said and believe the outcome of our lives is in His control. Those who choose to trust God and the promises He has made to them can be confident that their lives will be found acceptable to God, now and in the afterlife. The apostle Paul speaks a great deal about our salvation. Our salvation is based on the belief Jesus has done all that is necessary for us to stand justified before God. Justification simply means God will not hold us accountable for our sins on Judgment Day because Jesus has already paid the price for every sin committed in the past, currently being committed, or committed in the future. All that is required of a person is to activate his or her faith by believing his or her sins are forgiven, and begin to live in the righteousness that God has provided through Jesus.

Our salvation has nothing to do with our own efforts to keep the Law. Paul explains how an active faith can release the grace and mercy which God extends to us: "'What does Scripture say?' Abraham believed God, and it was credited to him as righteousness.' Now to the one who works, wages are not credited as a gift but as an obligation. However, to the one who does not work but trusts God who justifies the ungodly, their faith is credited as righteousness" (Romans 4:3-5).

Faith is not simply the assent of the intellect to revealed truth. It is the practical submission of the entire person to the guidance and control of the truth. If faith were simply a stated confession to the truth, then the devil and his minions would have assurance of heaven. The Bible says, the devils believe Jesus is God and it causes them to shudder (James 2:19). So, cognitive assent is not enough. There must be more. If we do not act on our faith through obedience to the One we say we place our trust in, then we have no more than what is possessed by the ultimate enemy of God.

What Does the Bible Say About Faith?

In Hebrews 11:1 Scripture says, "Faith is the substance of things hoped for. It is the evidence of things not seen." It is important for us to understand the meaning of the word "hoped" in this passage or we will be in danger of misinterpreting the intent of the author. The word "hope" today often is associated with wishful thinking. The Bible does not use the word "hope" in this manner. The word "hope" is a word of assurance for the person who believes. When we use the term "blessed hope," referring to the Second Coming of Jesus, we do not understand Jesus's return as wishful thinking. Rather, we use the term "blessed hope" to speak with assurance Jesus will return someday and our future is secure. With this concept in mind, the author of the book of Hebrews says our trust demonstrates our belief God will do what He said He will do even when we do not see the fulfillment of the promise in our lifetime. We can believe Jesus will return; even if we never witness His return. We can believe Jesus has gone to prepare a place for us, even though we have no physical proof of this truth. We can believe our salvation is secure, even though we do not feel saved at times. Just as Abraham believed God's promise that he would have a dedicated homeland and many children, even when he only had a handful upon his death, we must believe what God promises will materialize.

Faith is not an option for those who have witnessed the evidence of Jesus. First John 3:23 expresses the expectation of those who have seen the evidence that Jesus is the son of God: "And this is His commandment, that we believe in the name of His son Jesus Christ and love one another, just as He commanded us." Individuals, who have had the opportunity to examine the claims of Jesus, and fail to submit themselves to His Lordship, place themselves in great peril. During Jesus' ministry on earth, He did many miracles which people refused to acknowledge. This frustrated Jesus because He was doing all He could to help them see and understand. But they refused to put their trust in Him. Listen to His pain as He calls out to them: "Woe to you, Chorazin! Woe to you, Bethesda! For if the mighty works done in you had been done in Tyre and Sidon, they would've repented long ago in sackcloth and ashes" (Matthew 11:21). The same peril awaits those today who refuse to recognize Jesus for who He truly is.

The Bible declares faith is a gift of God. The apostle Paul clearly believed faith was not something we earned, but something God has given to us. Paul believed some individuals have greater faith than others because they have been exposed to more revelation from God, so they have more to base their faith on. We must remember, when Paul wrote his letters the New Testament had not been recorded. People did not have equal exposure to the evidence of Jesus' Lordship, as we have today in most parts of the world. Those who had more exposure to Christ's life and ministry were not to consider themselves more spiritual than those who had limited exposure. In Romans 12:3, Paul puts this in perspective. He states, "For by the grace given to me I say to everyone among you not to think of himself more highly than he ought to think, but to think with sober judgment, each according to the measure of faith that God has assigned." We must never judge one another based on where we are in our spiritual life. If we wish to take steps toward God, we will attempt to increase our exposure to the character and nature of God.

In the letter to the Ephesians, Paul explains the entire salvation process is initiated by God and is a gift from Him. He states, "For by grace you have been saved through faith. And this is not your own doing; it is a gift of God" (Ephesians 2:8). Paul's letter to the Philippians provides even more evidence Paul believed faith is a gift from God as he speaks about the troubles Christians may face as a result of their faith in Jesus. He states, "For you have been given not only the privilege of trusting in Christ but also the privilege of suffering for Him" (Philippians 1:29).

The Bible teaches that faith is the work of God. It cannot be generated by a preacher, although a preacher is often used in the process. The book of Acts shows us many examples of individuals finding faith in Christ. The report in Acts 11:21 is clear concerning the initiator of the conversions that took place in Antioch. "The hand of the Lord was with them, and a great number who believed turned to the Lord." The apostle Paul made it a point to not allow people to think he was the source of their faith. In 1 Corinthians 2:5, Paul explains his actions regarding his failure to baptize believers there by saying, "[I did this] so that your faith might not rest in the wisdom of men but in the power of God." No matter how effective you are in communicating the gospel, or no matter how powerful you are in demonstrating the miracles of God, be very careful to understand faith must be attributed to the works of Christ and not to the works of man. It is vital you understand you are simply an instrument being used by God.

The Bible also teaches there should be an outward evidence of the faith we declare. Works does not produce faith, but faith does produce works. One cannot read the book of James without recognizing he believed, if there are no spiritual results of one's faith, then there is no real faith. James declares, "But someone will say, 'You have faith and I have works.' Show me your faith apart from your works, and I will show you my faith by my works" (James 2:16). He was not making a distinction between faith and works to demonstrate one as better than the other. He was simply declaring it is impossible to truly have faith without it revealing itself through our expressions of love to God and to others. This is the reason James argues, "Religion that is pure and undefiled before God the Father is this: to visit orphans and widows in their affliction, and to keep oneself unstained from the world" (James 1:27).

The Bible teaches faith is accompanied by repentance. Repentance is a willful decision to turn away from a self-focused life and turn toward a God-focused life. Our faith in God demands us to relinquish control over our lives and our destiny and give ourselves to His purposes which bring Him glory. One of the first declarations of Jesus recorded in the Gospel of Mark directs His listeners to make a commitment to not only believe the gospel, but to turn their lives in a new direction. He states, "The time is fulfilled, and the kingdom of God is at hand; repent and believe in the gospel" (Mark 1:15). And some of the final words in the Gospel of Luke (24:47) undergird the linkage between faith and repentance. Jesus explains why He had to suffer, die, and be raised on the third day. It was so people of all nations would repent and be forgiven of their sins. He commissioned His disciples to communicate what they had seen and what they had experienced for a foundation of belief for others.

Conclusion

We have now returned full-circle to the beginning of this chapter. Hopefully, if you face a situation someday like I faced after preaching in my home church, you will have the information necessary to correct misguided theology which is often offered as truth. Faith is not based on a fable, or something that we hope to be true. God is sovereign. Faith does not change Him. It recognizes who He is and provides confidence in His decisions. Faith is grounded in truth. Jesus died and rose again. The resurrected Christ was witnessed by more than 500 people (1 Corinthians 15:6). The disciples responded to the truth and shared that truth with others who would listen and consider their testimony. But faith is incomplete without repentance. Believers must turn away from their self-centered, egotistical lives and turn towards a selfless, others-oriented existence. Our faith must be more than a creed. It must shape the way we live, love, and serve others.

Study Guide Questions

1. How does poor theology about faith cause spiritual damage?

2. How much faith is enough?

3. What was Jesus teaching when He told His followers that mustard see faith was enough to move a mountain?

4. How does a person gain faith?

5. What was the point of the author telling a story about a person in a wheel chair?

6. What is the primary idea expressed by the word "faith"?

7. What is the difference between "knowledge" and "faith"?

8. What does the word "hope" mean in Scripture?

9. What role do preachers play in the development of faith in people?

10. What does "repentance" mean and how does it relate to faith?

FIVE

FREEDOM ROOTED IN FAITH

Christianity has lost much of its luster in our current culture. If you asked the average person living in Western society to describe an evangelical Christian, you would discover most non-believers would use unflattering terms. A survey was done a few years ago in which the author asked average individuals on the street to describe an evangelical Christian in one word. The words that were given included the following list: conservative, right wing Republican, hypocritical, no sense of humor, and judgmental. Whether or not we believe these things about ourselves, it's important for Christians to realize this is how we are perceived by those outside of the Church.

Understanding the perception of people helps Christians understand why evangelism is more challenging today than it has been in the past. Can you imagine going up to somebody who views Christians in the way just described and asking them if they would like to meet someone who could make them like us? No one in his right mind would want to take that deal. So what is the answer to help individuals recognize that Christianity is a vehicle to freedom and real joy, rather than a means to live a life less fulfilling than the one they already live?

The key way to allowing individuals who do not know Jesus to get a proper perspective of what Christianity looks like is to introduce those individuals to real, living, breathing Christians. But these believers must be individuals who have embraced Jesus as their Savior, and who have learned to walk according to the Spirit of God. Once an individual sees a truly victorious Christian, it will help them understand their perception of Christianity has been skewed. They will realize Jesus truly does offer the hope they desire. But this can only occur if the individuals who claim to be followers of Jesus have found that freedom themselves.

Conditions of Freedom

The essence of the gospel can be reduced to two basic principles. The first principle is that we must love God with all of our hearts, minds, and strength (Matthew 22:37-38). The second principle is we will love others as a result of our love for God (Matthew 22:39). When we begin to see people the way that God sees people, the natural result will be that we will fulfill the Great Commission to go into all the world and preach the gospel, leading individuals to Jesus, and helping them to grow in Him (Matthew 28:19-20).

One of the problems which we face in Christianity today is many individuals have substituted a set of religious rules for a dynamic relationship with God. We find absolutely no problem in believing our salvation was a result of the work that Jesus did on the cross and the resurrection that followed three days later. We know we were sinners, unable to appease God in our own ability. We acknowledge it is by faith that we receive salvation. Unfortunately, we have much more difficulty accepting the fact we remain saved as a result of Jesus' death and resurrection.

The Galatian believers struggled with the idea that faith was all that was necessary to stay saved. When Paul realized this, he asked the Galatians who had tricked them into believing they had to do "work" to maintain their faith (Galatians 3:1). The Galatians had started out so well in their faith. They had found freedom in Jesus Christ. But shortly after their salvation, they began to live according to a set of rules which they were told would keep them in right standing with God.

Although living right might seem admirable on the surface, it can be damnable. Living righteously is a goal all Christians should attain to, but it never should be viewed as the criteria of maintaining one's salvation. It is a matter of cause-and-effect. If the cause is Jesus' death and resurrection, than the effect will be our salvation and righteous living. But if the cause is living according to a set of rules, than the effect will be bondage and personal destruction.

The Galatians had begun to believe if they ate the right thing or withdrew from certain activities, then they would be secure in Christ. Paul explains this type of mentality negates the effect of their faith in Jesus and relegates salvation to personal achievement that no one can attain. Today this is called legalism.

Legalism is a philosophy which teaches that living up to a legal standard will provide freedom. In society this is true. If we drive at the speed limit, we will be free from speeding tickets. If we avoid stealing, we will be free from the jail cell. If we stay faithful to our marriage vows, we will avoid the pain of divorce. Legalism works well to maintain a society, but it is the antithesis of what Jesus desires for His Church. Jesus came to fulfill the Law. When we accept Him, and His sacrifice on our behalf, we do not have to fulfill the Law. As a matter of fact, there is no longer any Law to maintain, other than the law of love. "Love does no wrong to a neighbor; therefore love is the fulfilling of the law" (Romans 13:10). We no longer have to work to fulfill the law, for if we do, we are saying what Jesus did was not enough to sustain our spiritual lives. (See Hebrews 10:1-18.)

Although what I am going to say next will cause some of you to scratch your heads, I believe positive activities such as praying, reading your Bible, going to church, fasting, and giving money in the offering can all be vehicles to lead you away from freedom in Christ. These activities can stem from a person's relationship with Jesus or they can become activities which are seen as a means to earn the right to be in relationship with Him. The apostle Paul told the Corinthian believers activities such as speaking in the tongues of men and angels, and even giving one's body to be burned for the cause of Christ are meaningless, if they are not done with the right motive (1 Corinthians 13:1-3). In another place, Paul told the Corinthians many of the spiritual activities individuals undertake during their life will be of no value on the Day of Judgment because they were done with the wrong motivation (1 Corinthians 3:10-15). So it really isn't a matter of if you read your Bible or not, it's a matter of your motivation for reading it.

Hindrances to Freedom

One of the struggles with maintaining a proper relationship with Jesus is the relationship we had with our parents. Even though our parents should have loved us unconditionally, in all reality, unconditional love is beyond the reach of humans. Most of us can remember times when we pleased our parents by doing what they asked us to do in a timely manner. We were rewarded for this effort. We also remember times when we were asked to do something and we failed to do it. Our parents punished us. Sometimes they made us feel they were greatly disappointed in us.

The natural reaction of an individual who wants to please their parents is to try to live up to every request their parents make. They hope to gain their approval and to live in harmony with them. Unfortunately, none of us are able to accomplish this, so each time we fail, we begin to feel undeserving of the love of our parents. The child who is not inclined to be a people pleaser will not even try to earn their parents' love. They rebel against, what they consider, the unrealistic expectations of their parents.

The same attitude we have towards our parents often follows us into our relationship with our Heavenly Father. If we see His love for us as conditional, we will either do whatever we can to earn His love, and end up feeling like a failure because we can never achieve the expectation that we imagine He has for us, or we walk away from the relationship bitter and rebellious.

It is crucial for us to understand our Heavenly Father has the capacity to love unconditionally. He proved this by sending His Son to give His life for us while we were still sinners (Romans 5:8). There was nothing we did that could earn His love before we knew Him, and there is nothing we can do to earn His love now that we do know Him. He cannot love us any more than He loved us before we knew Him. When we begin to fully understand God's love for us, we can live righteously as a result of the transformation He made in our lives through our faith in Jesus.

When we comprehend the love of God, we will begin to read the Bible because we want to, not because we are seeking God's approval. We will pray because we want to know Him more, not because we think it will elevate us in the eyes of God. We will give because we want to be generous with people as God has been generous with us. And we will go to church, not to achieve a spiritual merit badge, but so we can fellowship with like-minded believers and worship God from our hearts.

Face of Freedom

A stinging accusation made by those who do not follow Christ against Christians is that most Christians are hypocrites. Most Christians bristle at this accusation. We do not believe we are hypocrites. But I'm sure the Pharisees, in the first century, bristled when Jesus accused them of living hypocritical lives (Matthew 23:27-28). It is important for us to assess ourselves to see if there is any truth in the accusation.

So what is a hypocrite? Jesus took a common word from first century language and infused it with new meaning. The word "hypocrite" was a theatrical term in the New Testament era used to describe actors who covered their faces with masks so the audience would not see the person behind the mask. The actors wanted the audience to only see the characters they were portraying. If the actors could accomplish this, they were viewed as excellent hypocrites.

Jesus said the Pharisees were excellent hypocrites because they were showing a character for their audience, but it was not reflective of what was truly going on in their lives. Jesus cites a verse from the prophet Isaiah and applies it to the Pharisees, "Woe to you, scribes and Pharisees, hypocrites! For you are like whitewashed tombs, which outwardly appear beautiful, but within are full of dead people's bones and all uncleanliness. So you also outwardly appear righteous to others, but within you're full of hypocrisy and lawlessness" (Matthew 23:27-28).

Jesus' sarcasm would have been obvious to the Pharisees. He was clearly angry with the religious people because they claimed to be one thing when they really were something totally different. The reason Jesus was so angry with the Pharisees was because they officially represented everything that was right about the kingdom of God, but lived in opposition to it. They believed in the Bible. They believed in prayer and fasting. They believed in the resurrection of the dead. They believed in giving to the poor. They believed all the right things. But believing in the right things, and even doing the right things, does not make a person right with God. The Pharisees were interested in others seeing them as righteous, but they were not concerned about developing a relationship with the only One who could truly make them righteous.

None of us want to be known as excellent hypocrites today. But the question must be asked, "Are we putting on a front for people to see which is not reflective of what's going on in our spiritual lives?" If we have been around the church long enough, we know what is expected of us. We know the right words to say. We know how to sing the songs. We know how to act in front of people to make them think we are spiritual. But are we religious actors or is this authentic activity?

It is crucial that we live outwardly in the same manner we are living inwardly. Those who live hypocritical lives will either become extremely prideful and judgmental towards others, following the example of the Pharisees, or they will live empty lives filled with shame and dishonesty. Neither of these extremes is the desire Jesus has for our lives. He wants us to live an abundant life, full of freedom and full of joy (John 10:10).

Fraudulent Freedom

The opposite extreme of legalism is libertinism. Libertinism is the belief that since we can do nothing to maintain our salvation, then it follows, there is nothing we can do to lose our salvation. Those who embrace this belief think they can live their lives any way they wish with total disregard to the express desires of God. The apostle Paul anticipated this rationale. When considering this thought process, Paul's response was, "By no means! How can we who died to sin still live in it?" (Romans 6:2). When talking to the Galatians concerning this topic, he stated, "For you were called to freedom, brothers. Only do not use your freedom as an opportunity for the flesh, but through love serve one another. For the whole law is fulfilled in one word: "you shall love your neighbor as yourself." (Romans 5:13-14)

Paul left no room for the idea that we could live ungrateful lives and ignore the desires of the One who loved us so much that He provided a way for our freedom. To live in libertinism is like spitting in the face of someone who just paid our bail to free us from a jail cell. God does not desire for us to work for our salvation, but common decency would say we should be appreciative of the sacrifice He made so we could be free. It only makes sense we would use the freedom we have achieved to honor God and to help others who are in captivity to find their freedom as well. To live unrighteous lives, while declaring ourselves righteous before humanity, works against the very purposes of God and His desire to see the whole world set free through the power of Jesus Christ.

Discovering Balance

So, how do we find a balance between legalism and libertinism which will lead us to victorious Christian living, rather than living as hypocrites? Fortunately, we are not left to try to discover this on our own. The apostle Paul gives us guidance through his conversation with the Galatians. He states, "But I say, walk by the Spirit, and you will not gratify the desires of the flesh. For the desires of the flesh are against the spirit, and the desires of the spirit are against the flesh, for these are opposed to each other, to keep you from doing the things you want to do. But if you are led by the Spirit, you are not under the law" Galatians 5:16-18.

The secret to living a victorious Christian life is to learn to listen to the Holy Spirit and respond to Him as He guides and directs our lives. The Holy Spirit will never ask us to do something that is displeasing to the Father. The Holy Spirit will always help us to see life events the way God sees them. The Holy Spirit will encourage us to respond to situations as the Father would have us respond to those situations. The Holy Spirit will also help us to avoid situations and activities that would bring displeasure to the heart of God. If we will listen to the Spirit and respond as He directs, we will have the fruit of the Spirit in our lives as naturally as an apple tree produces apples and a grapevine produces grapes. We will not have to try to have love, joy, peace, patience, kindness, goodness, faithfulness, gentleness, and self-control if we are walking according to the Holy Spirit (Galatians 5:22).

It is not beyond reason, from time to time, a follower of Jesus will find themselves tripped up spiritually. Sin should not be a natural part of the Christian's life, but as long as we struggle with the temptations that the world places in front of us, there will be times when well-meaning Christians yield to temptation and find themselves spiritually distraught.

Paul anticipated Christians would fall into sin on occasion. While writing to the Galatians on the subject of freedom in Christ, he provided wise counsel on how to assist those who find themselves ensnared by sin. Paul did not criticize these individuals for their missteps, but rather, he devised a plan that would offer hope, and restore them to spiritual health.

Paul addresses his instructions concerning spiritual restoration to the spiritually strong in the church. He says those who are living in righteousness should offer a helping hand to the person caught in sin. Paul's instructions are designed to encourage restoration within the protection of community (Galatians 6:1). It's easy to ridicule an individual who has claimed to live a godly life and then is caught in the trap of sin. We may wonder if they ever were truly godly people. The cruelest individual might say they are just getting what they deserve for living disobedient lives and they should suffer the consequences of their sin.

As I write this page, a very prominent conservative pastor has just resigned his large church after having been charged with possession of illegal drugs. I must admit, when I first heard the news, I was shocked. I quickly became judgmental. I wondered if his strong ultraconservative proclamations over the years were a cover up for activities he had been involved in. But then the Holy Spirit convicted me and told me it was not my place to condemn this individual. As a fellow brother who is currently doing okay in his spiritual life, it was my responsibility to pray for my fallen brother and to attempt to lift him up so he can one day be standing in confidence, proclaiming a testimony concerning the healing, merciful, and gracious God who we both serve. God reminded me the same thing Paul reminded the Galatians, don't be arrogant because I might be the next to fall into sin and need help to find forgiveness and freedom.

Paul indicates it is my responsibility to treat the fallen person the same way I would want to be treated if I had been the person who fell. Paul tells us when we do this, we have fulfilled the law of Christ (Galatians 6:2).

Paul concludes his message to the Galatians concerning the freedom that can be found through faith by reminding us what we sow is what we reap. If we sow to our flesh, we will reap the destruction of the flesh. If we sow to the Spirit, we will reap spiritual rewards. Paul leaves little room for a fleshly Christian.

Paul presents a clear distinction between those who live without Christ and those who live with Christ. Those who live without Christ will be characterized by impurity, hatred, jealousy, selfish ambition, and drunkenness. This is a natural outcome of a fleshly person (Galatians 5:19-21). None of these things should be common in the life of a Christian because we live according to a different standard. Our behavior should reflect our relationship with Jesus. Paul proclaims this results in love, joy, peace, goodness, and self-control among other characteristics (Galatians 5:23). The world will never respond to the gospel if the message does not make a difference in the lives of those who claim that they have been affected by it.

Conclusion

If modern Christians truly desire to reach the whole world with the gospel so that people will experience the freedom which is available through Jesus Christ, they must resist the temptation to impose legalistic standards which are impossible to live up to on those who attend our churches. At best, the legalistic rules present a false sense of holiness. At worst, they display an arrogance reminiscent of the Pharisees who Jesus justly rebuked. Legalistic rules are meaningless in regard to enhancing spiritual vitality.

Modern Christians must take off the mask of hypocrisy and live transparent lives. This will sometimes reveal messiness that can only be cleaned up through on-going submission to Jesus Christ. Modern Christians must also put off fleshly living which disregards the supreme sacrifice made by Jesus. This can only be accomplished through a humble life as we walk according to the Holy Spirit. When we accomplish these things, we will see vitality in our lives and the kingdom of God will be expanded in the earth.

Study Guide Questions

1. What is the opinion of Evangelical Christians by the average non-believer?

2. What is the key to changing the non-believer's view of Evangelical Christians?

3. What are the two basic principles of the gospel?

4. How does a Christian "stay saved"?

5. What is "legalism"?

6. How do people's relationship with their parents impact their belief system regarding God?

7. How did Jesus change the way the word "hypocrite" is used?

8. What is "libertinism"?

9. What is the secret to finding balance between legalism and libertinism?

10. How should a strong Christian respond to a believer who has become entrapped in sin?

UNIT TWO

ENHANCING YOUR PERSONAL RELATIONSHIP WITH GOD

SIX

SPIRITUAL FORMATION THROUGH HEARING GOD'S VOICE

The idea that God speaks is problematic for some people. There is a segment of the Christian community who believe God stopped talking when the New Testament was complete. Many non-believers ridicule Christians who say they hear God speak to them. As I write, a controversy is brewing in the nation because a television talk show host cruelly ridiculed the Vice President of the United States because he said he hears God speak to him. She stated it was okay for us to talk to God, indicating it really is not much more than us talking to ourselves, but she said it was troubling when somebody says they hear God talk back to them. She suggested anyone who hears God's voice is mentally ill. Since her ill-fated comment, she privately apologized to the Vice President for her rudeness, but has yet to recant her words publicly.

Many Christians who believe God still speaks do not attempt to hear His voice nor do they believe they will ever hear Him speak to them. A recent Pew Research poll indicates that 75% of Christians report they talk to God, but only 28% say God talks to them. Part of the reason for this discrepancy is a misunderstanding of what it means to hear God's voice and an unrealistic expectation of what His voice sounds like. In this chapter, I will explore what the Bible says concerning the way God speaks to humans and provide examples of how God has chosen to speak in the past. From there we will be better prepared to hear Him today.

Understanding How You Hear

God does not talk to everyone in the same way. God has wired us different from one another. Some people have been wired to process communication primarily through our emotions. Other individuals tend to process primarily through their analytical abilities. The way God wired us sets up a level of expectation regarding how God talks and our receptivity to it.

I will always remember the day my daughter came home from a series of religious gatherings at her university. She walked into the dining room area of our home. She looked very serious. She asked me, "What's wrong with me?" She told me she had attended each of the chapel services and was open to the move of God. She stated all the people she sat near were talking about hearing God, and feeling His presence. She told me she had not heard God or felt Him during the entire week, no matter how hard she tried. She repeated her question, "What is wrong with me?"

I assured her there was nothing wrong with her. I explained we all respond to God differently. My daughter is a lot like me. We are both analytical by nature. Analytics tend to process first cognitively. We hear things, think about things, and in time we are moved to do something about what we have heard based on the rationality of the message we have heard. People who process through their emotions tend to feel things and sense things and eventually act on what they have experienced. It is important to realize one of these is not good and the other bad. They are just different. Churches must make opportunities for both the emotional worshiper and the cognitive worshiper. If a church only makes room for one type of person, it is likely they are excluding a large portion of the population. God created the affective and the analytical person and desires both to be a part of His kingdom and accomplish His purposes through their lives.

Understand How God Talks

The stories found in Scripture reveal a variety of ways God talked to people. Few will hear God in all the ways God used, but everyone can hear Him in some manner. The list which will follow is not exhaustive, but every way addressed was used by God with at least one person in the Bible.

When I teach about this subject, I love to begin by showing a picture of a donkey. The picture always gets the attention of the class. Most who have a background in the Bible know I am drawing their attention to the story of Balaam's donkey. In the story, Balaam wouldn't listen to God, so God spoke to Balaam's donkey who was willing to listen to God and obey. I always state if God could speak to a donkey, He can certainly talk to us.

Let's look at some ways God has spoken in history.

A Broadcasted Voice

God spoke occasionally in a loud-broadcasted voice. God spoke to Jesus in this manner. The Father spoke from heaven and the crowds heard it (John 12:28-29). Jesus had this experience of hearing an audible booming voice from the Father on other occasions. (See Mark 9:7; Luke 3:14-22.)

If you ask the average person how they think God sounds when He talks, many of them would tell you they believe He always speaks in a booming voice. Perhaps they get this idea from watching too many movies. But if you ask the same people how many of them have heard a booming voice from God, very few will tell you they have heard a loud voice from heaven. As a result, they believe they have never heard from God.

Why do so few people hear a booming voice? I have a theory. Perhaps it is because they don't need to hear God in this fashion. Think about the reason Jesus may have needed to hear God's booming voice. First, we must keep in mind Jesus was not only fully God, but He was fully human while on earth. As a human, Jesus felt everything we feel. He would have felt loneliness, pain, and heartbreak. Now think about Jesus in the garden of Gethsemane. He left His disciples after asking them to pray for Him and went deeper into the Garden to pray. We hear a portion of Jesus' prayer recorded in the Gospel of Luke. Jesus knelt down and prayed these words, "Father, if you're willing, remove this cup from me. Nevertheless, not my will, but yours, be done" (Luke 22:42). If we continue to read Luke's account, we will see Jesus was in agony to the point where He sweat "like great drops of blood" were falling on the ground. Jesus was willing, but not desirous, to go to the cross. I wonder if Jesus, who was fully aware of the story of Abraham and Isaac on Mt Moriah, anticipated the Father would at the last moment provide a substitute to take His place as well. Could this have been the removal of the cup Jesus requested?

So, what was it that kept Jesus on the path of obedience at this trying time in His life? I'm sure there were a lot of factors, but one of the things that kept Jesus faithful to accomplish His assigned task was the numerous occasions He had heard a booming voice from heaven identifying Him as the son of God. He was the promised Messiah who alone could accomplish the task of paying the price for the sins of the world. Jesus could not deny who He was or what His task was because He had heard an undeniable proclamation from heaven with His own earthly ears.

One reason God restricts His booming audible voice is most people will never face anything in their lives which will require that kind of confirmation. I would suggest those individuals who do hear a booming voice from heaven probably do not need the voice at the moment they hear it. It will be at a future time when they face extreme challenges and desire to walk away that the booming voice they heard will keep them solidly planted because they know who they are and they know the task to which they were called.

A Gentle Whisper

Another way God talks is through a whisper. A biblical example of God whispering to someone is recorded in the book of First Kings. The prophet Elijah had just run from the threat of persecution from Jezebel. God asked him why he was hiding in a cave. God told him to stand on the mountain and listen for His specific word. Elijah anticipated God would speak in a dramatic way. But God chose to speak in a low whisper (1 Kings 19:12).

Many more people will identify with the experience of Elijah than they will with the experience of Jesus. It is common to hear people share of times when they heard an audible voice which was very quiet. I personally have never heard the loud booming voice of God, but I have heard the low whisper on a few occasions. The first time I remember hearing God's whisper was in the fall of 1974. I had started my studies at a Christian University, majoring in psychology. I had really become intrigued with the idea of spending my life counseling those with psychological needs.

My vocational direction changed in a little prayer chapel in the center of campus. In a dimly lit room, I knelt alone. I had not entered the room anticipating anything special other than an intimate time with Jesus. But during that time of prayer, I heard an audible whisper directing me to pursue vocational ministry. I didn't get the indication I had to forgo my psychological studies, so I continued those. I added a major that would equip me to pursue vocational ministry. God's hushed voice, over 40 years ago, has guided me through many avenues of vocational ministry keeping me focused on accomplishing God's purpose for my life. Much like the undeniable booming voice of God, the gentile whisper is an anchor to keep us where God wants us to be and provides confidence we are in His will.

Impressions

God also speaks to us through impressions. An impression is a feeling we get that directs us to do something. It is more than likely if you accepted Jesus as your Savior, you came to that decision because the Holy Spirit spoke to you through an impression. Jesus explains it this way; "Behold, I stand at the door and knock. If anyone hears my voice and opens the door, I will come in to him and eat with him, and he with me" (Revelation 3:20).

Impressions may be one of the most common ways God speaks to people. Often we miss hearing God because we do not equate impressions with God's voice. As a result, often we brush aside the impression and fail to respond to God's desires. God speaks to me through impressions regularly. It's not uncommon for me to be walking down a hallway at our university and feel God impress me to encourage a student. When I recognize God speaking to me, I will go to the person, speak to them, and offer encouragement. In many cases, the person will say they needed the encouragement I had given to them. God will also communicate with me through impression when I am counseling someone. Often an individual will come into my office and start talking about some mundane topic. As I listen, the Holy Spirit will impress me to ask a question which is somewhat off-topic, but in many cases, it will be the key that unlocks the heart of the individual. The individual will begin to pour out his or her heart and we will begin to talk about what is actually troubling them.

Be aware of and sensitive to the impressions you receive, and assess them to see if they are from God. Questions you may wish to ask include, "Do I have peace in my heart to follow the impression, even if I may be scared?" "Is the action something that will encourage and build up the person I am approaching?" "How does the person respond when I follow through on the impression?" The more we step out in obedience to impressions, the easier it will be to determine God's voice in this important fashion.

If you determine the impression is from God, take the risk of following through on the impression so you can be used of God. Impressions will not necessarily direct you to a face-to-face ministry encounter. Sometimes, we are impressed to pray for people who are distant from us. I may feel impressed to pray for my daughter who lives 500 miles away because God knows she needs spiritual encouragement at that moment. Perhaps God will wake you up in the night so you will pray for a missionary in another part of the world, or a friend from your past. Please do not ignore impressions. It could very well be God speaking to you.

Revelation

Another way God talks to us is through revelation. The Bible teaches that no one can have faith in Jesus's death and resurrection without God's revelation. The apostle Paul, writing to the Corinthians, explained it this way, "'No eye has seen, nor ear heard, nor the heart of man imagined, what God has prepared for those who love him'—these things God has revealed to us through the Spirit. For the Spirit searches everything, even the depths of God." (1 Corinthians 2:9-10). Paul goes on to say, "The natural person does not accept the things of the Spirit of God, for they are folly to him, and he is not able to understand them because they are spiritually discerned" (1 Corinthians 2:14).

So how does revelation work? Some people might use the word illumination rather than revelation, but in either case, it is bringing to light or unveiling a truth that already exists, but has been hidden from the mind of the person. Revelation can occur in a variety of different ways, but in any of these ways, it results in an "a-ha" moment. It could occur while you are reading the Bible. Most Christian have had the experience of reading a passage of Scripture and suddenly a verse will jump out at them and take on special meaning for the moment. They will see the passage in a new light and provide opportunity for direct application to our lives.

God has revealed himself to me through music on occasion. Much like when we read the Bible, we will hear a lyric that speaks to us in an unnatural way. One day, God gave me a revelation while I was driving. A song came on the radio. As I listened to the words of the song, it reminded me of the sacrifices made by the President of the University where I serve. His sacrifices often go unnoticed. After listening to the words of the song, I saw his ministry in a new light. I felt impressed to send him a note thanking him for what he does. In that case, a revelation led to an impression, which led to ministry, which hopefully was received as a word from God to him. Revelation is not limited to time spent reading the Bible or listening to Christian music. Revelation can happen while listening to a sermon, reading a piece of fiction, or looking at art. The avenues used by God to reveal himself are limitless.

Dreams and Visions

God also speaks through dreams and visions. I must confess, I have never had a vision, and the way that I process life, visions seem a little bit spooky. But my mother is a person who fully embraces visions and can tell you how God has directed her through visions. But it really doesn't matter what I think about visions, or even what my mother thinks about them. Visions are one of the most common ways God spoke to people throughout the Bible. The Bible proclaims visions are a primary way He will communicate with His people in the last days. Luke quotes the prophet Joel stating, "And in the last days it shall be, God declares, that I will pour out my Spirit on all flesh, and your sons and your daughters shall prophesy, and your young men shall see visions, and your old men shall dream dreams; even on my male servants and female servants in those days I will pour out my Spirit, and they shall prophesy" (Acts 2:17-18).

Some of the most notable visions/dreams in Scripture include Pharaoh's dream of fat and skinny cows (Genesis 41:1-36); Nebuchadnezzar's vision of the statue (Daniel 2:1-45); Ezekiel's vision of a field of dry bones (Ezekiel 37:1-14); Cornelius' vision concerning the apostle Paul (Acts 10:1-8); Peter's vision of unclean animals (Acts 10:9-16); and of course, the visions in the Revelation recorded by John.

Each semester I ask my students to share stories of visions and dreams they have experienced. Probably the most compelling stories came from a young man who approached me after class one day. He was excited I had endorsed visions and dreams as a way God speaks. He began to tell me about numerous times God had given him a dream, and just a few days after the dream, the very things that occurred in the dream occurred in his life. Then he shared a dream he had the night before. I did not attempt to interpret his dream. I simply listened to him. About a week later, the student came up to me after class with excitement in his eyes and in his voice. He excitedly told me about an event that had occurred the day before which was nearly identical to the story he had told me the previous week. He shared his excitement of being able to respond to the person in need because God had already shown him what to say during the dream. I rejoiced with him and encouraged him to continue dreaming dreams and trusting God.

Inspired Thought

God spoke to people in the Bible through inspired thought. Often we do not consider our cognitive processes as a means by which God communicates with us. One of the most important communications of God to humanity was made through a cognitive process. Acts 15 records the events of the Jerusalem Council that occurred in 50 A.D. At this official gathering, a controversy was coming to a head.

Standing on one side of an issue were the Judaizers, who argued a person could not accept Jesus as their Savior until they had first become a Jew. Their rationale was that in the Old Testament period, a Gentile could only become a follower of God if they would submit to all the rules of Judaism. This included requiring all males to submit to circumcision. If a person was willing to live like a Jew, they could worship the God of the Jews.

On the other side of the issue were people who believed like the apostles Peter and Paul. During the apostles' ministry to the Gentiles, they had witnessed uncircumcised people not only finding Jesus as their Lord and Savior, but they were also baptized in the Holy Spirit with the evidence of speaking in tongues. (See Acts 15:7-18.) They argued that if God was okay with saving people and baptizing them in the Spirit before they converted to Judaism, they should not require people to adopt Jewish customs in order to follow Jesus.

After the arguments went back-and-forth, a decision was made that would change the face of Christianity forever. This decision was not a result of a vision, or prophecy, or revelation, but it was made through a thoughtful process directed by the Holy Spirit. After careful consideration, James, speaking on behalf of the leaders at the Jerusalem Council, declared, "Therefore my judgment is that we should not trouble those of the Gentiles who turned to God, but should write to them to abstain from the things polluted by idols, and from sexual immorality, and from what has been strangled, and from blood" (Acts 15:19-20). These words have allowed multitudes of non-Jews to be able to access the kingdom of God without having to live in a manner designed to show people their need for God.

There are many times God guides our minds through deliberation to arrive at decisions which are God's will. Often, we do not recognize it is the voice of God until we look back and see the decision we made was beneficial to the kingdom of God. Hearing God through this means is predicated on an individual carefully considering all the facts and asking God to give wisdom as He promised. James tells us, "If any of you lacks wisdom, let him ask of God, who gives generously to all without reproach, and it will be given to him" (James 1:5). I would encourage you to not overlook this very important means of hearing from God.

The Bible

The final biblical example of God speaking to humans that we will explore is the one probably used most often by all segments of the Christian Church. This means of communication is the Bible. We will spend an entire chapter on the importance of reading the Bible and studying it for our spiritual development, so I will limit myself to saying that God carefully designed the Scriptures to contain the essence of His heart, His will, and His emotions toward humanity. By studying the Bible, we can hear God speak to us in an unquestionable fashion as He tells us His priorities for our lives and for the world we live in.

No one valued God's voice through Scripture more than Jesus. He used what He heard to confront Satan (Matthew 4:1-11); to combat the religious leaders (Luke 11:37-54); to teach His disciples (Matthew 24:1-51); and to gain personal direction (Luke 22:37). As a Jewish man, Jesus would have known the Scriptures of His time thoroughly. His perfect life indicates He took God's voice expressed through the prophets and the Law to heart.

If the Bible doesn't address every issue people face in a specific manner, it does provide principles that can be applied to every aspect of our lives. The Bible may not talk specifically about the use of illegal drugs, but it provides a principle concerning the lack of wisdom associated with not having full control of one's behavior. We may not find a specific passage about transgender individuals, but the Bible clearly teaches that God knew what He was doing when He assigned our sex at birth and we should trust God with the design of our lives. These are just a couple examples of how biblical principles can be applied to situations that were not in existence in the first century. God continues to speak to us through the Bible. I encourage you to make Bible reading a regular part of your spiritual development.

Hearing God with Confidence

God desires to speak to people. It is up to them to prepare themselves to hear Him when He speaks. In the preparation process, it is important for believers to discern if what we are hearing is actually from God or simply a personal desire they attribute to God. Let's examine principles that will help us to have confidence in our communication with God.

Prepare to Hear God

We must truly believe God will talk to us if we are going to hear Him. If you do not believe God will talk to you, there is very little chance you will hear His voice. The Bible asserts that God intends to speak to us forever. The Psalmist proclaims, "He will guide us forever" Psalm 48:14.

Next, we need to prepare our hearts to hear God's voice. Jesus told a parable of the soils. He said the "seed" was the word of God. The sower went about casting seed upon the ground. Some seed fell on hard soil, and it found no ability to take root. Other seed fell on the ground that was a little looser. The seed began to take root. It shot up quickly, but when the sun hit it, the roots were not strong enough to sustain its growth. It withered and died. A third type of soil was much better than the first two. The seed took root and grew up, but weeds were allowed to grow alongside the good seed. The weeds ended up choking out the fruit of the good seed. Jesus explains this represents people who allow the cares of life to choke out their spiritual vitality. But then Jesus tells of a fourth type of soil. He calls it the good soil. The good soil received the seed. The seed took the nutrients from the ground, combined with the water from the clouds and the warmth from the sun and produced fruit. The good soil allowed the full potential of the seed to come forth. Jesus explained this parable to His disciples. He told them that the good soil is, "Those who, hearing the word, hold it fast in an honest and good heart, and bear fruit with patience" (Luke 8:15).

If we want to hear from God on a regular basis, we must prepare our hearts to receive it. There really is little sense in God speaking to us if we are unwilling to hear His instructions, or to apply them to our lives. Ask parents how they feel when they talk to their child and the child either won't listen, or they listen and then quickly forget, or worse yet, they act in a rebellious fashion. Many parents just give up. But how grateful are parents who shares information with their children and they listen and apply it to their lives!

A third principle for hearing God is to expect His voice. The writer of Proverbs instructs, "Hear instruction and be wise, and do not neglect it. Blessed is the one who listens to me, watching daily at my gates, waiting beside my doors. For whoever finds me finds life and obtains favor from the Lord, but he who fails to find me injures himself; all who hate me love death" (Proverbs 8:33-36). In this passage, the author is speaking about wisdom specifically, but it is wisdom that comes from God. The question that I must ask myself is whether or not I anticipate God is going to speak to me each day. Do I stand waiting with expectation of God speaking to me every day, or am I surprised when He does?

Right now there are many types of waves whipping past you that you do not see. There are television waves. There are radio waves. There are internet waves. There are telephone waves. And the list could go on. You really don't know they are there unless you have a receiver designed to capture the waves and translate them to produce their intended purpose. So if you have a radio with you right now, and you turned it on, you would be able to prove the existence of radio waves by the sound emitted from the radio's speakers. If you have a telephone, you can prove whether or not there are "telephone" waves in the room by making a call. Without those devices, with their appropriate antennas, you could never benefit from the vast amount of information swirling around you at this very moment.

In a similar fashion, God is speaking to us all the time. You and I will never know if He is communicating with us, if we do not have our antennas up and our equipment tuned to His frequency. If we want to hear from God on a regular basis, we must expect that He will speak and prepare ourselves to receive what He has to say. It's not that God is not talking, it's generally that we don't listen because we don't expect Him to say anything to us.

Another principle for hearing God is to be willing to obey Him when He speaks to us. God is not in the business of repeatedly telling us to do something and having us ignore Him. If we say He is the Lord of our lives, we are saying that He has the authority to tell us what to do. James states,

> But be doers of the word, and not hearers only, deceiving yourselves. For if anyone is a hearer of the word and not a doer, he is like a man who looks intently at his natural face in a mirror. For he looks at himself and goes away and at once forgets what he was like. But the one who looks into the perfect law, the law of liberty, and perseveres, being no hearer who forgets but a doer who acts, he will be blessed in his doing (James 1:22-25).

The best way to hear more from God is to obey what we've already heard from Him. God is taking us on a path of spiritual growth. As we have seen, each segment of the trip requires us to be transformed in various aspects of our lives. This transformation occurs when we hear God's voice, identify areas holding us back in our development, and act on God's instructions to get victory in those aspects of our lives. Often we want to hear more from God before we are willing to do the things He has already told us to do. He knows the steps required to arrive where He wants us. We must be patient as God shapes our lives.

A final principle I will address is the importance of humility. The Psalmist states, "He leads the humble in what is right, and teaches the humble his way. All the paths of the LORD are steadfast love and faithfulness, for those who keep his covenant and his testimonies" (Psalm 25:9-10).

Some people view humility as a negative word. They view it as a put down. But humility is not a word that implies I should feel less about myself than I do, but rather it is to view myself honestly. I can say that I am a great piano player while still acknowledging there are greater piano players. The fact there are greater piano players does not mean my skill as a piano player is diminished. I simply acknowledge others have more developed skills as a piano player than I do at this point. Paul cautions us to not become arrogant, but to see ourselves through the eyes of God's grace. "For by the grace given to me I say to everyone among you not to think of himself more highly than he ought to think, but to think with sober judgment, each according to the measure of faith that God has assigned" (Romans 12:3).

The reason humility is crucial in order for us to hear God is that we need to recognize God is greater than we are, wiser than we are, and more powerful than we are. If we will humble ourselves, and submit ourselves to a greater wisdom and power than is resident within us, we will open ourselves to hearing God and be receptive to the words that He has to say. A proud person is one who thinks they know everything and can be taught nothing. The Bible says God opposes the proud because they refused to recognize who He truly is (James 4:6).

Confirm it is God

So the ultimate question is "How do I know if what I'm hearing is God and not just the pizza that I ate last night?" This is a very important question because the answer to it will keep us from falling into heresy or taking unwise steps in our spiritual walk. So although this is not an exhaustive list, let's look at three guidelines that can be employed to help keep us on the right track.

The first guideline is to ask, "Does what I am hearing match with the clear teaching of Scripture?" There is no authority greater than the word of God. One of the basic tenants of the Protestant belief system is our only authority is the Bible. It is the premise of the Protestant church that God will never violate His word expressed in the Bible.

There are some who will argue that the decision of a community of believers can supersede (or adjust) the truth of Scripture. These individuals will often justify lifestyles and attitudes based on what they want to be true, rather than what the Bible clearly declares. If what you are hearing does not line up with what the Bible teaches, then what you're hearing is not from God. God is not going to tell you to steal, to kill, to have immoral relationships, to do something to hurt others, or to abandon your family. Some will say the Bible is harsh toward some people who practice behaviors such as homosexuality. They would argue we must adapt to modern realities as an act of love and acceptance. Adapting the Scriptures, to justify immoral behavior is not love. Telling people the hard truth is sometimes the greatest form of love (1 Corinthians 5:1-13).

The second guideline is to ask, "Does what I am hearing sound like God?" The Bible teaches we can learn to discern whether the voice we hear is Christ's or if it is someone else's. Jesus said, "My sheep hear my voice, and I know them, and they follow me" (John 10:27). Those who are part of Jesus' flock are able to discern His voice because they know His character. Jesus never condemns those who follow Him. He convicts and corrects His followers, but there is a vast difference between conviction and condemnation. Conviction is designed to turn someone around and set them on the correct path. Condemnation is designed to stomp someone down and keep them in a subservient place. Condemnation is the tool used by Satan to continually keep people feeling defeated. If you are hearing a condemning voice, you can be sure it is not Jesus. Jesus speaks with love, encouragement, guidance, and with the best outcome of His followers in mind. The story of the prodigal son demonstrates the heart and attitude of God. (See Luke 15:11-23.)

The final guideline is to ask, "Is the word confirmed by others?" God does not speak in isolation. If God has truly given you a word, it will be confirmed by someone. Sometimes this confirmation comes before we step out and sometimes it comes after we step out in obedience. I believe we should be cautious when another believer gives us a word from the Lord, but words of confirmation are to be treasured.

It is important for Christians to have a circle of individuals around them who love Jesus deeply and love them fully. If we can have individuals who we trust to share the things we feel God has spoken to us, and we can be assured the individuals we are talking to will give us honest feedback, we will avoid many pitfalls in our lives. It is never wise to go against the wise counsel of godly friends because they often see things to which we are blind. If our friends give us poor advice, God will be faithful to speak to us again in a clearer fashion, but in most cases, if our friends are committed to Jesus and committed to their relationship with us, their words can be trusted.

Conclusion

A person can't read the stories of the Bible and deny God desired to have a relationship with His creation. A key to any relationship is communication. He still wants to talk to us today as much as He ever did. It is up to us to listen for His voice. God takes the initiative in the communication process. Sometimes we miss His overtures toward us because we are not listening for them. We must purposely prepare to hear God's voice daily.

We can know with confidence it is God who is speaking to us. Don't forfeit your opportunity to hear from God because you think He only talks to the super spiritual people. God wants to talk to you as He did to the people in the Bible. The writer of Hebrews reminds us; "Jesus Christ is the same yesterday and today and forever" (Hebrews 13:8). When we anticipate His voice, and obey His words, we will take steps toward God.

Study Guide Questions

1. How do analytic and affective learners hear God's voice differently?

2. List the ways, identified in this chapter, by which God spoke to people during biblical times.

3. List the principles the author suggests will prepare a person to hear God.

4. Why is it important to live obediently if you desire to hear from God on a regular basis?

5. Why is humility a prerequisite for hearing God's voice?

6. What is the difference between conviction and condemnation?

7. Why is it important to have a circle of committed Christian friends when you are attempting to hear God?

SEVEN

SPIRITUAL FORMATION THROUGH PRAYER

The Bible records a myriad of incidences of people praying to God. Some of these prayers are formal, some are made in desperation, and others seem to reflect a level of intimacy often reserved for best friends. In the Scriptures, we find many of these prayers recorded in the book of Psalms, yet the Bible records Jesus' prayers, as well as many of the prayers of the apostle Paul.

As a Christian, you have probably been exhorted to pray on many occasions. Our pastors tell us to pray. Our parents prayed with many of us when we were children. We feel guilty if we don't pray when we eat a meal. If you attend a Christian University, you are challenged to pray often; in class, during chapel, in dorm devotions, and prayer meetings scheduled throughout the week.

So, why do we pray and what does it really accomplish? If God knows everything and is sovereign, why do we need to voice our concerns, provide God guidance as to what He should do regarding our situations, or simply communicate our ideas through prayer?

Why Pray?

As with most spiritual disciplines, prayer is not designed to benefit God, but rather to benefit the individual doing the spiritual activity. The primary purpose of prayer is for the human to take time to hear God's voice to determine His desire concerning the situation and then to come into alignment with God's will and His desired outcome for the situation. As we determine His will in a situation, we then pray not so much that He accomplish the work, but that we will discover what He wants us to do to accomplish what He desires through us.

An example of how this works is when an individual begins praying for a situation, such as praying for those who are trafficked sexually, or people in a particular region of the world, or even for friends we grew up with who desperately need to know about the love of God. Our prayer may start out rather formal in nature, but the more we pray with passion for God to reveal the answer to the situation, we will discover that God will show us the answer.

Do not be surprised when after God shows you the answer, He will request you become actively involved in being a part of the answer to the situation you have been praying about. So, if you desperately pray for the women who are caught in the sex trafficking trade, don't be surprised if you become involved in freeing these women in one manner or another. If you have been praying for a specific region of the world, or a specific people group in that region, do not be surprised if God asks you to go to that part of the world and reveal the love of Christ to those people who you have learned to love through prayer. And do not be surprised if you are praying for friends who have no hope for eternity when God asks you to rekindle relationships and lead those individuals to a new hope only found through a relationship with Jesus Christ.

I discovered this truth personally one day as I was taking a stroll through the community Civic Center in our city. There is a large mural depicting the history of Waxahachie, Texas hanging on a wall of the Center. Half of the mural is done in black and white which depicts our city 100 years ago. The other half of the mural is in color and depicts the city in more recent years. As I stood there looking at the mural, I heard the Holy Spirit speak to my heart. He told me I was focused well on the people I associated with presently, but I had disregarded the people from my past. He quickened my heart to begin to pray for the people I had grown up with who needed a relationship with Him.

I began to pray on a regular basis for my old schoolmates that day, especially those I associated with in my junior high and high school years. As I began to pray for them, I began to wonder what they were doing. I discovered that some of them had become Christians, some had unfortunately passed away, but some were still in need of an encounter with Jesus. God began to ask me to reestablish relationships with many of these people. Through the wonders of social media, I began to have conversations with many of them. I did not preach to them, but simply showed an interest in their lives. I hoped they would feel my love for them. As social media friends, they would also be exposed to my heart as they read my posts, and eavesdropped on my conversations with fellow Christians.

For most of my adult life, I ignored any invitation to reunions that were held for my class. When I went back to my home town to visit family, I seldom showed any interest in what my old classmates were doing. When I began to pray for them, and began to feel God's love for them, it birthed something in me that made me want to get together with them. I didn't want to meet with them as an evangelism opportunity, but to love them as Christ would love them. Now each year when I return home, it becomes a highlight of my trip to eat a hamburger with a group of old friends.

Obviously, it is my desire to see each one of them in heaven, but that will ultimately be a decision between them and God. My job was to align myself with God's purposes and to show them His love through my relationship with them and take opportunities presented to me to help them understand the grace and mercy of God.

What Does It Mean to Pray in Jesus' Name?

The Bible tells us to pray in the name of Jesus. Some people have taken this to mean if they end their prayer by saying "I ask this in the name of Jesus," they will get whatever they prayed for. This manner of thinking is not far removed from the child-like thinking that occurs in malls each Christmas. Children climb on Santa Claus' knee and read the list of gifts they prepared to share with him. They get off Santa's lap fully expecting to get everything they just asked for only to be disappointed on Christmas morning when many of the items he promised are not under the tree. They believed the myth that if they claim it, they can have it because the powerful Claus must provide their wishes. Much like the disappointment misguided children face on Christmas morning, Christians who pray with an expectation that they will get whatever they want because they add "in the name of Jesus" to the end of their spiritual wish list will be disappointed on a regular basis.

This is not to say God does not answer our prayers. What we must understand is to pray in the name of Jesus requires us to determine what Jesus desires and then to pray according to His desires. When we do that we can be guaranteed our prayers will be answered according to His will and not according to our will.

So, how can you explain what it means to pray in the name of Jesus? The best way to illustrate this concept is by thinking of an ambassador who goes to another country to represent his homeland. When an ambassador from the United States goes to China, the ambassador has the right to speak to the Chinese government with the full authority of the United States backing each word he/she communicates. But an ambassador cannot speak any words he/she desires to speak. Ambassadors can only speak the words they have been authorized to use from the ultimate power of the United States; the President. So, when the ambassador speaks, he/she is speaking as if the President of the United States was present and speaking those very words. When an ambassador speaks outside of the authority given to him/her by the president of United States, the ambassador can cause confusion, and ultimately can cause great damage.

The same is true for Christians who pray without the authority of Jesus. If Christians make assertions which have not been initiated by the Holy Spirit, it will lead to disappointment. If Christians guarantee a person will be healed as a result of prayer without confirming it is God's will, and that person is not healed, it leads to confusion. Many well-meaning Christians have caused people to question God because their prayers were not answered in the manner promised by well-meaning Christians who overstepped their authority. On the flipside, if we determine what God desires, and we pray according to what God has said, the confidence level of both the person praying and the person prayed for will be heightened as they see God work in their lives.

In January 2011, I was diagnosed with cancer. As with anybody who has been given a diagnosis of cancer, I was numb. I knew God would take care of me in one fashion or another. As a Christian who had preached the gospel all his adult life, I was convinced if the cancer lead to my death I was going to heaven. But that still did not take away a series of questions I had about my short-term and long-term future. Many of the students on the college campus where I teach began to pray demanding God to heal me. I appreciated the zeal, but I knew passion and volume was not going to force God to intervene in my situation. Some may say that is a lack of faith, but I would rather view it as a realistic assessment of the situation.

There were at least three individuals on the University's campus that took the time to hear God and then share with me what God said to them. One student left a note on my door anonymously that simply said, "This will not end in death." Less than an hour later, I was walking down the hall and a student I had never met before asked me if I was Dr. Hayes. When I told him I was, he said God had spoken to him and said to tell me, "This will not end in death." I asked him if he had left a note on my door and he told me he hadn't. This made me a bit curious. Later that week, a faculty member came to me and told me she had been on her knees crying out to God on my behalf when God stopped her and said, "Why are you so sad? This will not end in death."

Three times words came to me that said the cancer I had would not result in my death. I did not know how God was going to take care of my situation, but I had confidence I would live. My faith was not because of wishful thinking, nor because I had commanded God to heal me, but because it was God's will to not allow the cancer to take my life.

Just four months earlier, one of my close friends who loved and served God had died as a result of the same type of cancer. We can argue all day about the fairness of God, or about the reasons why one person gets healed and another person doesn't get healed, but if I believe God is truly good, and He does not hold back His blessings to those He loves, then I must believe there is a greater purpose behind His decision to heal one person and not another. As difficult as this is to accept from a human standpoint, it's crucial for me to embrace God's love and His goodness.

Why Don't I Always Get What I Desire?

One of the dangers involved in prayer is we can attempt to usurp God's authority. Some people come to believe we have the power to tell God what to do. They believe they have more wisdom than the Creator of the universe. They look at situations, assess them from their vantage point though their filters, and demand God do things as they desire. When people tell God how to do His job at best their solutions are shortsighted, self-centered, and only minimally likely to result in benefits for the entirety of the kingdom of God. It's essential when people pray that they have a level of humility that displays their understanding that it is not their will, but His will which must be done.

This is not to say we don't have the privilege to ask God for anything we want in prayer because we do. I have two children that I love very deeply. When they were small, they could ask me for anything they wanted. As a five-year-old, my son could look into my eyes, and with the deepest sincerity, ask me for candy and a toy, for a knife and a semiautomatic weapon, for a car and a motorcycle. When he was done with his list, he might have told me that he loved me. He may have even declared he had asked for all of these things in the name of his father.

Now if my son had made these requests (which he didn't), there would have been absolutely nothing wrong with him doing so. As his father, it was my responsibility to listen to the request. But as his father, it was not my responsibility to give him everything he asked for. Rather, my responsibility as his father was to assess what would be best for him and to give him those things which would be useful and beneficial to him. It would also be my responsibility to withhold from him those things that could be harmful to him. Even though he might want a vehicle to drive at five years old, or a weapon to brandish, as his father who loved him deeply, it would be irresponsible for me to give him those items no matter how much he cried for them. He wasn't ready for them. He was not equipped to use them. They would do harm to him and others. So, as a good father, I would listen to his requests, I would sort out the beneficial from the harmful, and I would grant him the things best for him.

If my son fully understood my love for him and my superior knowledge, he would not get angry with me because I didn't give him everything on his list. Instead, he would rejoice in the gifts I did give him and trust that his father would not withhold any good thing from him. As a good father, I would use my wisdom to protect him from himself when his desires were out of line with what was best for him.

Christians have the privilege to ask for anything when they pray, but they must trust God, who loves them deeply, to give them what is best for them and say "No" to those things that do not align with His purposes or their best interest.

How Do You Sound to God?

The bottom line assumption required for Christians when they pray is that God is truly good. If Christians believe God is good, He loves them, and He withholds no good thing from them, then they will view prayer from a very positive and productive vantage point. They will take the time to attempt to determine what God's will is for their situation and pray according to His will. They will feel free to pour out their hearts passionately expressing their understanding of the situation and their desires for the situation, but be content with His responses to those prayers. Christians who understand God is good will not walk away from prayer despondent or frustrated when they don't get what they have requested. They will trust Him to make the right decision for their lives.

In some Christian communities, you will hear people talk about praying with authority. The Bible is clear the Christian does have authority, but that authority is over darkness not over the God of the universe. It is never appropriate to demand God give you what you desire. It is equally inappropriate to use prayer as a bargaining tool where we tell God we will do something, if He does something in return. It is also unsuitable for us to arrogantly demand God do something because His Word promises He will do it. If God has promised He will do something, He will do it without us having a condescending attitude toward Him. As stated before, Christians have a right to ask their Father for anything, but asking is much different than commanding God to answer their prayers. God is faithful to accomplish what He has promised, in His time, and in His way.

The book of Job provides a great example of God doing things in His time, and in His way. After Job had all he seemed to be able to take, he began to lash out at God. But when Job was finished venting, God put him in his place by asking him a series of questions concerning where he was when God was putting the universe together. God corrected Job by telling Job that when he became God, then he could do things in his timing and in his way.

Be very careful about your tone toward God when you pray. People would never go to their earthly parent who they respect and speak in the same tones often used when individuals make demands on God in prayer. God wants Christians to pray with confidence, but He does not want them to act like spoiled children when they pray.

Keys for Effective Prayer

The point of communication is to be understood. It is important to remove as many barriers to effective communication as possible. It is important to use the best technology and resources available to us when we attempt to communicate with others.

When I travel overseas to preach and teach, there are some assumptions I must make. The first assumption is if I do not know the native language, I will need an interpreter to assist me. The second assumption is if I do not learn a little bit about the culture, it is likely I will unintentionally offend someone in the audience. The third assumption is that my American idioms will not always translate into the language of the country I am visiting. It is even possible the interpreter will not understand what I'm trying to say. When this occurs, it causes confusion for everyone involved.

A few years ago, I was ministering in the Dominican Republic. I speak no Spanish, and my interpreter was an American who had little interest in sports. I was aware baseball was a big deal to the people of the Dominican Republic. In an attempt to build a bridge between me and my audience, I told them how impressed I was with a native son of the island who was playing major league baseball on my favorite team; the Boston Red Sox. I thanked them for loaning "Big Pappi" to the Red Sox organization. My translator looked at me with a quizzical expression on his face as he attempted to translate my words. He asked me to repeat myself. I said "Tell the people, thank you for giving us Big Pappi." He continued to look perplexed. It was clear he didn't have a clue what I was trying to say. I was perplexed because I thought everyone knew who "Big Pappi" was.

The people sensed the tension occurring on the stage. The people in the audience started to shout, in English, "Big Pappi; Big Pappi." They understood what I was trying to say even though my interpreter was at a total loss. I explained to my interpreter that "Big Pappi" was David Ortiz, a famous baseball player from the Dominican Republic. This confusion could have been avoided entirely if I had effectively communicated my intentions to my interpreter before taking the platform.

In the remainder of this chapter, I want to identify some ways to fine tune our communication with God. It is not like God is not going to understand us. He does not need an interpreter, but the Bible reveals conditions and attitudes that help our communication to be more effective with God. The Bible also warns us of conditions and attitudes that put up blockades to our ability to have open and unhindered access to Him through prayer.

Conditions of Successful Prayer

The first condition of successful prayer is humility. Believers must be aware that if a breach exists between them and God, it is their fault. When people are contrite, they take responsibility for their actions.

Your first action when preparing to pray should be to ask God if there is any sin in your life. If you discover sin, it is your responsibility to repent of that sin to clear a path to God. When the sin is removed, you can approach God unashamedly and with integrity.

The people of Israel were known as the people of God. Unfortunately, they were not always good representatives of God. They often neglected His mandates and ignored the prophets who spoke on His behalf. The result of this disregard for God resulted in the nation being overtaken by enemies. When Israel got into trouble, they would cry out to God, and on many occasions, He rescued them.

There came a point in Israel's history when they began to take their chosen status as a ticket to act any way they wished with no expectation of repercussions. They believed it was God's duty to protect them simply because they were Israel. They believed God made His home in the Temple in Jerusalem. They reasoned He would always assist them when they called on Him, regardless of their attitude and behavior. But God had other ideas. It wasn't that He was unwilling to hear them. But He did put a condition upon His willingness to listen to them and to respond.

Second Chronicles 7:14 is a famous passage of Scripture that lays out God's condition for His relationship with the Israelites: "If my people, who are called by my name, will humble themselves and pray and seek my face and turn from their wicked ways, then will I hear from heaven and will forgive their sin and will heal their land."

God still considered Israel His people, but God was not satisfied with the heart condition of the Israelites. They had become arrogant. They no longer honored God, but rather saw Him as someone who was there simply to service their needs. God instructed them to humble themselves. It was vital for the Israelites to recognize the greatness of God and to submit themselves to Him. If they would just humble themselves, God was ready to reestablish a healthy relationship with them.

It naturally follows that if Israel submitted themselves to God, they would honor Him rather than dishonor Him among the nations through living immoral. The people desired that God would save them and restore their land. He was willing to grant Israel's request if they would accept His reasonable conditions.

Today Israel is no longer God's primary vehicle of displaying himself to the nations. This does not mean Israel no longer has any value in the eyes of God, but it does mean the promise given in 2 Chronicles 7:14 has been extended to include the Church. Christians can be equally guilty of viewing God as their personal possession expecting Him to provide a quick fix for their problems, rather than them living humbly before Him. If Christians today wish to have effective prayer lives, they must be contrite people. This act of humility is not intended to belittle individuals, rather it is to exalt God to His rightful place in their sight. Those who fail to recognize the supremacy of God will almost always live in opposition to the righteousness that God desires for His followers. If we will live humble lives, admit our arrogance, and seek to eliminate it, God will hear our requests and respond to them.

The second condition of successful prayer is passion. When we seek God passionately, we are more likely to communicate clearly and reach the heart of God. Passion is not measured in the volume of our voice, but in the longing of our heart. In Jeremiah 29:13, it is written, "You will seek me and find me when you seek me with all your heart."

If you are not passionate about what you are praying for, there is very little reason for God to see the seriousness of your request. I have watched haphazard prayers go up during class time and church services because the person who was praying really had no personal investment in the situation they were praying for. I am not saying this in condemnation. Why should there be passion for somebody we know little about or a situation that doesn't touch our lives? True, we all should be concerned about the general welfare of all humanity, but our prayers take on an added dimension of urgency when the request revolves around someone we love, or a situation that touches us personally. It is important before we pray to learn a little bit about the condition of the person or the seriousness of the situation, and then seek to put ourselves in the shoes of the person for whom we are praying.

This principle hit home for me many years ago. While working in Springfield, Missouri, my office building sat across the street from a hospital complex. Every day during break time, a friend of mine and I walked the blocks around our office building which took us past that hospital. I seldom gave a thought to the individuals suffering in that infirmary; that is until the day one of my children became a resident. I remember how my attitude and perspective changed. Now, as I walked next to the hospital, I would look at the rooms where my child was confined and cry out with passion for God to heal him. No longer was the building just a place that held random people in various states of health. Now it housed my precious child. When I prayed, it was not perfunctory. I knew what I wanted God to do and I single-mindedly expressed my desire to Him.

A third condition for successful prayer is faith. Faith is a crucial part of successful prayer because it demonstrates our trust in the only One who has ultimate control over every situation. Jesus answered many requests while He was on earth. He healed people both physically and spiritually. They believed Jesus was the son of God and He had the capacity to do what they asked Him to do. This does not mean they had no doubt about the outcome. Mary and Martha both questioned Jesus' timing and His ability to heal their brother once he had died. As we saw earlier in this book, we must not have faith in faith, but we must have faith in God. If we ask God for anything, according to His will, we can be assured we will receive what we have asked for. Mark 11:24 states, "Therefore I tell you, whatever you ask for in prayer, believe that you have received it, and it will be yours." The key is knowing the request is God's desire before we utter the prayer. This requires us to spend time listening to God for directions regarding the focus of our prayer.

A fourth condition of successful prayer is righteousness. Righteousness is something all Christians possess. This does not mean we make no wrong choices in our lives. We have been made righteous through the death and resurrection of Jesus Christ. The Bible tells us our own righteousness is like filthy rags (Isaiah 64:6). If left in our unredeemed condition, we would all be eternally lost. But the letter to the Romans teaches us we have been justified. As a result, we have access to God through Jesus Christ. James 5:16 states, "The prayers of the righteous man are powerful and effective."

A fifth condition of successful prayer is obedience. John explains this straight-forward condition. "Dear friends, if our hearts do not condemn us we have confidence before God and receive from Him anything we ask, because we obey His commands and do what pleases Him" (1 John 3:22).

Communication is a two-way street. If prayer is communication with God, we should anticipate He will speak back to us if we are patient enough to listen to Him. Just as we request things from God, He is likely to request things from us. He is never in need of what we have. He does desire that we live in a manner that builds the kingdom of God and enhances our own well-being. We should be prepared to respond positively to these requests if we desire Him to respond positively to our requests. This is not a conditional concept which places God in a box. This is a heart condition that says "I want to honor God, just as God wants to bless me."

What Causes Failure in Prayer

The first condition that causes failure in prayer is disobedience. One of the greatest failures of all time is recorded in the Pentateuch. Moses led the people of Israel victoriously out of Egypt. The people watched God part the Red Sea, so they could pass through on dry ground. As they looked over their shoulders, with the approaching Egyptian army catching up to them, they watched God release the sea which engulfed the Egyptian army allowing Israel to live in freedom.

After only a few weeks, spies were sent into Canaan to scout out the land. They were to determine what it would take to possess the land which God had promised to them many years before. When the 12 spies returned, they reported the land contained vast wealth in terms of resources. But they also reported the challenges of the walled cities and intimidating residents.

When Moses heard the report, he asked for an opinion from the spies as to the viability of conquering Canaan. Two of the spies, Joshua and Caleb, assured Moses and the people the land could be conquered with God's help. They were confident the same God who had delivered them from Egypt could help them to obtain the land He had promised to them. The remaining 10 spies had quite a different story. They drew a picture for the people which struck fear in their hearts. After hearing the spies, the people were not convinced God was powerful enough to overcome the Canaanites. The people refused to trust God.

After the people made their decision to walk in disobedience, God pronounced His judgment upon them. All the adults 20 years and older would die in the desert; only Joshua and Caleb would see the Promised Land. Once the people heard God's sentence upon their lives, they had a change of heart. They decided they did not want to die in the desert, so they pushed towards the Promised Land, this time against God's will, only to be soundly defeated. When they returned, they confronted Moses and asked why God did not fight on their behalf. Moses' response is telling:

But the LORD told me to tell you, "Do not attack, for I am not with you. If you go ahead on your own, you will be crushed by your enemies.' "This is what I told you, but you would not listen. Instead, you again rebelled against the LORD's command and arrogantly went into the hill country to fight. But the Amorites who lived there came out against you like a swarm of bees. They chased and battered you all the way from

Seir to Hormah. Then you returned and wept before the LORD, but he refused to listen (Deuteronomy 1:42 – 45).

People cannot expect God to work on their behalf if they refuse to listen to Him when He gives them instructions. God will not be mocked. If He has clearly told us something and we go against His wishes, we cannot expect Him to try to clean up our messes. This is not to say He will not forgive our sins if we are remorseful, but we will often have to suffer the consequences of our willful disobedience. We cannot use God as a safety valve for the consequences of our arrogance. If we ask God to remove the consequences of direct disobedience to Him, it is only because of His grace and mercy that He will occasionally respond to those requests. He is not obligated to do so.

A second cause for failure in prayer is hidden sin. Hidden sins are offenses against God that the person is well aware of, but masked from others. Hidden sins could range from hatred in one's heart towards another, to sexual sins, to selfish motives. In Psalm 66, the writer rejoices that God is listening to his prayer, but he tells us that God is only listening because he had confessed his hidden sin.

Come and listen, all you who fear God, and I will tell you what he did for me. For I cried out to him for help, praising him as I spoke. If I had not confessed the sin in my heart, the Lord would not have listened. But God did listen! He paid attention to my prayer. Praise God, who did not ignore my prayer or withdraw his unfailing love from me (Psalm 66:16-20).

You can't miss the excitement that oozes out of the Psalmist as he considers the wonder of God's mercy in his life. The exclamation that God listened to him and "paid attention" to his prayer can only be explained by the depth of disappointment he had in himself for carrying around his hidden sins for so long.

Christians cheat themselves out of many of the blessings God intends for them if they harbor secret sin in their lives. But beyond the blessings they miss out on, they miss out on developing an intimate relationship with God. If you happen to be harboring some hidden sin in your life which is keeping you from effective communication with God, you can follow the lead of the Psalmist and confess the sin. Once you do, you can approach God with confidence.

A third cause for failure in prayer is minimizing God. The writer of Proverbs describes God's response to those who view God as incidental to their lives. He states, "Then they will call to me but I will not answer; they will look for me but will not find me, since they hated knowledge and did not choose to fear the Lord. Since they would not accept my advice and spurned my rebuke, they will eat the fruit of their ways and be filled with the fruit of their schemes" (Proverbs 1:28–31).

We live in a day when God has been minimized in the eyes of many in the Western Hemisphere. They may give God lip service, but their lives reveal they have no respect for Him. Is it no wonder that our world is in the condition that it is in today? Many people ask the question, "How can a good God allow so many terrible things to occur?" A better question may be, "Why won't humankind submit themselves to a sovereign God who loves them and has their best interest at heart?" The prayer of the indifferent person will never produce spiritual results for there is no faith associated with their prayers.

A fourth cause for failure in prayer is neglect of mercy. During biblical times, there were no governmental safety nets to protect the welfare of the poor. It was the responsibility of those who had great resources to assist those who had little because of the situations of life that prevented them from caring for themselves. Often we hear these people referred to, in Scripture as "the orphans and the widows." These individuals had no extended family, no land, and little, if any, money. Most of these people were relegated to begging or prostitution to eke out a meager existence.

From the very beginning of God's relationship with the people of Israel, carrying forward to His relationship with Christ followers in His Church, God has declared His greatest desire is for people to love Him and because they love Him, they would love others. Unfortunately, many of the Israelites who had the ability to meet the needs of the poor, failed to reach out and demonstrate God's love to the needy. God's attitude towards those who neglected to show mercy was clear to the Israelites. The writer of Proverbs states, "Whoever shuts their ears to the cry of the poor will also cry out and not be answered" (Proverbs 21:13).

In the politically charged environment that exists in our culture today, it is easy to align ourselves with one political party or the other. If you are a conservative in the United States, it is common to believe the poor should pull themselves up by their bootstraps, get a job, and take care of their own needs. If you are a liberal, it is common to believe the government should take money forcibly from the rich and give it to the poor with no expectation that the poor will ever have a better station in life. In the kingdom of God, neither of these extremes is acceptable. Indeed, the rich should make provision for the poor, but it should be an act of love and generosity, not an act of extortion. Equally, in the kingdom of God, we must not ignore the plight of those who are less fortunate and leave them to fend for themselves with no tools to succeed. To do so jeopardizes our relationship with God who assures us He will not respond when we find ourselves in need. If we wish for God to answer our cries, we must be willing to respond to the cries of the "widows and orphans" in our society.

A fifth cause for failure in prayer is self-indulgence. It is not wrong to present your needs to God and to trust Him to meet your needs. The problem arrives when your motivation is wrong when you pray. If you demand God increase your possessions while others around you are suffering, it is unlikely that God will grant your request. People will point to the prayer of Jabez and argue that it is appropriate to demand that God give you more possessions (1 Chronicles 4:10). It is true that this short prayer received a positive response from God, but it must be remembered that Jabez was not praying for personal accumulation. He was calling on God to help him accomplish the promises of God.

James asks his audience a profound question, "Why do we fight and quarrel among ourselves?" (James 4:1) He answers that arguments come from desires that battle within us. He goes on to say, we desire something we do not have, so we fight to get it. "So you kill. You covet but you cannot get what you want, so you quarrel and fight" (James 4:2a). James explains, "You do not have because you do not ask God" (James 4:2c). But interestingly, James doesn't stop there. He says, "When you ask, you do not receive, because you ask with wrong motives, that you may spend what you get on your pleasures" (James 4:3).

God answers prayers based on a person's motives. When our prayers are designed to benefit the purposes of God and His people, God will respond. God does not want us to be paupers, but neither does He expect us to live lavishly with no concern for the welfare of others. God wants us to be conduits of His blessings. If you find yourself frustrated with God because you do not have as much as someone else, this is a sure sign that your motives are incorrect.

Conclusion

Prayer is a key component in the Christian's spiritual development. Prayer is for the development of the believer. Prayer is a process by which believers can communicate with God and learn about themselves. It is crucial to maintain a correct attitude during prayer and to allow God to shape us into the vessel He desires.

Dr. Paul Brooks states, "Prayer is for the purpose of alignment with our King and His Kingdom. As believers develop in their spiritual formation, they become kingdom-centric."

God desires to hear us, to respond to us, and to provide us blessings. Examine yourself and determine how well you are doing in the areas described in this chapter. A loving relationship cannot be sustained without effective communication. It is my desire that you will develop a robust relationship with God through an effective prayer life.

Study Guide Questions

1. What is the primary purpose of prayer?

2. What does it mean to pray "in the name of Jesus"?

3. What danger does the author point to concerning people who pray?

4. What attitude should a person have when they pray?

5. What is the bottom line assumption people should make when they pray?

6. What does the word "contrition" mean?

7. How is passion measured?

8. What must a Christians do if they have a hidden sin but want God to respond to them?

9. Why do Christians argue and fight, and what is the solution to this problem?

10. What role does "mercy" play in a believer's prayer life?

EIGHT

SPIRITUAL FORMATION THROUGH THE BIBLE

Christians would wander aimlessly if they didn't have a standard by which to measure themselves. Fortunately, we have the Bible as our standard. If Christians are going to grow in their faith, they must engage in Bible study as well as in devotional reading of God's Word.

This chapter is not designed to defend the authority of Scripture or explain the canonization process. If you are interested in these concepts, there are many good resources that can assist you. This chapter assumes you believe the Bible is the Christian's standard for faith and conduct. After completing this chapter, you'll have a better understanding of various views concerning the importance of reading the Bible and discover ways to help you make Bible reading and Bible study a priority in your life. Bible reading, along with prayer, are the primary tools God uses to transform you into the person He desires you to be.

Historical Approaches to Bible Reading

The Early Church embraced a concept called *lectio divina* to help guide their Bible reading. *Lectio divina* instructed people to read the Bible to hear God's voice. The emphasis was on contemplation, rather than content. Origen of Alexandria, the most important theologian and biblical scholar of the early Greek Church, was one of the first to emphasize this way of reading the Bible. Origen believed when a Christian reads the Bible, they are able to encounter Jesus Christ personally as the Holy Spirit speaks to them through the written pages. Origen used the word "mysticism" in referring to the way a person can find Jesus in Scripture. Origen taught meditation as a way to encounter Jesus personally, align themselves with His will and purposes, and to avoid temptations that entice the soul.

Augustine of Hippo, another major theologian in Church history, took Origen's thoughts a step further. In his *Confessions*, Augustine argues that God calls to us through the Scriptures. God beckons to the reader and in response to His voice, God changes the believer's heart which results in a desire to seek Him more. Augustine argued when a person hears God's Word, they can have a face-to-face epiphany with God.

John Calvin, the great Reformer, argued the motivation behind studying Scripture should be to learn what God wanted us to do and then to do it. Although Calvin would not deny encountering Jesus on the pages of Scripture was a valid quest, of greater importance was to rightly interpret the biblical text and then apply it to the believer's life.

John Wesley saw the spiritual disciple of Scripture reading quite differently from Calvin. Wesley did not see the primary purpose of studying Scripture as a discovery and imposition of rules. Wesley saw Bible study as a means of developing intimate knowledge of God. He believed the more we knew God, our relationship with Him would grow. This would result in transformed living. For Wesley, the goal of reading Scripture was spiritual transformation.

Dietrich Bonhoeffer, famous for his work *The Cost of Discipleship*, saw Scripture reading as a discipline that should take place corporately, as well as personally. Bonhoeffer believed a person could only understand God's Word fully within the context of community. For Bonhoeffer, reading the Scriptures was a way to identify with Christ; a way to get into His flesh, and to understand life as He understood it.

Richard Foster, a leader in the modern spiritual formation movement, places Scripture reading under the spiritual discipline of "study." Foster makes a clear distinction between devotional reading and study. In devotional reading, the disciple immediately looks for application. In study, the reader seeks to be controlled by the intent of the author. Foster's approach to Bible study is exegesis. He believes our job is to draw out meaning rather than read our priorities into the Scriptures.

A growing number of Christians have embraced a postmodern view of Scripture which argues there are no universal standards. As a result, the Bible is under the interpretive control of communities of believers. Postmodernism argues that two people could view a passage of Scripture diametrically different from one another, and they would both be right. The assumption lies in the idea that no one is able to truly get into the mind of the original author of the text. At best, they would argue, we can make a good guess at what the author intended. And if it is only a guess, then who is to determine which guess is right. This philosophy of interpretation is the basis of modern society's dismissal of traditional morality which formerly was built on a commonly held belief in the authority of Scripture. Ultimately, this approach (often called reader-response) allows the reader to determine the meaning of the text, thus transforming Scripture, rather than it transforming the reader. Evangelicals, who hold a high view of the authority of Scripture, reject this manner of interpretation.

General Principles for Bible Study

Avoid Legalistic Thinking

There is no "one size fits all" Bible reading system that works for everyone. Some people argue since Bible reading should be a priority for a Christian, it should be the first thing a person does in the morning. Reading the Bible in the morning has many positive benefits. It focuses a person's mind on God at the beginning of the day and sets a tone for the rest of the day. The strength a person draws from the Bible passages consumed early in the morning can provide nourishment throughout the day. Also, reading the Bible first thing in the morning assures nothing will get in the way of this important spiritual transaction.

Reading the Bible first thing in the morning works well for early risers, but it becomes problematic for those who resist getting out of bed until the last possible minute. Another struggle for many young families is the busyness of the house in the morning as both parents and children attempt to get out of the door. Some people tend to do better with Bible reading in the evening before they go to sleep. At the end of a long hectic day, with the kids put in bed, some Christians find it settling to pull out their Bible and reflect on the goodness of God. There was a period of time when this was my favorite time to read.

If early morning or late night doesn't work for you, find a time that does. It is important you have a designated time to read or it is likely that your reading will be hit or miss. When this occurs, you will discover you are missing way more often than you are hitting.

Many Christian leaders will challenge you to read through the Bible in a year. This can be a good way to make sure you know what is in all of the books of the Bible. But reading the Bible through in a year can be very daunting for many people. It is kind of like using a credit card; it is wonderful until you miss a payment. If you are required to read eight chapters each day to complete the task, and you miss a day, you have to read 16 chapters the next day just to catch up. If you miss a few days, it will seem like an impossible task to get back on schedule. Many people who try to read through the Bible in a year give up. Another negative aspect of attempting to read through the Bible in a year is you never have time to stop and study a passage that is of interest to you. There is nothing wrong with reading through the Bible in a year, but there is also nothing wrong with lingering in a book of the Bible. It is important to expose yourself to a variety of genres of the Bible, but there is no system you have to follow. Remember, Bible reading is designed to help you grow. It is not a competition between you and others. God is not going to award you a Bible reading badge if you read through the Bible in a year. Enjoy your spiritual journey as you augment your Bible reading with commentaries, Bible dictionaries, and Bible atlases. Purchasing Bible software is a great way to have a variety of tools at your fingertips.

Prioritize Bible Study

Studying God's word is a deliberate process. You will have to want to read your Bible to make it a daily activity. Spiritual disciplines are just that, disciplines. Moses knew how important it was to study God's word. He told the Israelites studying the Law would be a key to their success as they entered the Promised Land. "You shall therefore lay up these words of mine in your heart and in your soul, and you shall bind them as a sign on your hand, and they shall be as frontlets between your eyes" (Deuteronomy 11:18). Moses told the people to actively engage the Word of God. Listen to his words; "lay up," "bind," "create frontlets." The people of Israel took this command literally. Not only did they internalize the Word of God, they externalized it through their clothing.

Today's Christians are not required to wear frontlets to demonstrate their commitment to the authority of Scripture, but they are still required to internalize it, if they wish to take steps toward God. There are many ways to internalize the Bible. Some people memorize a verse a day. I have a friend who regularly memorizes entire books of the Bible. I believe he told me he has memorized 14 books of the Bible, at this time. Other people internalize the Bible by committing the basic themes of each book of the Bible to memory. Others reread portions of Scripture until they are deeply engrained in their minds and hearts. It is said that the great evangelist Billy Graham read a chapter of Proverbs, which corresponded to the day of the month, each day for most of his adult life. Each of these examples of internalizing Scripture is predicated on a decision by the person to be consistent in Bible reading.

Respond to the Bible

Studying the word of God is an active process. When we study the Bible, it's unlike reading a novel or poetry. Reading a good book is very enjoyable. Reading the Good Book demands response on our part. The writer of Hebrews describes the Bible this way, "For the word of God is living and active, sharper than any two-edged sword, piercing to the division of soul and spirit, of joints and marrow, and discerning the thoughts and intentions of the heart (Hebrews 4:12).

The Bible is not intended to leave you the same way after you read it as you were before you open its pages. The Bible, infused by the power of the Holy Spirit, has a way of seeing inside of the reader. It brings to light areas of hidden darkness. It brings life to places of death. It unmasks hurts, challenges, and sin. If the reader resists making adjustments highlighted by the Holy Spirit while reading the Bible, the effectiveness of Scripture will be lost for that individual. The Bible must never become simply a history book which records interesting facts about the Jewish people. Neither is it a textbook one masters in order to discuss deep theological concepts found within its pages. Although we can find history and theology, and these things may be extremely interesting and exciting, if we do not allow the words found in Scripture to make a significant impact in our lives, we will be no better off than atheists who study the Bible to support their ungodly beliefs.

Each time we open the word of God, we should start with a prayer that God would speak to us through its pages. We should ask God to open our hearts to receive what the Spirit wants to say to us during our time of study. Finally, we should request God to give us strength to implement the principles we discover. When we do this, we can be assured we will be refreshed, challenged, and shaped more closely into the likeness of Jesus daily.

Consume the Bible

Those who are passionate about God will find time to study the Bible. One of the most passionate individuals about God and His word was Jeremiah. The passion of Jeremiah can be seen in his words recorded in Jeremiah 15:16, "Your words were found, and I ate them, and your words became to me a joy and a delight of my heart, for I am called by your name, O Lord, God of hosts." The imagery of this verse shows a man who so loved the word of God he wanted to place it in his mouth, to savor it, and to ingest it.

As I read Jeremiah's words, I imagine myself sitting at a table in a fine steak house. The waiter places before me a well-marbled 20-ounce ribeye steak, a large baked potato filled with sour cream, chives, and bacon pieces, and a mix of steamed cauliflower and broccoli. As I pick up my fork and cut through the steak with my knife, I dip the rich red meat into horseradish sauce. I place it in my mouth. As I chew this delightful morsel, I thank God for such a delightful experience. The difference between Jeremiah and myself is when I swallow my steak, it will sustain me for 24 to 36 hours. The food Jeremiah longed for would sustain him for a life time. May my passion for the Bible outweigh my passion for perishable food!

We show passion for what we love. When I was in high school, I met a cute redheaded girl. We dated for two years. When it was time for college, I moved 1500 miles away from home and away from my girlfriend. This was in a day when there were no cell phones or social media. The idea of Skype or FaceTime were relegated to fantasy comic strips.

My girlfriend and I would coordinate a time each Sunday when she would call the only payphone on my dorm's hall. But she also wrote me a letter every day that I was away at college. Each morning I would wake up, go to class, and then to chapel. On the way back to my room after chapel, I would stop at the mailboxes, which were located in my dorm, to see if I had any mail for that day.

At first, I was excited to get a letter each day. After the first few days of finding her letters and reading them, I didn't get as excited. After making sure it was a letter from her, I would toss the unopened letter onto the top portion of my closet. They remained unopened and piling up for about two months.

One day my roommate asked me if I was ever going to read the letters my girlfriend had sent. I told him maybe someday, but there really wasn't a reason to read them because I already knew what they said. I explained she always told me how much she loved me, she would tell me what her day was like, and she would tell me how much she looked forward to spending quality time with me when I came home. Since I knew what was in the letters, why waste my time unsealing them?

Before somebody throws this book across the room and declares that I am a horrible person, let me assure you, most of story I just told you is not true. The portion of the story that is true is she wrote every day and I picked up the letters from the mailbox. But it's at this point the story strays from the truth. See, the truth is, once I pulled the letter out of the box, and I recognized my girlfriend's penmanship on the envelope, I would pull the envelope close to my nose. I would sniff deeply trying to gain her scent. (Little did I realize, I was probably smelling the scent of the post man.) I clutched the letter in my hand and rushed to my room so I could read my girlfriend's words and picture her beautiful face as I thought about her composing the letter.

Much, of what my girlfriend wrote, was repeated from the day before, but I didn't care how many times she said she loved me; I never got tired of it. (By the way, I wrote her every day for two years, as well.) Over 40 years later, I still have some of those handwritten letters from that young girl who would become my wife.

Why did I tell you this story? Because some of us treat the Bible with the same lack of passion I describe in my fictitious story. We toss the Bible aside because we don't think there is anything new we can gain from it. Sure, we know it will tell us God loves us. But why waste our time reading it? It is interesting that some people who were upset about my made up story concerning my girlfriend's letters feel no remorse about ignoring God's communication with them.

My desire is your story concerning your Bible reading will be like my true story regarding my (now) wife's letters. The Bible may be predictable after a while, but how many times is too many to hear God say, "I love you"? You may know the stories of the Bible by heart, but you can find joy in discovering a detail or two you didn't know. As you read the Bible, think about how much God loved you, as He superintended the writing of Scripture. May you become so passionate about Scripture, you will be disappointed if you miss a day of reading it.

If you find yourself lacking passion for God's word, heed the words of Jesus to the church located in Ephesus:

> I know your works, your toil and your patient endurance, and how you cannot bear with those who are evil, but have tested those who call themselves apostles and are not, and found them to be false. I know you are enduring patiently and bearing up for my namesake, and you have not grown weary. But I have this against you, that you have abandoned the love you had at first. Remember therefore from where you have fallen; repent, and do the works you did at first. If not, I will come to you and remove your lampstand from its place, unless you repent (Revelation 2:2-5).

Benefits of Bible Study

The Bible Provides Direction

Studying God's Word will guide your path. The Psalmist declares, "Your word is a lamp to my feet and a light to my path" (Psalm 119:105). Who wouldn't want to avoid stumbling in the dark? But so many people go through this life stumbling and falling. If they would just read God's word and live according to its wisdom, they could stay on their feet and walk uprightly.

Studying Scripture can help us to avoid many of the events in life which cause us to become bruised and broken. The Bible opens our eyes to the dangers many do not see in their paths. If we read the Scriptures, we can learn how to avoid sexual sins by viewing men as fathers and brothers and women as mothers and sisters rather than as sexual beings to sexually conquer (1 Timothy 5:1). We can avoid spending time in jail, if we will just learn the consequences of lying, stealing, and murder (Romans 13:1-5). We will not face challenges from the IRS if we will just obey the biblical commands against dishonesty and deceit (Romans 13:6-7). We will avoid many bad decisions, if we heed the words in Scripture about drunkenness and addiction (Ephesians 5:18; 1 Corinthians 6:12). We will be able to live harmonious lives, if we will learn what the Bible teaches about dealing with anger, conflict, and hatred (Ephesians 4:26; Colossians 3:8). So many of life's problems can be avoided, if we will study the Bible, accept its guidance, and walk in a manner that pleases God.

Some people want God to tell them the details that await them in life. They want a blueprint for the next few decades. God seldom gives us the entire map of what our lives will look like. Instead, He gives us direction a step at a time. This can be frustrating to those who want to be in control of their lives, but it is freeing for those who are willing to trust God with their future. It is a joy to not have to worry about tomorrow!

God's will for your life is clearly declared in Scripture. His will is for you to love Him and to love others. We love others by sharing hope with those who do not know Him and edifying our brothers and sisters in Christ. If you will simply do these things, you will not only be fulfilling the will of God for your life, but you will be living a fulfilled life.

The Bible Provides Hope

Studying the word of God provides hope. The apostle Paul wrote to the Romans concerning this purpose. He explains, "For whatever was written in former days for our instruction, that through endurance and through the encouragement of the Scriptures we might have hope" (Romans 15:4).

The word "hope" in the New Testament is not wishful thinking, nor is it an unfounded expectation. Hope is assurance a promise is going to be fulfilled, even when it doesn't look like it will happen.

During the New Testament era, there was a great deal of persecution faced by the young Christians. Many of them wanted to give up and go back to their Jewish roots or perhaps even walk away from any relationship with God. The apostle Paul reminded the Romans that no matter how bad the situation becomes, the hope they had for future victory was based, not in their circumstances, but on the faithfulness of God. God has proven himself faithful throughout history when individuals seemed to have no hope.

The Bible promises believers they can have joy and peace, but it does not promise them they will be in a continual state of happiness. Happiness is based on happenings. Joy is based on the hope we have through Jesus Christ. I am not going to be happy when bad things happen to me, but I can have joy when bad things are happening to me. I am not going to be happy if I'm in an oppressive country and I am forced to sit and watch my wife be raped, but I can still have joy in my heart knowing the God of the universe is in control even in moments such as those. Happiness is based on my understanding of the situation. I can have joy and peace even when I don't understand.

It's easy to read stories about Abraham, Joseph, Job, and Daniel and walk away not fully feeling the tension found in these stories. It takes us just a few hours to read through all of the experiences of Abraham's life. It is hard to grasp the level of faith Abraham needed to navigate his life considering the condensed nature of Scripture. We can whisk through the story of Joseph in a setting and miss the fear, misunderstanding, and disappointment Joseph must have felt when he was imprisoned and forgotten. It may take us a little longer to read through the book of Job, but we don't have to live through the endless days he endured as he lost his family, his health, and his wealth while listening to self-righteous friends. And while it takes very little time to read through the book of Daniel, it can be easy to miss how this young man felt as he was being torn away from everything he knew. When we read the Bible, we get to see the end of the story. We see that Abraham got to keep his son, Joseph saved a nation, Job had everything restored to him, and Daniel walked out of the lion's den without a scratch. The end of their stories show us we can have hope for the end of our story. No matter how bad our circumstances are currently, we can look beyond the circumstances and trust God with our future.

The Bible Provides Strength

Studying the Bible is the source of moral strength. Throughout history, most leaders who brought change to help enslaved people were individuals who drew strength from the Bible. William Wilberforce, Abraham Lincoln, and Martin Luther King Jr. are examples of people who fought for the civil rights of oppressed people. Each man was grounded in the principles declared in the Bible on the topic. Each faced much persecution for their beliefs. Ironically, each died as a result of their effort. Wilberforce died three days after the law banning slavery in England was passed. Lincoln died months before the official ending of slavery in the United States. King died as the leading spokesperson for the Civil Rights movement in the 1960s. None of these leaders could have made the difference they made, in the cause of justice if they were not men who loved the Bible.

The apostle Paul explains that learning more about Jesus has a way of enriching a Christian's life. "Let the word of Christ dwell in you richly, teaching and admonishing one another in all wisdom, singing psalms and hymns and spiritual songs, with thankfulness in your hearts to God" (Colossians 3:16). Reading the Bible plants seeds in the follower of Jesus. Over time, the fruit of those seeds emerge and are used by God to reflect His love to the world.

Studying God's word provides spiritual strength. Psalm 119:11 states, "I have stored up your word in my heart, that I may not sin against you." Jesus regularly set aside time for communion with God which would have included interaction with the Scriptures. Whenever Jesus faced a difficult moment, we see that He points to the Scriptures to find victory. When He was in the wilderness being tempted by Satan He used Scripture as a means of spiritual battle. (See Matthew 4:1-10.) When He was betrayed, He refers to what He had learned through Bible study. (See Matthew 26:47-56.) When He taught the crowds, He used what He had learned in Bible study to challenge them. (See Matthew 5:17-48.)

If we only read the Bible on rare occasions, we will find ourselves spiritually weak. If we desire spiritual health, we must have a regular diet of spiritual food. Jesus and His Word provide the nourishment needed for our spiritual growth (John 6:32-33).

Studying God's word provides emotional strength. The Psalmist explains the source of joy in a Christian's life. In Psalm 19:8, we read, "the precepts of the Lord are right, rejoicing the heart."

On most college campuses, you'll find a large percentage of the students enrolled in courses leading to a degree in human services. The need for counselors and social workers is great as more families are disintegrating. Statistics indicate that more people are depressed and receive prescriptions for drugs that were once reserved for a very small portion of the population. Emotional instability is rapidly increasing in modern society.

While emotional instability rises in the Western world, the number of those who regularly attend church and seek to enhance their spiritual lives decreases. Numerous studies show a direct correlation between emotional stability and church attendance. This should come as no surprise to those who have studied Scripture. The Bible teaches that emotional well-being can be obtained through a healthy relationship with God.

The word *shalom* in the Hebrew is translated in English as "peace." It has the meaning of wholeness or a sense of well-being as a result of having peace with God. The Bible says we can have *shalom* if we will keep our minds focused on God and trust Him (Isaiah 26:3).

Jesus assured His disciples He would provide His followers with peace: "Peace I leave with you; my peace I give to you. Not as the world gives do I give to you. Let not your hearts be troubled, neither let them be afraid" (John 14:27).

Not every depression will be remedied through Bible study because some depressions are chemically based. But some depression results from people dwelling on the troubles they face in their lives. For those, Bible study can provide *shalom* by getting to know God better through studying the Bible. Understanding God through Bible study will help us embrace Jesus' command recorded in the Sermon on the Mount. "But seek first his kingdom and his righteousness, and all these things will be given to you as well. Therefore do not worry about tomorrow, for tomorrow will worry about itself. Each day has enough trouble of its own" (Matthew 6:33-34).

I encourage you, if you have felt emotionally drained, spend some time reading the Psalms. Nearly two-thirds of the Psalms are laments. Laments are Psalms written by people who were going through a tough time. These writers could've thrown in the towel, but they chose to put their focus on God and trust Him. If you are facing dark emotional moments, you will begin to see the light as you study God's word and allow Him to minister to you.

Psychologists, counselors, and social workers have a role to play in society today, but there will never be enough of them to solve all the problems people in this world face. Much of their labor could be lightened if those who follow Jesus would spend more time in His Word finding His encouragement.

Conclusion

Reading the Bible is an extremely important element for a Christian's development. We must not do it to earn spiritual points with God, but when we do study the word of God, and take it seriously, we will become more like Jesus. Bible study helps us to see the heart of God, His attitude towards humanity, and His desire to assist all of His creation to come into a place of fullness through Him. If you are not currently reading Scripture on regular basis, I encourage you to take a step toward God through Bible study.

Study Guide Questions

1. What is the standard that unifies all Christians throughout time?

2. What is *lectio divina*?

3. Which church leader argued that we should be motivated to read the Bible to learn what God wants us to do and then do it?

4. What does postmodernism teach about the authority of Scripture?

5. What four principles were provided in the chapter for Bible reading?

6. What is the best time of the day for a Christian to read the Bible?

7. What personal story does the author tell to illustrate passion for the Bible?

8. What Bible character is mentioned as a person who had passion for God's word?

9. What five benefits of Bible study were discussed in the chapter?

10. What is the difference between happiness and joy, according to the author?

NINE

SPIRITUAL FORMATION THROUGH WORSHIP

Worship is foundational to the Christian experience. Unfortunately, over the years it has been relegated to a segment of a church service when the congregation sings together. As a result of this emphasis, worship tends to be relegated to the arena of music. Although music is an important aspect of worship, it must never be limited to musical expression.

Defining Worship

William Temple, who was a bishop in the Church of England, provided a very thought-provoking definition of worship in the book *Nature, Man, and God*. I will use this definition to begin our study of worship. I believe it will help us discover its true meaning. Temple states, "To worship is to quicken the conscience by the holiness of God, to purge the imagination of the beauty of God, to open the heart to the love of God, to devote the will to the purpose of God."

Temple's definition begins by implying that anything which turns our minds toward God to see His holiness is worship. This broad view of worship helps us to remove the line between sacred and secular, and allows us to see worship in the greatest context possible. The "anything" can include words from a song, phrases from poetry, a beautiful painting, stained-glass windows, beautiful architecture, or the robes on choir members. But the "anything" can also include watching a baby crawl across the floor, or an athlete skillfully using his or her body to perform great feats, the trees lining the sidewalks, the stars shining in the night skies, or the fragrance emitted from flowers. The "anything" can also include the concepts found in a science textbook, the lectures from a business teacher, watching the skillful hands of a mechanic, turning on a light switch, or attempting to understand the components of a computer. "Anything" includes everything that helps us think about God and appreciate who He is and see Him in His supreme context.

Observing the ordinary elements of life can initiate worship. Unfortunately, many of us go through the day and see the great creation God has made, or the skills He has invested in people, and totally ignore His role in these great accomplishments. We begin to take His creation, His gifts, and His love for humanity for granted. Often this is a result of our busyness, but sometimes it's a result of our arrogance. We can begin to see the gifts, talents, and accomplishments we possess as our accomplishments. Worship occurs when we recognize God for who He is.

So the first step in learning to worship is to slow down enough to appreciate the wonder that is around us. When we do this, we will develop an intensified appreciation for God and give Him the honor He deserves. God has given us five senses to help us to be worshipers of Him. We must use the senses with intentionality. Allow your ears to hear the cry of a baby and worship God, the giver of life. Use your eyes to see the trees and worship God, the creator of all things. Draw deep breaths and smell the cinnamon rolls that just came out of the oven and worship God for fragrances. Touch the shoulder of a loved one and worship God, the author of relationships. And slow down to enjoy the taste of your food and worship God, the provider of an array of wonderful culinary options.

I encourage you to think of the little things in your life which are truly large things, if we did not have them. Allow a good night's sleep to lead you to worship. When you blink your eyes, allow the fact God thought about lubricating our eyes and keeping them free from dust lead you to worship Him. Worship must begin with an intentional desire on our part to recognize the great gifts that God has given to us and His involvement in every aspect of our lives. Worship must extend to all aspects of our life.

The next portion of Temple's definition is "to purge the imagination of the beauty of God." We touched on this to an extent in the previous point, but I would like to develop it just a little bit further. I would like to focus on the wonders of God's creation. Anything that is beautiful should draw our attention to the holiness of God.

The apostle Paul encourages us to stay focused on the beautiful things: "Finally, brothers, whatever is true, whatever is honorable, whatever is just, whatever is pure, whatever is lovely, whatever is commendable, if there is any excellence, if there is anything worthy of praise, think about these things" (Philippians 4:8). If our minds are focused on the beautiful, they will be ultimately focused on the Source of all beauty.

Satan has attempted, since his rebellion against God, to pervert anything that is beautiful. In the Garden of Eden, he took a good tree and used it as object of envy. He has taken the beauty of music and turned it into an avenue for hatred and abuse. He has taken the gift of sex and turned it into a meaningless immoral activity. He's taken the blessings of God and convinced people to hoard it while others suffer. Our world is filled with crime, debauchery, immorality, hatred, and violence. We can think about those things and allow them to dominate our lives. When we do, we will be filled with worry, stress, and soon we will be drawn into depression. We may even begin to take part in the negativity of our world. If we are going to be worshipers of God, we must move our focus away from the ugly we see around us and place our eyes on the Source of all good things.

One of the most important steps we can take "to purge our imagination by the beauty of God," is to turn off our televisions, avoid the newsfeeds on the Internet, and refuse to be dominated by fear. I'm not suggesting we stick our head in the sand ignoring the world's problems, but I am suggesting we spend at least as much time reading God's word and looking at the beautiful things in life as we do spending time consuming reports concerning contaminated humanity. Those who spend time focused on the beautiful things, and talking about the beautiful things God has accomplished, will naturally become more positive in their outlook and more worshipful in their lifestyle. It is crucial, if we desire to be a worshiper of God, that we affirm the words of the apostle Paul and focus our minds on the positive and allow those things to shift our attention toward God which is the essence of worship.

The next portion of Temple's definition seems straight forward, but it might be the most difficult step for a Christian to take. He states, "Open the heart to the love of God." So why is receiving God's love important, and why is it difficult for some people to do?

Many people don't feel they are worthy to be loved by anybody, let alone to be loved by God. They feel inferior and filled with shame because of their background and the poor choices they have made. Increasingly, people no longer have supportive families of origin. God designed a family to consist of a mother and a father who would bring children into the world and help them to understand His love through the love they receive from their parents. This type of love is unconditional and in many cases unwarranted. But when people have not experienced this type of love from their own parents, it becomes increasingly difficult for them to receive the unconditional love God has for them. People, who don't understand love, tend to reject genuine love or spend their life trying to earn love from the significant people in their lives. If a person is not able to receive God's love, they will not be able to worship. If a person believes their works produce God's love, than there is no need to worship because the love was earned.

It is important for us to open our hearts to God's love, if we truly want to be worshipers of God because it is only after we feel His love unconditionally, that we are able to return love through adoration, appreciation, obedience, and holy submission which are hallmarks of worship. Once we begin to accept God's love for us, we will experience a freedom in His presence, rather than an expectation of judgment from Him. A child who questions the love of the parent is always in fear of the next punishment they will face if they do something that displeases their parent. They live in a constant state of confusion, frustration, and uncertainty. There are too many Christians who live in the same confusion, frustration, and uncertainty in relationship to God because of their lack of understanding of His love for them. Worship must never be an appeasement to God. Worship must always be a willing, free expression of one's esteem of the Creator of the universe.

The last portion of Temple's definition is a natural outflow of the previous components. He says the result of worshiping God is "To devote the will to the purpose of God." If we have worshiped God, then we have recognized who He is and who we are in relationship to Him. If we fully understand who He is, then we will live in submission to Him. His agenda will be our agenda. What He says is what we will do. Where He says to go is where we will go. No longer do we live to fulfill our desires, but we live to accomplish His desires. The Bible tells us when we worship God we can have the mind of Christ (1 Corinthians 2:16).

It is impossible to truly worship God and to live in rebellion to Him. There are some people who attempt to live mindless to God throughout the week and then come to church on Sunday and attempt to worship Him. But they're only fooling themselves when they do this. The true sign of worship is submission. We cannot say that God is worthy of our honor and worship, if we insist on living according to our own standards and limit our relationship with God to a form of spiritual fire insurance which will keep us out of hell. Worship is foundational to Christianity. If we live in rebellion to God throughout the week and still come to church and sing songs of praise, we may be expressing some kind of religious activity, but it is not authentic Christianity, and it is not pleasing to God.

Practicing Worship

Worship is not an activity created by man. God has taken the initiative to build a relationship with humans. Not only did He create people, but the Bible tells us He walked in the Garden of Eden in order to have fellowship with them (Genesis 3:8). God initiated fellowship and relationship with humans throughout Scripture. We see God approached Noah (Genesis 6:11-21), Abraham (Genesis 12:1-3), Jacob (Genesis 28:10-15), Joshua (Joshua 1:1-6), Saul (1 Samuel 9:14-27), and many other people who were not thinking about Him or engaging Him at the time. God continues to reach out to humanity in an attempt to have a relationship with them. It is God who seeks, draws, and persuades individuals (Luke 19:10). Worship is simply the human response to the divine initiative. When we respond to God, we recognize who He is and agree to a relationship in which He takes the lead.

Worship provides an ever-expanding view of God. Each time we sing a song, read a book, look at God's creation, or engage in any other activity which draws our attention to God, our view of Him increases as our appreciation for Him increases.

As stated before, holy worship leads to holy obedience. Anything less than an obedient life emanating from worship, will support the idea purported by Karl Marx many years ago. Marx, an atheist/socialist, was famous for saying religion was simply an opiate for the masses. He believed the way people dealt with the pain in their lives was to engage in religious activity that would numb them and provide a means to tolerate life. He argued people went to church to be medicated. He went on to argue it's only weak people who needed religion. The strong could survive on their own.

As a Christian, we argue against the proposition made by Karl Marx, but sometimes we live as if Marx was correct. Those who go to church, week after week, simply to survive the pain in their lives, use God as a medication rather than responding to Him as God. The worship experience must not simply be a way to fix our lives, rather, it must be a time of recognizing who God is regardless of our circumstances. Worship is not a medication. It is a recognition of the One who created us and cares about our situations in life. We can trust Him to care for us because He is God. Because He is God, we worship Him.

How Can We Prepare to Worship?

Since worship is our response to God's initiative, it's important for us to prepare ourselves to respond to God in an appropriate fashion. Let me share just a few ways I have found that helps me prepare to worship God throughout the week, but specifically, to worship God within the congregation. I discovered many of these practices through advice provided by mentors and the wealth of spiritual formation literature that I have read.

The first way you can prepare to worship God effectively is to come to church with expectancy God is there and wants to meet with you. Often we miss God when we go to church because we do not look for Him. God is always present, but often not recognized. Just as we can walk beside beautiful trees and not think about God, we can go to church and sing songs about God without engaging Him. If you will go to church with an expectation you are going to hear from God and experience Him, it is more likely a connection will occur which will result in true worship.

God will reveal himself in many ways during a typical church service. He may reveal himself through the music, the sermon, and during a time of prayer. He may reveal himself through the stained-glass windows or other architectural features of the church building. He may reveal himself through a person who is worshiping beside you. He may reveal himself during Communion or the offering. The list could go on and on, but suffice it to say, God is drawing you into worship each time you go to a church service. It is your responsibility to respond to Him.

The next way I have found to increase the likelihood of the occurrence of worship is by listening for His voice daily. If you are in the practice of worshiping God on a daily basis, it will be very easy for you to worship Him in the sanctuary. God is as real on the streets of your city as He is in the chairs in your church. If you learn to hear God daily and to obey Him regularly, worship will not be an event. It will be a lifestyle. The natural transition from your weekday behavior into your church day behavior will be seamless. It is sad that some churches feel like they have to prepare their people to worship God through a set of songs, rather than being able to assume believers walk through the doors already in an attitude of worship. If the church is ever going to be an example of what Christ desires it to be, then worship will have to take place both inside the doors of the church, as well as outside of the church building.

A third way to prepare to worship is to practice obedience. There is no sense for you to seek a deeper relationship with God through worship, if you are living in disobedience to what He's already told you. The Bible teaches if you have heard something from God, yet refuse to obey it, you are living in sin (James 4:17). It is illogical to think someone who is living in sin can effectively worship God. It is the responsibility of the believer, who is living in rebellion, to repent of their sin, turn from their wicked way, and then be prepared to worship God (2 Chronicles 7:14).

Richard Foster suggests a way to enhance your worship experience in a local church setting is to arrive in the sanctuary at least 10 minutes early. Use this time to focus on the greatness of God. Resist the temptation to talk to your friends. Rather, close your eyes or lift them heavenward and think about all God has done in the past, His goodness to you, and the privilege you have to serve Him. After spending these 10 minutes focused on God, it will become much easier for you to continue your worship when the songs begin, prayers are offered, and the word of God is declared. You will not have to be revved up or encouraged to worship, as if it is a foreign activity.

Another practice suggested by Foster to maximize your worship experience in church is to spend time praying for the leaders of the church service. Pray that they will be instruments of God, to reveal himself to you and to others in a significant fashion. God has placed individuals in various roles in the church in order to assist followers of Christ in their pursuit of Him. Regardless of how you feel about the particular leaders in your church, it is your responsibility to pray for them. Ask God to magnify the message the person is sharing, with the congregation. Pray for each member of the "worship" team. Ask God to help them use their musical talents to reflect the glory of God. Pray for the person leading prayer and those who are giving the announcements. Ask God to use their words to bring encouragement. And pray for the person who is delivering the sermon. Request God to give the person clarity of thought and speech in order to declare His word in an effective fashion, so everyone will be able to see God more clearly and enhance their worship of Him.

Another thing you can do, when you show up to church early, is to pray a prayer of intercession for someone who needs God's special help. Intercession is a form of worship which closely reflects the heart of God. The Bible tells us that Jesus is at the right hand of the Father making intercession for us (Romans 8:34). Jesus understands there are times we cannot pray for ourselves or perhaps we don't even know what we should pray. It's at those times that we need somebody to stand in the gap and pray for us. It may be somebody in the church gathering who needs our prayer. It may be a friend or family member. It may even be somebody we've never met but God places the person on our heart leading us to pray for them. Many of us miss the opportunity to intercede because we don't quiet ourselves long enough to be aware of the needs of others. When we begin to intercede on behalf of others, we will be accomplishing the commandment of Jesus to love God and love others. When we obey God, we are worshiping God.

Conclusion

Does worship lead to spiritual formation or does spiritual formation lead to worship? Spiritual formation cannot take place until an individual begins to worship. It's not until an individual understands who they are in relationship to God that they will have the ability to live in obedience to Him. And it's not until we begin to live in obedience to Him that we will grow in our Christian walk. But, as we grow in our Christian walk, we learn more about Him and will be able to worship Him even more effectively. Spiritual formation is a process. Worship, likewise, is a process. Trusting Jesus for our salvation is only the first step. The more we learn about God, the more we will understand the depth of His love for us. But we will also more fully understand His desires. Worship is not an option for the Christian. It is the recognition that we are not enough and will never be enough. Worship helps us to identify our purpose, and to live the life intended for us when God designed us. We must worship God in spirit and in truth (John 4:24).

Study Guide Questions

1. What is worship?

2. What can cause a person to worship?

3. Where can worship take place?

4. What does it mean to "purge one's imagination by the beauty of God"?

5. How does a mother and father's love prepare us to worship?

6. What role does obedience play in the worship experience?

7. How is worship initiated?

8. List the ways the author suggests that a person can prepare to worship God in a church setting.

9. How does worship develop a person's spiritual life?

TEN

SPIRITUAL FORMATION THROUGH SOLITUDE

The practice of solitude has a long history within the Christian Church. In the Roman Catholic tradition, the monks devote great periods of time to being alone with God. During these times of solitude, they seek to soak up as much engagement with God as humanly possible. To do so, they live in monasteries set aside for silent reflection. Monasteries also function as retreat centers for priests who wish to engage in shorter periods of solitude.

Solitude has lost its emphasis in many Protestant circles. Protestants tend to be more like the biblical character Martha who was busy doing the work for Jesus rather than, being like Mary who spent time fellowshipping with Jesus. Interestingly, when given these two extreme options, Jesus revealed He would rather have us spend time in fellowship with Him than to have us work for Him (Luke 10:41-42). Obviously, it is important for Christians to fulfill their purpose and accomplish the goals of Christ, but too many Christians attempt to accomplish the tasks of Christianity without experiencing the power to accomplish them through deep encounters with God.

Many Christians set aside moments in their day to pray and read the Bible. These moments are very important for enriching the soul. But extended periods of solitude allow the believer to come away from the stresses of life and focus their full attention on their relationship with God. These periods of intense intimacy will provide Christians to be better equipped to do the work of the kingdom of God.

One of the reasons solitude is so difficult for those who live in the Western world is that we are very uncomfortable with silence. Consider how many times you drive your automobile without turning on the radio. And how many times do you immediately turn on the television when you walk into your house? I notice around our campus, people seldom walk down the hall or across our campus without having earphones blasting music into their craniums. It has gotten so bad in our society that we cannot even exercise without having noise. Most of us feel very uncomfortable being alone and sitting in quietness for extended periods of time.

A reason for the discomfort associated with loneliness is a lack of self-esteem. People are afraid to be alone with their own thoughts. No one knows us better than we do. We know our faults, our deceptions, and our weaknesses. It is natural for us to want to block those realities out of our minds through busying ourselves. Solitude is scary to individuals with a low self-esteem because they do not want to face the shame and the guilt they know resides within them.

The good news concerning solitude with God is He is never going to condemn you for who you are or for what you have done. He loves you in the condition you come to Him. He will not allow you to remain in that condition, but rather than condemning you, He will help you to see a way of escape so you can live in the freedom you desire. Solitude is the real solution to low self-esteem because when we're in the presence of God, He reveals to us our true value.

Practicing Voluntary Solitude

Practicing solitude is an intentional activity. You don't just happen on significant periods of time in the busy life you lead. A person who practices solitude must be willing to set aside everything to achieve this valuable time with God. The time necessary for significant spiritual intimacy to develop will not be achieved by setting aside five minutes here and five minutes there. For solitude to be effective, it must occur in time blocks you cannot fill up with your own words. Anyone can spend five minutes with God and fill that time with personal prayer requests. Few individuals can spend a couple of hours talking to God without running out of things to say. This is why I suggest the minimum amount of time you should set aside for solitude is two hours. In a two hour block, you will run out of things to say, and you will be forced to be quiet and listen for God.

When you go into solitude, resist the temptation to take music with you. Many people, who are learning to practice solitude, will take music with them into the period of solitude. Instead of listening to God, they find themselves listening to the lyrics of their favorite songwriter. It is true, God can speak to us through music, but this time should be dedicated to hearing God's word in new and powerful ways. I recommend, when you go into a time of solitude, you should limit yourself to a Bible, a journal, and a writing utensil. I suggest the Bible which you take in with you be a paper Bible, rather than an electronic Bible. I am not arguing one is superior to the other, but if you take electronics into your time of solitude, you will be tempted to engage with technology, rather than engage with your Creator. Having a Bible with you will be valuable because God will often prompt you to turn to a passage of Scripture. You don't want to lose any of the valuable insights you gain during your time of solitude, so having a journal with you to write down insights and discoveries will serve to enrich, not only the time you're spending in solitude, but also you will be able to reflect back on the time and draw strength in the future.

When you are in your time of solitude, don't be surprised if you feel extremely uncomfortable at first. As with any new experience, you come to the experience with expectations. Don't be surprised if your expectations are not fully met. God does not work according to our expectations, but according to His purposes. He realizes what is needed in your relationship, and He will take the lead if you quiet yourself. It is not unusual for you to spend the first two hours in solitude and walk away feeling you did not receive anything. This can be discouraging if you are not warned in advance that this is normal. Often, in the first session God will teach you that you have to set your expectations aside and be satisfied with the encounter He wants to offer to you. This is why I recommend a minimum of 10 hours of solitude spread over a period of five sessions. If you will do this, you will discover by the third two-hour session that you are experiencing God in a new and special way. Most individuals, who actually accept the challenge of spending 10 hours in solitude, say they want to make solitude a regular part of their Christian experience.

If you quit practicing solitude in disappointment after the first two hour session, it says more about you than it says about God. We live in a consumer society. We want to expend our money and in exchange receive a product. We can carry that consumer mentality into our spiritual lives. We may feel if we expend our time with God, then He should respond by giving us the product we anticipated. One of the most difficult things Christians have to release is their perception that they deserve something from God because of the sacrifices they make on His behalf. Solitude forces us to let go of the consumer mentality we possess, and embrace the reality that God is the giver of all good gifts. But, as the giver, He gets to choose what gifts He provides.

You will learn many lessons when you practice solitude, but among the greatest lessons you will learn is how to make God a priority in your busy life. Blocking out two-hour periods can seem virtually impossible. There is homework to be done, laundry to be folded, children to be fed, and apartments to clean. The list seems to be endless. How on earth can a person set aside these tasks to have the luxury of spending a couple hours alone with God on a regular basis? The real question should be, "How on earth can a person accomplish all of the tasks they have in their lives without setting aside time with God on a regular basis?"

It is easy to make the "immediate" the most important thing in our lives, rather than allowing the most "important" to take precedence. Those who read these words may immediately object. They probably think I don't live in the real world. If you have that response, I would suggest you have determined your priorities. Nothing is wrong with doing homework, cleaning the house, or feeding one's children. They only become wrong when they become more important than spending time in the presence of God.

We all have the same 168 hours in a week. We must prioritize the time God has given to us. God has asked us to give Him one full day per week. On the Sabbath, people were instructed to do nothing but focus on Him. Our society, for the most part, has rejected the idea of giving God one day a week. Our world has taken its eyes off from Him and placed them on the material blessings He created for them. As Christians, we must never adopt the world's standards. One of the ways, we can stand against the enemy of our souls, is to give God the proper priority in our life.

Forced Solitude

Not all solitude is chosen. There are times God forces us into solitude. These times are often identified by periods when we no longer feel God or hear Him. These times can lead to depression and frustration if we do not understand what God is attempting to do in our lives. If you have gone through extended periods of spiritual dryness, you are not alone. Most Christians will find themselves at one time or another in these periods of spiritual darkness. St. John of the Cross coined the phrase, "the dark night of the soul" to help Christians articulate what they are feeling during these periods in our Christian life.

Probably the most famous biblical character who experienced the dark night of the soul was Job. Job was a faithful follower of God. Unbeknownst to Job, God agreed to withhold blessings from him to demonstrate his level of spiritual commitment.

The first thing we learn from the story of Job is if God puts us into a dark night of the soul, it is His choice and there is nothing we can do to get Him to resume responding to us. Many people who experience a period of spiritual darkness begin to negotiate with God. They make promises to entice God to begin to speak to them as He normally had. We must understand, God is not going to change His mind until He has fulfilled the purposes He has set out to accomplish in our lives. On the surface, this may seem uncaring. Nothing could be further from the truth.

The second lesson we learn from Job's story is God will never withhold His Word or His blessing from our lives, unless we can make it through the test victoriously. The Bible says God knows how much we can take and also what we need in our lives in order to continue to mature in Him. Paul assured the Corinthian church, "No temptation has overtaken you that is not common to man. God is faithful, and he will not let you be tempted beyond your ability, but with the temptation he will also provide the way of escape, that you may be able to endure it" (1 Corinthians 10:13). As difficult as it may be to understand, when God puts us into a dark night of the soul, He is paying us a compliment concerning the condition of our spiritual life. Just as a parent would not jeopardize the well-being of their baby by withholding food from the child, God will not put a person into a dark night of the soul unless they are capable of surviving this very important transaction.

A cautionary note needs to be made here. It is possible to enter a period of spiritual dryness, not because God placed us there, but because our sin placed us there. The Bible identifies a variety of conditions that will keep God from responding to us. Among these conditions are rebellion (Isaiah 59:1-2), mistreating your loved ones (1 Peter 3:7), sowing discord among believers (Proverbs 6:19), sinful acts (Psalm 66:18; Jeremiah 14:10-12), and hypocrisy and insincerity (Isaiah 29:13; Malachi 1:7-9). When you face a dark night of the soul, the first thing you must do is determine if you have done something that has drawn you away from God. If you discover something in your life is causing the breach, it is your responsibility to repent and take responsibility for your sin and reestablish your relationship with God. The Bible repeatedly teaches God will never leave us nor will He ever forsake us (Hebrews 13:5), but it never promises that we will not drift away from Him.

If we determine we have done nothing to separate ourselves from God, we can make the assumption the dry period is God's desire to do something in our lives that will eventually pay great dividends. God uses this period to perform spiritual surgery on our lives. During this time, He cuts spiritual cancers out of our lives that we may not even know exist, but He knows if it remains, it will eventually destroy us.

Earlier I mentioned my bout with cancer in January 2011. After months of being badgered by my wife, coerced by my doctor, and the death of one of my best friends from colon cancer, I submitted myself and went to have my very first colonoscopy. In early February 2011, after performing the procedure, the doctor informed me that I had a tumor the size of a golf ball attached to my colon. He told me it was cancerous and I would need to have surgery as soon as possible. The following week, I went in for a consultation and he told me he did not know if the cancer had spread. All he would say to me was that he needed to go in and cut out the disease.

I walked in to have my colonoscopy with no idea there was an invader living inside me, seeking to destroy me. In the same way, there are things in our lives which we may not even recognize that God can see. As our Great Physician, He does not want us to be destroyed by those things. He takes it upon himself to cut those things out of our lives, so we can live in spiritual victory. He knows there will be pain, but He also knows it will be worth it.

Some of the things causing spiritual harm are often the same things that were seen as positive when we were baby Christians. As baby Christians, we would pray and God would answer most of our prayers. As a more seasoned Christian, we pray and expect God to do what we tell Him to do. We become disappointed when He doesn't fulfill our wishes revealing a spiritual disease. As a baby Christian, we went to church and experienced the presence of God nearly every time we entered the doors. As more mature Christians, we go to church to feel His presence. If we don't "feel" Him every time we go to church, we feel like we've wasted our time. This attitude is another indication of a problem. As baby Christians, we read our Bible and we were thrilled when we discovered nuggets of truth. As older Christians, we read the Bible to earn a badge for spirituality. Slowly, and unintentionally, we replace a fascinating relationship with a transactional arrangement which reflects a consumer mentality. This is a dangerous condition for one's spiritual health.

God is well aware of the true motivation that drives our actions. He cannot allow us to continue down a path of spiritual consumerism. He loves us too much to allow us to repeat the mistakes of the Pharisees. We must not serve God for what we can get from Him. This attitude is a cancer which will destroy us if it isn't removed.

During the dark night of the soul, God cuts away the props in our life. God forces us to answer a single question. "Will you still serve me if you never hear from me again, never feel me again, and never receive additional blessings from me?"

This is a foundational question for every believer. Until we can answer this question in the way Job did, we are not ready to take the next step in the Christian maturation process. Job provided the correct answer when he proclaimed, "Though he slay me, I will hope in him yet I will argue my ways to his face" (Job 13:15). Job was not complacent in his faith, but he came to a point when he confessed that, even though he didn't understand what God was doing, he was okay because God was enough.

The loving nature of God will not allow Him to withhold himself and His blessings from us forever. We see, through the story of Job, there was a period of recovery after Job emerged successfully from his spiritual surgery. God began to reconnect with Job. God began to bless Job once again. God wants to pour out His blessings upon us when we appreciate them as gifts, rather items earned from a transactional relationship.

Once we awake from the spiritual surgeries and the disease has been removed, we can see Him with childlike awe and excitement again. Once we have regained this perspective, He will pour out His blessings abundantly. Jesus helps us understand how important a proper attitudes is to God when He states, "Truly, I say to you, unless you turn and become like children, you will never enter the kingdom of heaven" (Matthew 18:3).

Before the doctor could do surgery, he administered anesthesia. In the dark night of the soul, there is a numbness that comes upon us, but if we will simply trust the Great Physician, when we awake from the numbness, we will be in a much better spiritual condition.

Conclusion

Solitude is an important discipline in the maturing Christian's life. It can be by choice or it can be thrust upon us by God. Those who engage in regular periods of solitude may never have to face the Great Physician's scalpel. Regular periods of solitude serve as preventive medicine to keep us focused on who God is and who we are in relationship to Him. In those intentional times of solitude, we will hear His voice, experience His presence, and learn to live in proper relationship to Him. When we don't take care of ourselves properly, foreign entities can enter our relationship which must be removed so we can continue to live the life God has designed for us.

After I had my surgery, the doctor told me it was possible for the cancer to return. He told me I would have to change my lifestyle and my eating habits if I wanted to have confidence the cancer would not return. I now go in to see the doctor on a regular basis to be examined, and eat better because I do not want to have to face surgery again.

Those of us who have gone through the dark night of the soul and emerged on the other end successfully must not neglect regular checkups. If we do not regularly submit ourselves to scrutiny by the Great Physician, we will put ourselves in jeopardy of having to face another dry period in our lives.

I encourage you to use the delightful, yet somewhat uncomfortable, practice of intentional solitude to help you remain in a healthy spiritual condition.

Study Guide Questions

1. What is the purpose of spending time in solitude with God?

2. What is the minimum amount of time suggested in this chapter to practice solitude in a single setting?

3. What should a person have with them when they spend time in voluntary solitude?

4. Who is famous for the phrase the "dark night of the soul"?

5. What things can cause us to separate ourselves from God so that He does not respond to our prayers?

6. What biblical character experienced an extended dark night of the soul?

7. What is the purpose of the dark night of the soul?

8. How can one avoid repeated dark nights of the soul?

ELEVEN

SPIRITUAL FORMATION THROUGH
WATER BAPTISM

Both Protestant and Roman Catholic theology state water baptism is a vital part of the Christian experience. Although in theory water baptism is seen as important, I wonder sometimes if Protestants truly embrace its importance. Roman Catholics use baptism as a seal of spiritual protection until a child is old enough to confirm his or her salvation. Sometimes, it seems, Protestants use water baptism as an add-on accessory to their salvation. Many Protestants practice it as a required part of the Christian's spiritual clothing, but it does little other than fulfill a requirement of Scripture. These individuals would argue salvation is not complete until Christians check off the water baptism box. Once checked, they can go about their spiritual life without giving another thought to this transaction. While not embracing the Roman Catholic theology, I believe relegating water baptism to simply an act of obedience devalues the act and minimizes its intended significance.

Water Baptism: A Transformational Act

Water baptism is a transformational act which reflects a deliberate choice of the person being baptized. A definition of water baptism that captures this thought is presented by a 15th century Dutch thinker Desiderius Erasmus. In *The Colloquies of Desiderius Erasmus Concerning Men, Manners and Things*, Volume 3, Erasmus states:

I shall not here enter into the examination of the merit of man's dedicating himself wholly to God, when he is no longer in his own power. I take it that every Christian delivers himself up wholly to God in his baptism, when he renounces all of the pomps and vanities of Satan, and lists himself a soldier to fight under Christ's banner all of his life after. And St. Paul, speaking to those who die with Christ, 'that they may no longer live unto themselves, but to him that died for them,' does not mean this of monks only, but of Christians universal.

Reading Erasmus' words, reveals his assertion that all Christians surrender their lives completely when they become Christians. The idea that a person could be a Christian and not live in full surrender is outside of Erasmus' comprehension. He makes it clear this total surrender is not restricted to the religious elite. Everyone who has ever accepted Jesus as Lord must surrender personal ownership of themselves and submit every aspect of their lives to the lordship of Jesus.

Erasmus uses military terminology to illustrate what transpires at water baptism. Consider someone who joins the military today. The person is exposed to the pros and cons of making a commitment to a branch of the military during the recruitment stage. Once the recruit is convinced the military will be a good fit, the recruiter will gain a commitment from the person to join the military. Although committed to join, the person doesn't officially become a solider until he or she raises his or her hand and takes the oath of office. Once the oath is administrated, the person does not have a path out of the military until their contract is completed, they have a medical issue, or they are dishonorably discharged.

When a person makes a commitment to join the army of God, a similar process is followed. A person is exposed to the claims of Christ. The benefits of becoming a Christian are shared, as well as the cost of the commitment. If the person thinks Christianity is a good fit, the person sharing the gospel gains a commitment through a prayer of repentance. The commitment is formalized when a public declaration is made through water baptism.

When a person joins the military, they repeat an oath of office.

I, _____, do solemnly swear (or affirm) that I will support and defend the Constitution of the United States against all enemies, foreign and domestic; that I will bear true faith and allegiance to the same; and that I will obey the orders of the President of the United States and the orders of the officers appointed over me, according to the regulations and the Uniform Code of Military Justice, So help me God.

Notice what soldiers are promising in this oath. They are giving up their rights to direct their lives according to their will and preferences. They no longer get to call the shots of their lives. They promise to live according to a prescribed code of conduct established by someone else. They promise to defend an idea, philosophy, and rule of law. They promise to do whatever it takes to defend the country, even if it means laying down their own lives. They promise to live with integrity. They promise to live obediently to the Commander in

Chief. No wonder the oath ends with a prayer asking God to help them to fulfill this weighty promise.

Water baptism is the moment when a person takes a public oath declaring his or her intent to serve God with his or her whole heart, mind, and will. It is the moment when the convert seals the deal and makes a lifelong commitment to serve God, no matter the cost. Once a person is baptized in water, there is no turning back. Until a person is willing to make that stand, the person is not ready to be water baptized.

Perhaps there should be an oath of office given when a person is water baptized. It might go something like this:

I, _____, do solemnly swear (or affirm) that I will support and defend the Church of Jesus Christ against all enemies, spiritual and human; that I will bear true faith and allegiance to the same; and that I will obey the orders of the Father, Son and Holy Spirit and submit to the leadership appointed by God over me, according to the Bible, so help me God.

For those who prefer a football metaphor, water baptism is like a player being traded from one team to another. If one of the best players for the Dallas Cowboys was traded to the Washington Redskins, and he came out onto the field the next time the Redskins played the Cowboys wearing his old Cowboy's uniform, looked to the Cowboy's sideline for instructions, and attempted to help the Cowboy's win, it would be unthinkable. Unfortunately, this is what happens many times when people are baptized in water without knowing the price they are paying to wear the new uniform of salvation. They may say they are on God's team, but they continue to try to live like they did when they were living according to their own standards. Their actions tear down the kingdom of God, rather than build it up. And they don't look much different than they did before they made their declarative statement through water baptism.

Water baptism is a big deal. Every Christian should be water baptized because every Christian should fully submit themselves to the authority of Jesus. Jesus commanded His followers to them to take communion and He told them to be water baptized. This indicates Jesus saw water baptism as more than a ritual to be completed by the believer. Water baptism is a serious decision that should not be made to simply say we obeyed a command of Jesus. A person's priorities, allegiances, and affections should all be rearranged when a person submits to water baptism, as described in Scripture. In this chapter, I want to explore the significance of water baptism.

A Biblical View of Water Baptism

Let's take a look at what the Bible says about water baptism.

Water Baptism: A Command of Jesus

Water baptism is a command for both the new believer, and for the person leading that person to Christ. Jesus instructed His disciples, "Go therefore and make disciples of all nations, baptizing them in the name of the Father and of the Son and of the Holy Spirit, teaching them to observe all that I have commanded you" (Matthew 28:19-20).

It is not enough to lead someone to Jesus. We must also help them to understand the significance of salvation and help them to make the decision to take the public oath of spiritual commitment through water baptism.

The church fellowship which I belong to has had a significant disconnect between reported salvations and water baptisms. Each year churches in our fellowship (United States) complete reports that include the number of people who accepted Christ through their church ministries, and the number of people who were baptized in water (along with many other statistics). Each year nearly 500,000 new converts are reported while there are less than 150,000 people baptized in water during that same period. If these numbers are accurate, nearly 350,000 people are living "Christian" lives without making the essential decision to unconditionally submit their lives to the lordship of Jesus. My fellowship is growing, but not at a rate of 500,000 per year. Perhaps if more people were being lead to make a full-fledged commitment through water baptism, many more people would be attending our churches and additional workers would be available to further the kingdom of God.

Some people would say 150,000 out of 500,000 is not bad since it takes a long time to get people ready to be water baptized. Other denominations would shake their collective heads wondering why the number is so low. In their churches, a person is baptized in water the same day they accept Jesus as Savior.

So a question must be considered, "When should a person be water baptized?"

Perhaps the best way to answer this question is to avoid an artificial timeline, but state that when a person is determined to commit themselves to fully live for Jesus, surrender their will to Jesus' will, and become a productive part of a church family, the person should be baptized in water. This could happen quickly or over time, but in either case it requires someone to walk the new convert through a discipleship process.

New Testament writers assumed every Christian had been water baptized. To not be baptized was a sure indication the person was not a follower of Jesus. Jesus states this clearly: "Whoever believes and is baptized will be saved, but whoever does not believe will be condemned" (Mark 16:16).

Jesus was not saying water baptism was the source of salvation. He was simply saying, if you are a follower of Jesus, you will have been baptized. There is no excuse not to be baptized unless you have decided to reject the authority of God and live according to your own standards.

Some may be reading this and realize they were baptized in water, but it had no real significance in their life. If this is the case, don't resist the idea of being baptized again if you have made the decision to live a life of submission to Jesus since you were first baptized in water.

Water Baptism: A Sign of Submission

Water baptism is a sign of submission. Jesus thought water baptism was so important, He insisted on being water baptized (Matthew 3:14-15). Some may wonder why Jesus insisted on being baptized in water. There were at least two reasons for Jesus to go through this important activity. One reason was to set an example for all those who would come after Him. This example was to say, no matter who you are, it is vital that you identify with the kingdom of God through water baptism. A second reason was that during the first century it was a requirement for a person to be baptized before they could become actively involved in the ministry of the kingdom of God. Notice that Jesus did not actively minister until after He was water baptized. He was baptized, then went into the wilderness to spend time with the Father, was tempted by Satan, and then went full-fledged into his 3 ½ year ministry.

It would not have made any sense for an individual in the first century to not be water baptized, if they were going to stand in opposition to the religious culture, and function fully in the army of God. If a person would not submit themselves to God through the act of water baptism, and identify with the cause of Christ, they would be suspect among Christ followers.

Today, there are many Christians who have either willfully decided not to be water baptized, or have neglected this important act of submission, yet they still feel like they can function fully within the kingdom of God. It is true that water baptism does not save an individual, but failing to be water baptized indicates the condition of a person's heart. If we are not willing to be publicly identified as a follower of Jesus through water baptism, it indicates we wish to live our spiritual life according to our standards and our authority, rather than the standards set by Christ.

It's important for all of us to remember that if the only truly righteous person who has ever lived on this earth felt that it was necessary for Him to be water baptized, then it probably is at least as important for individuals who do not reach that standard in their own lives to willingly submit to water baptism.

Water Baptism: A Commitment to Share in Jesus' Suffering

Water baptism is also important for the believer because it demonstrates our commitment to share in the suffering of Jesus. The apostle Paul, talking about water baptism stated, "Do you not know that all of us who'd been baptized into Christ Jesus were baptized into his death? We were buried therefore with him by baptism into death, in order that, just as Christ was raised from the dead by the glory of the father, we too might walk in newness of life" (Romans 6:3-4).

When Christians are baptized in water, it symbolizes that their old life has died and they have been raised to new life when they emerged from the water. This death provides life, but also declares their willingness to suffer for the cause of Christ if necessary. Just as a soldier is willing to take a bullet to defend the nation, Christians must be willing to lay down their lives for the cause of the kingdom of God if necessary. When a person is water baptized, it is a serious decision because the consequences of that decision may be very serious. The majority of the people reading this chapter will never have to suffer intensely, for the cause of Christ, they must be willing to do so if called upon. Water baptism is a total commitment to do whatever is necessary to advance the cause of the kingdom of God.

Water Baptism: A Statement of Unity

When we are baptized in water, we must renounce all prejudice, pride, and bigotry. The apostle Paul helps us to understand this when he states, "For in one Spirit were all baptized into one body-Jews or Greeks, slaves or free-and all were made to drink of one Spirit" (1 Corinthians 12:13).

One of the concepts repeated throughout Scripture is the importance of unity among believers. From the very beginning of time, one of Satan's key methods to hindering the purposes of God is to cause dissension. We see it start with a breach between God and His creation when Adam and Eve chose to hide themselves from God after yielding to the temptation of Satan. Then in the very next chapter, we see Cain and Abel in conflict which led to the first recorded murder. Conflict can be seen throughout the entire Old Testament. Most of the New Testament letters written by the apostle Paul address conflicts of one fashion or another within the church. Paul repeatedly calls for Christians to learn to love one another and to live with one another in harmony. Jesus told His followers that people would know they were His disciples by the way they loved one another (John 13:35).

The tactics of Satan have not changed over time. The Church is as divided today as it was in the first century. We argue with one another based on our perceived superiority in regard to our theology, our station in life, our gender, and sadly, oftentimes, based on our race. The Bible teaches us when we are baptized in water we are holding hands with everyone who has ever been water baptized before us. Everyone who has ever been water baptized is equal. They have all been baptized into one body, which functions under a common head; Jesus Christ. When we take shots at each other, we are wasting our spiritual ammunition. Instead of focusing our energy towards defeating the powers of evil, we tend to shoot at other Christians who may have a different view than we have. This is leaving the Church wounded and humiliated. In the military, it doesn't matter what your background is, or what color you are, or your philosophy about the military. When the enemy attacks, those in the military can count on their fellow soldier to have their back. If we would turn our spiritual guns on the true enemy of our soul and do spiritual warfare with Satan and his army of demons, the Church would be much stronger than we are today.

There is absolutely no place in the kingdom of God for prejudice against a fellow Christian. If you believe you are superior to somebody else, and you treat them in an inferior fashion, you are not representing the King. When you are water baptized, you are clearly declaring that you are no better, or no worse, than any other foot soldier in God's army. Your task is to do the will of the Commander and to do whatever you can to protect and encourage your fellow brothers and sisters in Christ.

If Christians would ever embrace this concept, we could use this unified front to make major advances on the evil that we see in the world today. If you have been water baptized, and you are prejudiced toward someone, it is time for you to repent and recommit yourself to a spirit of unity. You might even consider being rebaptized to seal that commitment.

Water Baptism: A Uniform for Battle

Water baptism also proclaims the Christian has become one with Jesus. The apostle Paul says to the Galatian believers, "For as many of you as were baptized into Christ have put on Christ (Galatians 3:27). When we were saved, we became one with Jesus. Water baptism is the outward declaration of that truth. As a Christian, we clothe ourselves with Christ and wherever we go, He is there. When we wear Christ, it's much like a police officer who puts on his uniform. He is no longer Jack Smith, the citizen. He is now Jack Smith, the representative of the municipality in which he serves. When you see Jack Smith in uniform, you do not see an individual. You see a policeman. The uniform transforms our view of the person and helps us to understand what his purpose is. The same concept applies to the military soldier who puts on a uniform which removes individuality and provides purpose.

As Christians, we put on a uniform which is Christ Jesus. When people see us, they no longer see individuals who function according to their own agendas. We are seen as people who have a purpose, which is to advance God's kingdom.

Water Baptism: A Pledge of Faithfulness

And finally, water baptism is a pledge made to God in return for what He did for us. Peter explains, "Baptism, which corresponds to this, now saves you, not as a removal of dirt from the body but as an appeal to God for a good conscience, through the resurrection of Jesus (1 Peter 3:21).

Water baptism is similar to a man putting an engagement ring on a woman's finger. All the benefits of marriage are not bestowed at that point, but a serious commitment has been made. The man makes the following proposal to the woman, "If you will remain pure and committed to me, there will be a day when we will live together forever." If the woman accepts the proposal, she agrees to not share her love with anyone else. She will reserve her affections for him.

In a similar fashion, Jesus has made a proposal to us. He promises us eternity with Him if we will commit our lives to Him. We officially accept His proposal when we are water baptized. We are agreeing to commit ourselves to reserve our love for Him and not to compromise our lives by engaging with the world. There is no question that Jesus will keep His end of the bargain. Water baptism is our promise to keep our end of the bargain until the day of consummation, when we meet Jesus face-to-face.

Conclusion

Water baptism is a big deal. It is not a guarantee of salvation, but it is an act that declares we take our salvation seriously. If you have not been baptized in water, you need to do so if you intend to follow Jesus throughout your life. If you were water baptized and you were not ready to do so at the time, consider being baptized again to seal your commitment. Once you have been baptized in water, think about your baptism often, and let it remind you of your commitment to Jesus and the promises He has made to you that you will receive in the future.

Study Guide Questions

1. What is the premise of Erasmus in regard to water baptism?

2. What metaphor did Erasmus use to illustrate the power of water baptism?

3. Why does the author think water baptism is a "big deal"?

4. Why is water baptism commanded by Jesus?

5. Why should a person consider being rebaptized in water?

6. Why was Jesus baptized in water?

7. How should your water baptism impact your view of fellow a Christian who disagrees with you?

8. How is water baptism like a man and woman getting engaged to be married?

TWELVE

SPIRITUAL FORMATION THROUGH FASTING

The primary Hebrew term for fasting is *tsuwm* which means "to cover over (the mouth)." This word never occurs in the Pentateuch, but the indication is that the Hebrew phrase found in Leviticus 23:27 *innah nephesh*, refers to a fast. The phrase found in Leviticus 23:27 can be translated, "to afflict yourself: literally, 'afflict your souls,' but the meaning is 'fast' ('refuse to eat') or 'practice self-denial.'" Fasting has been practiced in various ways throughout history. This chapter will examine these various practices and discover what God desires when we engage in this practice.

Fasting in the Old Testament

Jewish tradition teaches the only required fast for all believers is on the Day of Atonement, referred to in Leviticus 23. The Day of Atonement is a national day of repentance and renewal. The Jews used the fast to demonstrate sorrow for their sins and their dependence on God for their future. The Jewish faithful refer to the Day of Atonement as "the day of fasting" (Jeremiah 36:6) or "the fast" (Acts 27:9).

Although the Law only required fasting once a year, fasting occurred much more often. Moses fasted at Sinai, while receiving the Law from God (Exodus 34:28; Deuteronomy 9:9) and once again, when he smashed the tablets (Deuteronomy 9:17). Leaders called for fasts when national tragedy was on the horizon (Judges 20:26, 1 Samuel 7:6, 2 Chronicles 20:3; Ezra 8:21-23, Esther 4:16; Jeremiah 36:9; Joel 1:13). The bereaved fasted as an act of mourning (1 Samuel 31:13; 2 Samuel 1:12; 3:35; 12:21; Esther 4:3; Psalm 35:13; Isaiah 31:13). The sinner fasted to seek forgiveness (1 Samuel 7:6; 1 Kings 21:27; Nehemiah 9:1-2; Daniel 9:3-4; Jonah 5:5-8). The desperate fasted to add power to their prayers (2 Samuel 12:16-23;

1 Kings 21:27; Ezra 8:21; Esther 4:16). The confused fasted to gain guidance from God (Exodus 34:28; Deuteronomy 9:9; 2 Samuel 12:16-23; 2 Chronicles 20-3-4; Ezra 8:21-23).

Four additional fast days were required during the Exile and became an ongoing part of the Jewish calendar. These fast days focused the exiles on the faithfulness of God throughout Jewish history (Zechariah 7:1-7; 8:19).

The first fast day occurred in the fourth month of the year. It commemorated the anniversary of the capture of Jerusalem by the Babylonians (Jeremiah 52:6-7). It also served to remind the Jewish believers of the rebellion against God when Aaron lead them in worshipping the golden calf (Exodus 32:1-35).

The second required fast day occurred in the fifth month of the year. This fast reminded the Jewish people of the day the Babylonians burned the city of Jerusalem and the Temple of God (Jeremiah 52:12-13).

The third day, which was set aside, occurred in the seventh month. This day reminded the people of the murder of Gedaliah (Jeremiah 41:1-2). Gedaliah was the governor the Babylonians had set over the Jewish people. Ishmael was hired by the Ammonites to kill the governor and to capture the Jewish people and take them to Ammon. This was a tragic day in Israel's history.

The fourth required fast occurred in the tenth month of the Jewish calendar. It was a day that reminded the Jews of the beginning of the conquest of Jerusalem by the king of Babylon, Nebuchadnezzar (Jeremiah 52:4; Ezekiel 33:21; 2 Kings 25:1)

Parameters of a Biblical Fast

A prescribed way to do a "proper fast" does not exist in the Old Testament (although there are rules given in the Talmud regarding fasts). The only uniform element of a fast is that it involves refraining from some type of food, for some length of time. Moses (Exodus 34:28) and Elijah (1 Kings 19:8) fasted for forty days. Daniel fasted for twenty-one days (Daniel 10:1-2). The fast on the Day of Atonement went from sunset to sunset (Leviticus 23:32). Saul's foolish fast lasted only one day (1 Samuel 14:24-28). Darius fasted for one night (Daniel 6:18). David's fast was indefinite, but ended on the seventh day after the baby died (2 Samuel 12:16-18). It seems clear no specific timeframe exists that sanctions a fast as legitimate.

In the same way, the Old Testament provides no guidance as to what types of food or drink people must eliminate during a fast. The fast, on the Day of Atonement, seems to be a total fast of all food and water. Those found guilty of doing any work or being in violation of the fast were cut off from the people of God. With this extreme consequence in play, it seems likely the true follower would not risk eating the wrong thing (Leviticus 16:29; 23:26-32). Daniel fasted rich food and meat, wine, and the use of fragrant oils (Daniel 10:3). During the foolish fast, called by Saul, even dipping a stick into a honeycomb and licking it was considered a violation of the fast. Total abstinence from food was seldom required, especially in a longer fast.

As with any discipline designed to help people draw closer to God, a danger lurks to turn a tool into a weapon. The Israelites began to use fasting as an attempt to manipulate God or to appear religiously superior to others (Isaiah 58:3; Zechariah 7:5-6; Malachi 3:14).

Isaiah 58 provides a pivotal examination of fasting which was embraced by pre-exilic believers, and the corrective instruction given by God through the prophet Isaiah. The chapter begins with God acknowledging the cries of His people who desire to hear from Him. The Jewish people do not understand why God is not responding to their fasting and self-denial (Isaiah 58:1-2).

The Jews display their theology of fasting when they declare, "Why have we fasted, and you see it not? Why have we humbled ourselves, and you take no knowledge of it? Behold, in the day of your fast you seek your own pleasure, and oppress all your workers" (Isaiah 58:3).

The Jewish believers had slipped into the mentality of their neighbors who thought God got His pleasure from watching His followers experience pain and suffering. They believed God would give them anything they desired, in exchange for the pleasure their pain gave Him. They couldn't believe God had not taken notice of their sacrifice.

God corrects the thinking of His people. God explains a proper fast is not primarily about denying oneself a pleasure or providing God with a personal sacrifice to gain His pleasure. This is the fast God desires:

Is not this the fast that I choose: to loose the bonds of wickedness, to undo the straps of the yoke, to let the oppressed go free, and to break every yoke? Is it not to share your bread with the hungry and bring the homeless poor into your house; when you see the naked, to cover him, and not to hide yourself from your own flesh? (Isaiah 58:5-7).

God desires a fast of the heart and attitude which aligns His followers' purposes with His purposes. God desires fasting to be a practice of selflessness. Fasting must not focus on what the person doing the fast receives through the fast. A fast approved by God focuses on producing His desire—ministry to the hurt and broken in the world.

The motivation of fasting is defined by God. The motivation must not be self-serving in any way. We do not trade something to get a blessing from God. To do so means we think we can force God to do our will if only we pay the right price. A biblical fast must be motivated from the Great Commandment given to us by Jesus; to love God and to love others. If we fast from this motive, we will be aligned with God's purposes. When we are aligned with His purposes, we will receive His blessings.

It is easy to get confused when God blesses those who fast. We can begin to think the blessings were a result of the fasting and then fall into the trap the Jews found themselves in. The blessings people get are not because they fast, but because of the outcome of the fast when the people realign themselves with God's purposes. As with many other spiritual principles, two people can do the same practice and end up with different results because of the motivation which prompts them to do the discipline.

A true fast will be transformative in nature. During the fast, we set aside time and resources to focus on our relationship with God. When we give our undivided attention to God, He will reveal areas in our lives that need to be adjusted. Often, God will point out areas where we lack in our love for Him, but more often He will point out a lack in our care for others. In the case of the fast mentioned in Isaiah 58, God challenges Israel concerning the way they were treating the oppressed (Isaiah 58:7-12). God would not bless Israel as long as they oppressed the poor. Until they changed their heart, He refused to give them His blessings.

Fasting in the New Testament

Jesus would have been very familiar with the practice of fasting as a young person. By the first century, the Jewish people had developed weekly fasts (Matthew. 9:14; Mark 2:18; Luke 5:33; 18:12; Acts 10:30). Fasts were performed every Monday and Thursday. These fasts were associated with the broken tablets containing the Ten Commandments. In addition to the public fasts, individuals performed fasts as they desired (Luke 2:37).

Jesus condemned the misuse of the fast by the Pharisees (Matthew 6:16) and He felt there was no need for His disciples to fast while He was in their presence (Matthew 9:14). Jesus does not reject the practice of fasting. Jesus' response to John the Baptist, when John sent his disciples to determine if Jesus was truly the Messiah, demonstrates Jesus' intent to restore the proper meaning of the fast. Jesus tells John's disciples to explain to John that He is doing all the things regarding an acceptable fast which are required by God in Isaiah 58 (Matthew 10:4-6).

Textual issues complicate the reader's ability to understand how the New Testament writers truly view fasting. Some of the most quoted New Testament verses, concerning fasting, cannot be supported by the most reliable manuscripts. The most reliable manuscripts do not include the phrase "and fasting" in Matthew 17:12; Mark 9:29; Acts 10:30; and 1 Corinthians 7:5. The fact the term made its way into later manuscripts indicates fasting was a valued spiritual practice, associated with prayer, in the Early Church.

Since the New Testament provides very little direct teaching regarding fasting, the best one can do is to learn from the examples of fasting found there. The disciples of John and the Pharisees performed the weekly fasts demanded by Jewish tradition (Matt. 10:1-3). At best, what can be learned from these fasts comes from Jesus' rebuke for the misuse of the fast by the religious leaders.

Although limited information is available, Anna's fast (Luke 2:37) provides some insight concerning her understanding of fasting. She serves through fasting and prayer. Dedication to God defines her entire life. Anna does not seek anything of a personal nature. Anna's fasting demonstrates a desire to be used more fully by God.

Jesus fasted for forty days before His temptation (Matt. 4:2). Many scholars believe Jesus did not intend to fast when He went into the wilderness to spend time with His Father. The first temptation indicates there was no food where He went to pray. The lack of food did not bother Jesus because He was focused on the Father during this time of dedication. Later in Jesus' ministry, we hear Jesus comment on His reliance on spiritual bread to sustain Him (John 4:32). It is possible that Matthew highlighted Jesus' fasting to place Jesus on the same stage as Moses, who fasted on the mountain 40 days before receiving the Law from God, in the minds of his Jewish readers (Exodus 34:28).

The apostle Paul went without food after his blinding encounter with Jesus (Acts 9:9), before his first missionary journey (13:2), when appointing elders (14:23), and for fourteen days during a storm at sea (27:33). Let's examine each of these events and see if they help us understand fasting a little better.

The first account gives no reference to a spiritual component associated with Paul's lack of eating or drinking. This does not help us much in our quest.

The second account provides more information concerning Paul's use of fasting. The Bible says, "They were ministering to the Lord and fasting." This terminology resembles the language used in Luke 2:27. In the context of fasting, the Holy Spirit instructs the assembly to send Paul and Barnabas on a mission to minister to the disenfranchised. Although it cannot be proven by this text alone, it appears fasting is a normal part of the first-century Church's worship, as it was in the life of Anna.

The third account records Paul and Barnabas "prayed with fasting" as they appointed leadership to the churches. Before Paul and Barnabas went on to the next city, they always spent time in prayer and fasting with the believers. Fasting was part of a worship time and not a means of demonstrating sorrow or seeking specific favor. It appears this type of fasting was an attempt to come into alignment with God.

In the final account mentioned (Acts 27:33), the subject is not fasting, but fear. The crew of the ship had been so consumed with navigating the storm, they had not taken time to eat. There is no indication the crew prays during their fast, or even that they were looking to God. Instead of encouraging the crew to continue fasting as a means of appeasing God, Paul tells the crew to eat, so they will have the strength necessary to carry on their mission.

The examples of fasting in the New Testament are few. We know it was a regular practice by the Pharisees, who used it inappropriately, and by the followers of John. We also know Jesus made the assumption His followers would fast after His ascension. The most we learn about fasting in the New Testament is what not to do. It is clear Jesus did not see fasting as a merit producing activity that manipulated God.

Fasting in Church History

Fasting takes on a greater emphasis in the Church after the New Testament era. One of the first things the Early Church does is to develop unique Christian expressions of fasting. One of these expressions concerns the practice of the weekly fast. The Jews had held two days sacred for some time. Now the Church set aside two fast days of their own. They wanted to not confuse their fasts with the Jewish fast days, so the Early Church set aside Wednesdays for a full day of fasting and Fridays for a half fast. On Fridays, Christians could not eat any meat. They believed refraining from eating flesh on Fridays would make people remember Jesus gave His flesh on a Friday. This remembrance would lead the believers to give thanks. Christians were allowed to eat fish on Fridays. The church felt compelled to fast regularly because of Jesus' words recorded in Matthew 9:15: "Can the wedding guests mourn as long as the bridegroom is with them? The days will come when the bridegroom is taken away from them, and then they will fast."

In the second century, the Church began to institute a 40 day fast leading up to Easter. This fast has become known as Lent. There were some countries that have variations to this Lent period with some limiting the fast to 40 hours, some a few weeks, but the standard was a 40 day fast to mimic Jesus' time in the wilderness. During the Lent period, believers would refrain from eating a particular food. In keeping with the concern for the poor associated with the Old Testament fast, the food that was not eaten was given to the disadvantaged. In addition to the lent fast, there were nocturnal fasts before the high festivals of the Church. A fast could be called at any time by the bishops when they saw a particular need that required extra resources. The result of these fasts was to help the Christians recognize the plight of the poor and to be a blessing to them.

By the sixth century, fasting was no longer an option for the believer. The Second Council of Orleans met in A. D. 541. At that Council, leadership made it mandatory for Christians to fast on a regular basis. The Council stated anyone who neglected to fast, at the required time, should be treated as an offender against the Church.

By the eighth century, fasting was taken to a new level by the Church. At this time the Church declared that those who regularly practiced fasting earned special favor from God. Those who refused to fast were excommunicated from the Church. Since an individual could not go to heaven if they were not a part of the Church, Church leaders were indicating fasting was salvific in nature. By the eighth century, the Church leaders were making the same mistake God had corrected through the prophet Isaiah.

The Reformation changed many things, but fasting was not one of those. Even though the Reformers argued that salvation was by faith alone, many of them still placed a high degree of importance on the practice of fasting. John Wesley, the father of the Methodist Church, insisted those who were a part of the church which he led return to the practice of fasting on Wednesdays and Fridays. Wesley made it a requirement for all ministers, ordained as Methodist pastors, to fast on those two days each week. If it was discovered that the minister was not fasting, or leading the congregation in the practice of fasting on these two days, their ordination would be stripped. Other Reformers, who promoted the value of fasting and made it of supreme importance in their theology included Charles Spurgeon, Martin Luther, John Calvin, Jonathan Edwards, and Charles Finney.

Fasting has lost some of its luster in recent years. In the Protestant church, very few religious traditions insist on fasting. Many will suggest people fast during Lent, but increasingly churches are not even emphasizing fasting during that time. Some churches will fast at the beginning of the year seeking to start the year aligned with God. Others will call for a special fast when they desire to hear God more clearly. But very few churches use fasting as a tool to address the needs of the poor in their communities. Even the Roman Catholic Church has relaxed its emphasis on fasting. Since the Second Vatican Council, Roman Catholics are only required to fast twice a year; on Ash Wednesday and on Good Friday. There are voices in the spiritual formation community who remind Christians of the value of fasting, but for the most part, fasting is an individual matter that receives little attention in most Christian gatherings.

Conclusion

Fasting has been an act associated with spiritual development throughout history. To ignore fasting as a spiritual discipline, including corporate fasting, is to ignore the potential it holds for spiritual development. Proper fasting redirects the believer to the priorities of God. When believers aligned themselves with God's priority, inevitably, they will become a more accurate reflection of the God they claim to serve.

One of the best statements made concerning fasting was adopted as part of the position paper crafted by the fellowship with whom I am ordained. This is a statement that crosses all denominational lines. They state: "Fasting should never be viewed as a merit-producing, manipulative, or in any other way an act of bargaining with God. The object of fasting is not to move God in closer alignment with us and our will, but rather to draw us in closer alignment with God and His will."

Let me encourage you to practice periods of fasting as a means of drawing closer to God and to become more aware of the needs of others. Allow fasting to propel you toward a deeper level of compassion for the poor and those who are in need of a relationship with God.

Study Guide Questions

1. What day was the Jewish "day of Fasting"?

2. What chapter of the Bible provides a pivotal examination of fasting embraced by the pre-exilic believers and corrective instructions given by God?

3. Describe a fast that God considers acceptable.

4. On what days of the week did the Jews fast?

5. What was the purpose of Anna's fast?

6. On what day of the week did the Early Church practice a half fast (abstaining from flesh)?

7. Since the Second Vatican Council, when are Roman Catholics required to fast?

8. According to the author, what does fasting accomplish when practiced properly?

UNIT THREE

ENHANCING YOUR PERSONAL
RELATIONSHIP WITH OTHERS

THIRTEEN

SPIRITUAL FORMATION THROUGH SUBMISSION

Submission has gotten a bad rap. For most people, the word "submission" has negative connotations. Women often feel like they're being put into subjection when they hear that they are to submit to their husbands. Some individuals ask how God could expect them to submit to a ruthless leader such as Adolf Hitler. The concept of submission can feel like we give up our rights so somebody else can have their rights, at our detriment.

Like so many other things, Satan has taken something God meant for good and has perverted it. A beautiful gift, given by God, has become tragically flawed. Submission will protect us if used appropriately. Rather than being a negative concept, it is an important positive practice which must be embraced, if we are going to live freely in the kingdom of God. Submission is a willful decision to sublimate one's own wishes and desires in recognition of the authority of another. I owe a great deal of my own formation in this area to material found in Richard Foster's *Celebration of Discipline*.

The Benefits of Submission

A person's attitude concerning submission reveals a great deal about the person. Submission is designed to help us understand we are not independent of one another and we cannot always have our own way. As a college professor, it intrigues me when I listen to students who are having struggles with their first college roommate. Most of these individuals have never had to share a bedroom before. Since they had their own room at home, they could live pretty much any way they wanted. They did not have to give consideration to another person's desires. It is a shocking experience when they realize not everyone wants to live like they do. It makes it even more difficult when the roommate decides they can use their roommate's clothes, rearrange their possessions, and help themselves to their roommate's toiletries. The whole idea of having to submit to the wishes of someone else becomes reality during the first few weeks of the semester. Some people can't handle it. They often insist on changing roommates, only to soon discover the new situation is not much better.

The apostle James points to the cause of the dilemma faced by these warring roommates. He states, "What causes quarrels and what causes fights among you? Is it not this, that your passions are at war within you? You desire and do not have, so you murder. You covet and cannot obtain, so you fight and quarrel" (James 4:1-2). Fortunately, we have not had any murders over the way toilet tissue hangs from the roll in the dorms.

Submission makes us face the fact we are not the center of our own universe. There are other people who must be considered as we live our lives. It is easy to think we are the star and everyone who comes across our paths are simply bit actors in our personal movie. In these personalized movies, we can do whatever we want to do, even if it negatively impacts somebody else. Learning to submit is God's way of teaching us how to live out His commandment to love God and to love others. Many of us have no problem with loving God, as long as His plans do not get in the way of our plans. We have no problem loving others, as long as they let us do what we want to do. Submission forces us to recognize God is greater than we are. When we do, we will be willing to live according to His plans. Submission also forces us to recognize other people are just as important as we are. As a result, we must take them into consideration as we make decisions in our lives. Submission is both a vertical exercise in regard to authority, and a horizontal exercise in regard to relationships.

Submission allows us to be free from a spirit of rebellion. Saul was the first king of Israel. He had the greatest privilege an individual could ever be granted. He was selected by God to lead His people. But Saul felt his thoughts were higher than God's thoughts. He openly disregarded God's directions. God would not tolerate the spirit of rebellion that lived in Saul's heart. When dismissing him from his role as king, God spoke these words, "For rebellion is as the sin of divination, and presumption is as iniquity and idolatry. Because you have rejected the word of the LORD, he has also rejected you from being king" (1 Samuel 15:23).

In the King James Version of the Bible, the word "divination" is translated "witchcraft." The question one must ask is, "Why is rebellion like witchcraft?" You might wonder how a refusal to obey authorities in one's life can be like worshiping Satan. Let's allow the apostle Paul to help us understand.

Paul states, "Let every person be subject to the governing authorities. For there is no authority except from God, and those that exist have been instituted by God. Therefore whoever resists the authorities resists what God has appointed, and those who resist will incur judgment" (Romans 13:1-2).

If all authority comes from God, then when we rebel against authority, we are actually rebelling against God. And what was the sin of Satan? The Bible teaches that Satan rebelled against God in his refusal to take his appropriate role assigned to him by God (Ezekiel 28:13-19). So when we rebel against authority, which was appointed by God, then we are participating with Satan in rebellion against God. When we cooperate with Satan rather than with God, it is little different than what witches do when they cooperate and promote the purposes of Satan.

Satan would like us to believe we will be free once we have cast off the restraints of authority. Like every other promise of Satan, the freedom that rebellion promises ends up putting us in bondage and captivity. The very restraints we cast off are the protections we need to allow us to live in true freedom. When we begin to do things our own way, refusing to submit to the authorities, we will suffer temporal punishments such as speeding tickets and jail sentences, but far worse, we will experience eternal suffering if we choose to live in rebellion to God. Peter explains the dilemma of listening to Satan. "They promise them freedom, but they themselves are slaves of corruption. For whatever overcomes a person, to that he is enslaved" (2 Peter 2:19).

Every human is enslaved, either by choice to God through faith in Jesus, or they are enslaved by choice or deception to Satan through rebellion. One enslavement results in loving kindness, freedom in our spirits, and everlasting life. The other enslavement results in hatred, destruction, and eternal damnation. We will all submit to either God or Satan. As a follower of Christ, we would be foolish to trade our freedom in Christ for perceived freedom.

Submission allows us to value other people. It is not until we see ourselves properly and appreciate how God has made us that we can see others properly and appreciate how God made them. Every person is unique and shaped in the image of God. He made each of us exactly as He desired to accomplish His plan and purpose within the body of Christ. The apostle Paul uses the imagery of a human body to describe how God sees each of us. "God arranged the members in the body, each one of them, as he chose. If all were a single member, where would the body be?" (1 Corinthians 12:18-19).

In a self-centered society, which ranks people according to their bank account or education, it is easy for Christians to adopt a secular mindset and begin to believe there are some people who are more important than others in the body of Christ.

A quick assessment of how you see people can be made by asking who you show more respect to, the janitor or the president of an organization. Most people in our society will show a great deal more respect to a person who has earned a degree and lives in a very nice home than they do for an individual working for low wages. This may be an acceptable way of valuing people in the world, but it is an unacceptable way of viewing people in the kingdom of God. Everyone within the church is equal in regard to value, even though some roles demand a greater level of responsibility and receive a larger paycheck in conjunction with that responsibility.

Submission also allows a person to treat those higher in an organizational chart with respect. In my job, I have four tiers of authority above me. I have my Dean, the Vice President for Academics, the President of the University, and the Board of Directors. There are decisions made in our organization I do not fully agree with, but that does not give me the right to disregard them or disobey them. God has not placed me in the position to create the rules. He has placed other individuals in roles of authority above me. They have the privilege and responsibility of determining the rules and regulations by which I function. I must honor God by honoring them, and living in accordance to their desires for this organization. If at some time God were to want my input to be considered in regard to these regulations, I believe He would insert me into a position of influence that could shape the rules in a different manner. We will address how we should respond in abusive situations later, but I am privileged to work in a place that is not abusive towards faculty, staff, or the students. Any objections I have are merely a matter of preference.

All of us have authorities in our lives. I have authorities over me, but I am in authority over others. The students I teach have various roles of authority such as residence assistants, student organization officers, and leaders of outreach teams. But at the same time, the students are under submission to the faculty advisors, administration, and resident life teams. Understanding submission helps an individual learn to respect the roles others possess and to respond to them in a way that honors their role, as well as God who authorizes those roles. I cannot expect people to submit to me if I have not proven I am willing to submit to others. Good leaders must first be good followers.

Submission allows us to give up the right to retaliate. It is natural for our response to be negative when a person in authority challenges a decision we make. When a police officer pulls us over for speeding, our natural reaction is to defend ourselves and to retaliate in some fashion. Most of us understand retaliating against a law enforcement officer is not the wisest decision, but we can still harbor anger towards these individuals if we are not careful. I've had students who have made poor decisions in regard to honesty when it comes to submitting assignments. As the teacher, it is my responsibility to all my students to punish those who cheat. If an individual is caught cheating in my class, I not only fail them for that assignment, I also fail them for the semester. To the person receiving the failing grade, it seems harsh and sometimes they lash out angrily. If the individual is truly repentant and seeking to draw closer to God, they admit their misdeed and overcome their anger. They recognize it would be unjust and unfair for them to be treated any other way since others worked diligently to earn their grades. Having a submissive attitude will not fix a mistake that was made, but it will open the door for God to use the lesson to help them see the value of living in accordance to God's standards, even when there seems to be an easier avenue to follow.

When facing a situation where you feel the authority has treated you unfairly, rather than retaliating, you must apply Jesus' directive, "But I say to you, Love your enemies and pray for those who persecute you, so that you may be sons of your Father who is in heaven. For he makes his sun rise on the evil and on the good, and sends rain on the just and on the unjust" (Matthew 5:44-45).

What Does Submission Look Like?

I will never forget the first time I had the privilege of going to Arlington National Cemetery, just outside of Washington DC. For anyone who has been there, you probably had the same first reaction I had when I saw the acres of simple white crosses. My first thought was how beautiful the crosses were against the backdrop of the rolling hills. My second thought was much more sobering. I thought about the men and women who were under those crosses, who willingly gave their lives so I could have the freedoms I enjoy in this country. These individuals swore allegiance to the country and to the Constitution. They considered their life an investment in the freedom of others.

The apostle Paul told the Philippian church their lives should be characterized by a selfless submission, much like that displayed by the soldiers buried in Arlington. But when Paul wrote his words, he was not thinking of soldiers who sacrificed their lives. He was thinking about Jesus, who gave His life unselfishly so we could experience spiritual freedom. Paul instructs the Philippians, "Let each of you look not only to his own interests, but also to the interests of others. Have this mind among yourselves, which is yours in Christ Jesus" (Philippians 2:4-5).

Submission requires a willingness to make a personal sacrifice for the good of others. Few people ever want to suffer. No person wants to be nailed to a cross. But some people alive today will be asked by God to lay down their life for the welfare of others. Throughout history there are many examples of individuals who have willingly gone where others would not go, paid the price many were not willing to pay, and have impacted the world in a way they never understood while still on earth. Dietrich Bonhoeffer refused to submit his will to Hitler. We do not fully know how his courageous decision shaped the resistance, but we do know that shortly after his execution the people remaining in the Nazi camps were set free. Jim Elliot was a father of a young family who felt compelled to go to the jungles of South America to share the gospel. While on his mission, he was cannibalized by the very people he sought to set free through the power of the gospel. Many years later, it was discovered his obedience and witness to the tribesmen of that village would be seed that sprouted spiritual vitality. These are just two individuals out of hundreds of stories that could be told of people who have laid down their life sacrificially so others could live.

The majority of individuals reading these words will never be asked to give their life for the welfare of others in a physical sense. But that does not remove the responsibility of living a submitted life of sacrifice, and reaching out to those who are suffering and lost in our communities. It may mean giving up some of our free time, spending some of our hard earned savings, or sacrificing a comfortable existence to minister to someone who is in desperate need of the love of God. Submission looks a lot like the crosses in Arlington National Cemetery and the cross on Golgotha. The apostle Paul helps us see this as he continues to talk about Jesus' sacrifice. "And being found in human form, he humbled himself by becoming obedient to the point of death, even death on a cross" (Philippians 2:8).

A person can suffer and spend his or her life complaining about it. The submission, which Christ calls for, is one which is victorious in nature. I like to say we should live a Cross life, rather than a Cross death. We should not begrudge any suffering which we have to endure in order to advance the kingdom of God. Instead, we should find joy in the midst of it. I'm not suggesting we adopt a masochistic lifestyle. I am simply arguing if we are willing to obey God at all times with joy in our heart, we will find fulfillment beyond the understanding of those who do not have a relationship with Jesus.

Humility and submission go hand in hand. Humility is not weakness, but a proper understanding of who we really are in relationship to God. Once we have humbled ourselves before God, we are in position to be used by Him however He wants, for the maximum good of the kingdom of God. When we are used by God fully, then we will be exalted in

His eyes. Jesus said, "Whoever exalts himself will be humbled, and whoever humbles himself will be exalted" (Matthew 23:12).

Those who embrace biblical submission know how to say "No" to themselves without feeling embittered by it. Attitude is huge within the kingdom of God. It is easy for workers to feel resentment toward their bosses, if things are not the way they want them. Likewise, they can have bitterness toward God if He makes a decision that is not in keeping with what they desire. They can feel life is unfair because their lot in life is not what those around them have experienced. But biblical submission helps believers see life through the prospect of eternity, rather than the quantity of their possessions or the comfort of their position on earth.

One of the people who lived a most tortured life for the cause of Christ was the apostle Paul. We read in Scripture that he was beaten repeatedly, left for dead, imprisoned without cause, chased from city to city, and eventually died in prison for his commitment to Christ. Paul's attitude during this suffering is amazing. Instead of seeing his plight as injustice, he saw his service to God as a privilege and an honor. Some of the last words we have recorded from Paul's life reflect the attitude we should have as we live in submission to God.

I have fought the good fight, I have finished the race, I have kept the faith. Henceforth there is laid up for me the crown of righteousness, which the Lord, the righteous judge, will award to me on that day, and not only to me but also to all who have loved his appearing (2 Timothy 4:7-8).

Paul was a man who lived a life of self-denial, but he had absolutely no regret. May each person reading this book conclude his or her life with the same proclamation!

Limits to Submission

Obvious questions that may be going through your mind as you read this chapter on submission are, "What about ruthless dictators who prohibit Christians from following God's will?" and "Should I obey laws which are in clear violation of biblical principles?"

There are two conditions the Bible presents when it is acceptable to disregard authorities and the rules they establish. The first condition is when the authority is requiring you to do something clearly in violation of biblical standards. An example of this is when Peter and John had just been released from prison for preaching the gospel. Upon their release, they were instructed to stop speaking about Jesus. Peter and John could have submitted to the authorities, but they made their intentions to disregard the instructions known. Their response sets a standard for Christians when told to do something they know God would not approve. They stated, "Whether it is right in the sight of God to listen to you rather than to God, you must judge, for we cannot but speak of what we have seen and heard" (Acts 4:19-20).

Peter and John made their decision with full awareness of the consequences. They knew the religious leaders would consider continued proclamation of the gospel an affront. Peter and John knew they would be punished. They were willing to face the consequences in order to do what was right in God's sight.

There will be time, in your life that you will be asked to do things by authorities that you know clearly violate Scripture. Like Dietrich Bonhoeffer, you may be asked to support an evil regime. More likely you'll face a decision like one a former student of mine faced. She was working in a medical facility and the authorities running the office told her to falsify paperwork to be submitted for reimbursement from Medicare. The administrator explained to her that there are so many claims submitted to Medicare, no one would ever discover it. He justified the action by saying, if they did not falsify information, they would not be able to continue to exist because of the low reimbursements Medicare provided.

My student knew her job was on the line. After thinking about the consequences of making the right decision, she told the administrator she would not do what he asked her to do. As she is suspected, he dismissed her from her job. When she left the job, she applied for many other jobs and was routinely turned down because of the bad references she received from the corrupt administrator. But it was a price she was willing to pay in order to keep her integrity. Please understand, if you take a stand based on God's word and the person in authority does not value God's word, there may be negative consequences you will have to endure for your righteous stand. The choice you will have to make is if you will submit to God and trust Him with your future, or if you will compromise your values and trust human resources to establish your future. The latter choice will result in you building your house on a very shaky foundation.

The second time when it is acceptable to say no to authority is less clear-cut. It is those times you are asked to do something which violates your conscience. Probably the most famous conscientious objector in Scripture is Daniel. When he was indentured by Babylon, he was groomed for service to the King. He was required to eat food in violation of his Jewish heritage. While many of the other young Jewish men compromised their values by eating the food, Daniel decided to take a different approach. "Daniel resolved that he would not defile himself with the king's food, or with the wine that he drank. Therefore he asked the chief of the eunuchs to allow him not to defile himself" (Daniel 1:8).

The chief of the eunuchs granted Daniel a period of time in which he could demonstrate that a Jewish diet could produce the results desired by the Babylonian king. At the end of the test, Daniel was stronger than those who ate the King's diet. Daniel was allowed to continue to eat what he desired. But the point of the story really isn't about the food. The Bible reveals Daniel was not going to compromise his beliefs, regardless of the consequences. We can see later in his life, he made other consequence defying decisions. In each case, God honored his decision, but Daniel was willing to make them, even if it meant death. He understood there was a higher authority he was responsible to in his life.

This type of decision was made often during the Vietnam War, when people were declaring their conscientious objection to the war. These people understood, if they took this stance they would go to jail or have to serve in some other capacity. Numerous individuals, during that time, left the country to keep their freedom without paying the cost for that freedom. This is not an option for the Christian. If a Christian makes a decision based on their conscience, they are free to do so, but a follower of Christ must be willing to take the consequences associated with the decision.

Conclusion

Biblical submission is an extremely important discipline as people take steps toward God. Submission is a willful act based on one's understanding of oneself and one's understanding of God. When Christians learn how to submit with the right attitude, it demonstrates their willingness to be used in the kingdom of God where God wants them, and how He wants to use them. Many people are religious, but few submit themselves to the Lordship of Jesus. Jesus says "Enter by the narrow gate. For the gate is wide and the way is easy that leads to destruction, and those who enter by it are many. For the gate is narrow and the way is hard that leads to life, and those who find it are few." (Matthew 7:13-14). My prayer is that you will see God for who He is, and be willing to be used in whatever manner He chooses.

Study Guide Questions

1. Define submission.

2. What does the Bible say is the reason people fight and argue?

3. Why is rebellion like witchcraft?

4. How does submission help us value others?

5. What attitude should a believer have toward authority when we disagree with that authority?

6. Name two people the author identifies as individuals who laid down their lives for the good of others.

7. List the two limits of submission listed in this chapter?

FOURTEEN

SPIRITUAL FORMATION THROUGH FORGIVENESS

Forgiveness is a concept we have learned from childhood. When we hurt someone, our parents reprimanded us. A part of our punishment was to tell the person we were sorry. In return for the statement, "I'm sorry," the other person was obligated to forgive us. We learned the phrase "I'm sorry" would get us out of trouble. It became a "get out of jail free" card we played every time we did something that hurt another person. Some people keep this philosophy into adulthood. "I'm sorry" might have made the individual who inflicted the pain feel better, but it seldom did anything to help the person who experienced the hurt. As a result of this convoluted way of looking at forgiveness, many people who have been hurt may say they forgive out of obligation, but they often hold onto the hurt and grow bitter as a result.

All of us have been hurt at one time or another. The degree of pain varies greatly, but it is highly likely you can recall something you have had a difficult time getting past.

In this chapter, I will be encouraging you to forgive those who have done you harm. Please understand I am not diminishing the pain you feel and the difficulty of letting the offense go. I believe, by the end of this chapter, you'll understand forgiveness is a gift you can give to yourself, as much as it is a gift that is given to the person who offended you.

Forgiveness Is Not Optional

Forgiveness is the key that unlocks bondage in a person's life. Many of us are stuck spiritually, and wonder why there is a blockage in our spiritual development. There may be a variety of issues at play that prevent us from maturing in Christ. The most common of these issues is a lack of forgiveness. Jesus made a striking assertion regarding forgiveness and our relationship with others. He stated, "For if you forgive others their trespasses, your heavenly Father will also forgive you, but if you do not forgive others their trespasses, neither will your Father forgive your trespasses" (Matthew 6:14-15).

At first glance, Jesus' statement seems unfeeling. To make my forgiveness from God conditional on my forgiving others seems to be asking too much. It's easy for me to rationalize that God is all loving and as a result, forgiveness comes easy to Him. But this type of thinking ignores the clear teaching of Scripture concerning the pain of the Father, as He had to make the decision to send His Son to die on the cross for the sins of humanity. But the Father was willing to make this decision, in spite of the fact that those who Jesus would die for had offended Him greatly. But forgiveness was a deliberate choice modeled by God, not based on the merit of the individual being forgiven, and not only after the person was sorry for what they did. God made the willful decision to forgive those who offended Him because He understood this was going to be the only way a relationship could ever be reestablished. The forgiveness God showed to us was just as costly, if not more so than anything we have experienced. God's requirement that we forgive those who hurt us, is not asking too much.

One of the reasons God requires us to forgive, as a condition of our forgiveness, is because anything less would be greedy. Jesus told a story of a man who owed a great deal to a king. The man who was in debt was called to the king's court to pay the debt he owed. The debtor didn't have the money to pay his debt. The king told him he would have to go to debtor's prison. The debtor cried out for mercy. The king showed mercy and allowed him to leave his presence debt free. As the servant got back on the street, he saw another man who owed the servant a very small amount of money in comparison to the great debt he had just been forgiven. He demanded the man to repay the loan. The man couldn't and cried out for mercy. The servant refused to grant his fellow servant mercy. He had the man thrown into debtor's prison. When the king heard what the servant had done, he recalled him and the king withdrew his forgiveness. He threw the greedy servant into a prison from which he would never be able to escape. (See Matthew 18:21-35.)

The point of Jesus' story is clear. Humans have offended God in a manner they would never be able to repay. The only way we are able to live in freedom is through God's mercy. If we are willing to accept God's mercy, and we are not willing to show mercy to someone who has hurt us, God is not obligated to continue to show mercy to us. God is not willing to show mercy to the merciless. James explains it this way, "For judgment is without mercy to one who has shown no mercy. Mercy triumphs over judgment" (James 2:13).

Forgiveness Is a Spiritual Discipline

One of the primary reasons we stop growing as Christians is because we don't trust God to take care of us. It's strange how we will trust Him with our eternal life, but we struggle to trust Him with our temporal life. It seems this applies to many different areas such as trusting Him with our money, our future relationships, and our jobs, but it definitely applies when we feel we have been mistreated. Until we learn to trust Him and forgive those who hurt us, we will never find the freedom Jesus told us is available to us. (See John 10:10.)

Jesus told His followers forgiveness supersedes other spiritual practices; even worship. He tells us if we are praying, and in the midst of prayer we realize we have not forgiven someone, we are to stop praying and start talking to the person who we need to reestablish a relationship with. (See Mark 11:25.) In another place, Jesus says if you are on your way to make an offering, which is another way of saying you are going to worship God, and you discover an offense, you are to put down your offering, go get the relationship right, then come back, pick up the offering, go to the Temple, and then make the offering. It will then be acceptable to God. (See Matthew 5:23-25.)

It is incongruent to say you love God, if you choose to remain in a broken relationship. We must remember there are two great commandments that go hand-in-hand; love God and love others. (See Mark 12:30-31.) There is a direct correlation between the amount of love Christians have for God and the amount of love they have for others. The more people love God and build a relationship with Him, the more they will see people the way God sees them. And if they see people who hurt them in the same way God sees people who hurt Him, they will forgive them, as He desires to forgive them. If they do not have the capacity to forgive people, it says a great deal about their true relationship with God.

God places a high value on healing broken relationships. The basic message of the gospel is God forgives and restores relationships. If Christians cannot put that into practice in their own lives, what does it communicate to those who are looking to us for hope?

Forgiveness is Limitless

One of the major reasons people present for not forgiving people is the fear the person will hurt them again. You may have heard the adage, "Fool me once, shame on you. Fool me twice, shame on me." Many Christians adopt this approach to forgiveness. They might be willing to forgive one time, but if the person ever does it again, there will be no forgiveness.

This mentality flies in the face of what Jesus taught regarding forgiveness. When asked how many times to forgive a person, Jesus replies in one place, "If he sins against you seven times in the day, and turns to you seven times, saying, 'I repent,' you must forgive him" (Luke 17:4), and in another setting He expands it to 490 times; "Then Peter came up and said to him, "Lord, how often will my brother sin against me, and I forgive him? As many as seven times?" Jesus said to him, "I do not say to you seven times, but seventy-seven times" (Matthew 18:21-22). Jesus was not saying on the 491st time a person hurts you, you are justified in not showing additional mercy. Jesus was saying forgiveness is limitless. Before you think Jesus was saying you should become a human punching bag, let me assure you, He was not. I will share some principles at the end of this chapter that provide protection in the midst of our vulnerability.

But what is the rationale behind Jesus' statement, concerning limitless forgiveness?

To answer that question, I must ask you a question. "How often have you sinned against God, in the last week? How many times have you sinned, in the last month? How many times have you sinned in the same way, in the last six months? And at what point did you stop believing that God was willing to forgive your sins, if you asked Him to do so?"

As Christians, we count on the fact God's forgiveness is limitless. If we approach Him with true repentance in our heart, He will forgive us. He understands we are prone to mistakes. It is important for us to remember, just as we are prone to mistakes, others are prone to mistakes, as well. If they are truly repentant, and have purposed in their hearts to not repeat the act, it is our obligation to offer them mercy, as we would want to receive mercy from God. One of the most hopeful statements in Scripture is found in one of the most hopeless books in the Bible. In the book of Lamentations, we hear the writer proclaim, "The steadfast love of the LORD never ceases; his mercies never come to an end; they are new every morning; great is your faithfulness" (Lamentations 3:22-23). If we want an endless supply of forgiveness from God, we must be willing to give an endless supply of forgiveness to those who hurt us.

Retaliation Is Not an Option

Retaliation is a natural reaction to an offense committed against us. What Jesus calls for is a supernatural reaction to offenses. Jesus tells us it's not a great feat to love those who love us. The real test of our Christianity is how we respond to the person who is hateful to us. (See Luke 6:32-36.) As a result, God commanded the Israelites, "You shall not take vengeance or bear a grudge against the sons of your own people, but you shall love your neighbor as yourself: I am the Lord" (Leviticus 19:18). This principle applies to fellow Christians, but I believe we can extend the principle to those outside of the Church, as well.

We can only take the supernatural step of not retaliating, if we learn to trust God to care for us. It is an act of faith to believe God will have our back. One of my favorite Scripture passages is found in Genesis 12. God is speaking to Abram (Abraham a little later). He tells Abram He wants him to take his family and go to a place he had never been before. God promises Abram a people and a place. But the part of the story that I love is another promise He makes to Abram. God told Abram He would bless those who blessed him and curse those who cursed him and that He would make Abram a blessing in the world. (See Genesis 12:1-3.) I believe this promise applies to all Christians today who live in obedience to God.

God had Abram's back. If people blessed him, God would bless them. If people cursed Him, God would curse them. Abram did not have to worry about defending himself because God would be his defender. We see this principle repeated elsewhere in Scripture. (See Psalm 5:11; 18:2; 31:2; 119:114; and Isaiah 31:5.) Because we can trust that God has our back, then we can rest in the fact He will exact vengeance if it is needed. Paul reminds the Roman Christians, "Beloved, never avenge yourselves, but leave it to the wrath of God, for it is written, 'Vengeance is mine, I will repay, says the Lord'" (Romans 12:19).

When we allow God to be our rearguard, we are able to look forward with hearts driven by love for all, regardless of their intent toward us. Paul explains how we should react to those who treat us poorly, "To the contrary, 'if your enemy is hungry, feed him; if he is thirsty, give him something to drink; for by so doing you will heap burning coals on his head.' Do not be overcome by evil, but overcome evil with good" (Romans 12:20-21).

In case you missed it, I said God will pay back the person who hurt me, if He feels it is necessary. This point makes some people upset. How could it be that God would ever find that a person who hurt me didn't need retribution?

I am so glad God has not made me pay the consequences of every sin I have committed. Jesus took all of my sins and paid for them on the cross. If I am repentant of my sins, and place my faith in the death and resurrection of Jesus, those sins are forgiven and forgotten. I will never have to pay a spiritual consequence. In like manner, if God has determined the person who hurt me has truly repented of the act, and has attempted to make our relationship right, there is no need for Him to take further punitive action.

Just because God has forgiven the trespass doesn't mean all earthly consequences will vanish. A number of years ago, a female murderer found Jesus while in a Texas jail. She became a model citizen. When the date of her execution neared, everyone felt she had reformed enough that she should no longer have to die. Even the family of the victim fought to get her released from her sentence. But this woman had a different perspective. She knew she had been forgiven by God. But she also realized she deserved to pay the price for her crime against society.

Onesimus was an escaped slave. He met up with the apostle Paul and became a follower of Jesus. Paul could have told him since his sins were forgiven, he could go his way. But Paul told him to go back to his owner, Philemon, and pay whatever price his crime against his owner warranted. (See Philemon 1:1-24.)

Probably the hardest part of practicing forgiveness is when the person seems to get away without suffering a consequence. Remember two basic principles: (1) God keeps good records. The consequences may come without your knowledge; (2) God knows the true heart of a person, and if He feels no punishment is needed, we must trust Him.

Don't Let Evil Control You

One of the most difficult passages of Scripture for many people deals with the subject of forgiveness. Jesus taught the crowd, "Do not resist the one who is evil. But if anyone slaps you on the right cheek, turn to him the other also" (Matthew 5:39).

I can hear someone who is reading this say, "There he goes again. I have to be a punching bag, if I want to be a follower of Jesus!"

Not so fast. Jesus was teaching an important principle, but the principle wasn't to allow yourself to be a victim. Jesus was teaching that we must not allow an evil person to dictate our response. In other words, aggression does not demand aggression.

If a person slaps you in the face, and you immediately hit him back, he is in control of you. It is a simple matter of cause and effect. His slap (the cause) creates an effect (your return punch). An evil act produces another evil act. But if the person slaps you in the face, and you do not slap him back, you are now in control of the situation. An evil response will escalate the problem. A decision to respond based in love will have a greater chance of bringing peace.

Now this does not mean you can't stop, think about it, and then act in self-defense. But if you do, that is your choice. And probably not a bad one, if the person is hurting you or your family members. I find little spiritual value in standing by while a person robs, rapes, or kills those I love.

In the society we live in today, many people are being controlled by others. The news media sets a contentious tone to increase viewership, and it makes people angry. Democrats hate Republicans and Republicans hate Democrats. A simple word from a member of one party creates a reaction in the opposition. Jesus may have chosen to use today's political climate as His sermon illustration instead of a slap in the face, if He was speaking today. It is time for Christians to stop allowing outside entities to control their attitudes and actions.

But closer to home are the people in our own faith and family communities that do things that control our actions and attitudes. Do you allow gossip, a raised voice, an unfounded accusation by a fellow Christian to change your approach to life? Do you look at the person who mistreats you with disregard and disgust, or do you still treat them with compassion? Much of the tension in the church, and in Christian homes, could be reduced if people would stop slapping back, take a step back, attempt to understand the situation, and then respond in a manner that is in keeping with their commitment to Christ.

Retaliation Has Consequences

If you chose to retaliate, it will provide momentary satisfaction, but it will do nothing positive for the kingdom of God. It will also usually result in you regretting what you said or did. Sometimes you will have to pay a higher cost than the person who originally hurt you. If you ever played football, you know it is seldom that the first punch is seen by the referee when a fight breaks out on the field. The same is true for Christians who retaliate. People will see your return punch and wonder how a person who claims to be a Christian could act that way. No matter how justified you feel in slapping back, it will never turn out well. This is one reason the apostle Paul instructed the Christians in Rome, "Repay no one evil for evil, but give thought to do what is honorable in the sight of all" (Romans 12:17).

The wise decision, for a Christian who has been hurt, is to follow the lead of Jesus when He forgave those who wanted to destroy Him. His rationale was that they really didn't know what they were doing (Luke 23:34). This did not justify their actions, but it gave Him a reason to not strike back. Jesus could have called an army of angels (Matthew 26:53), but He chose to suck it up instead, because it was for the greater good of the kingdom of God.

The apostle Peter gives additional rationale for accepting mistreatment rather than retaliating. He states, "Do not repay evil for evil or reviling for reviling, but on the contrary, bless, for to this you were called, that you may obtain a blessing" (1 Peter 3:9).

Peter deals with the flip side of the promise God gave to Abram (Genesis 12:1-3). God told Abram those who blessed him would get God's blessing. Here, Peter says that if we bless others, we will be blessed. It is also important to extend this logic. If people cursed Abram, they would be cursed. Perhaps we can also say if we curse others, we will be cursed. I don't want to take that chance. I would rather take a little abuse here, and have God's blessing and approval, than I would to enjoy the momentary satisfaction of cursing someone and suffer the curse of God in return.

Five Things Forgiveness Does Not Mean

It is quite possible you have read this chapter and you still have some questions about forgiveness. It is easy to read the verses, especially those spoken by Jesus, and walk away feeling like you are getting victimized again through the demand to forgive people who have hurt you in very significant ways.

I understand how you feel. My father left my family when I was 4 1/2 years old. I grew up not knowing what it was like to have a male figure in my life; one who would be there for me no matter what. God was faithful to put other men in my life, but they never fully replaced the loss I felt when my father left. I wish I could say I forgave him while I was a child. Throughout most of my life, I stuffed my feelings, masking the bitterness that raged within me. It wasn't until I was in my early 40s that I came to the point where I could forgive him. Unfortunately, by that time, he was dead. One of the things that held me back from forgiving my father, and perhaps one of the things that has prevented you from forgiving individuals in your life, is a misconception about forgiveness.

I want to conclude this chapter by talking about five things forgiveness does not mean. When I discovered these five principles, I was better able to understand Jesus' perspective on forgiveness. Once I was freed from my misconceptions, I could forgive without feeling victimized once again. I hope these five concepts will help you to understand forgiveness in a new way, and you will be able to find freedom in your own life. Once you find that freedom, you will be able to find full restoration in your relationship with God, as well.

Forgiveness Doesn't Mean the Offense Never Happened

One of the excuses people use for not forgiving is they feel it would minimize the severity of the offense committed against them. I hear people say that forgiving is simply excusing the action and admitting the offense really wasn't all that bad. Many people are afraid if they forgive an offense, they are simply stating they were the weak party, and confessing they should not have been offended in the first place.

This line of thinking could not be further from the truth. Forgiving a person who has hurt you does not mean the pain was not real. If you were abused as a child, forgiving the person who abused you does not mean you did not suffer abuse. If you forgive the person who raped you, that does not mean you were not raped. Your pain was real.

Forgiveness occurs the moment when you stop allowing the person who hurt you to continue to have control of your life. You do not have to choose between holding onto your pain in order to validate it and making believe it never really happened. Your suffering was real, but it doesn't have to define who you are for the rest of your life. When you learn to forgive the individual who has damaged you, you can turn ashes into beauty (Isaiah 61:3). Allow God to use your pain to demonstrate to others who have suffered greatly, the victory they can have through forgiveness.

Paul explained to the Corinthian church the benefit that can result from the suffering we experience. He states, "Blessed be the God and Father of our Lord Jesus Christ, the Father of mercies and God of all comfort, who comforts us in all our affliction, so that we may be able to comfort those who are in any affliction, with the comfort with which we ourselves are comforted by God" (2 Corinthians 1:3-4).

God does not bring suffering in our lives so we can help others who suffer. But because of the evil in the world, it is very likely most of us will suffer in some fashion. We can begrudge that suffering and become bitter, or we can use suffering in a positive fashion. But please remember, when you forgive the individual who hurt you, you are not minimizing the reality and the severity of the pain you endured.

Forgiveness Doesn't Mean You Will Forget the Offense

Another misconception that keeps people from forgiving is they believe in order to truly forgive, they must be able to forget the offense. I've heard many individuals say they thought they had forgiven a person, but they decided they really had not forgiven them because when they saw the person again, they remembered the offense.

This misconception is a lie from Satan to try to keep you in spiritual bondage. If you feel you have not forgiven somebody, even when you have tried, it is likely you will live in guilt and condemnation. Let me clearly proclaim to you, you will not forget what happened to you because you forgive the person who hurt you. The only individual who has the ability to forget an offense against Him is God. He has the ability to forget because He can do all things. Even then, the question might be asked, "Does He forget our sins or does He choose to no longer recall them, or to hold them against us?"

In the event nobody has ever told you this, you are not God, and you do not have the power God possesses. He created us with a mind that recalls events that occur in our lives. Some of the most vivid memories are the pains that occur in our lives. Pain is designed to help us avoid repeating harmful activities. To forget pain is to waste the experience. As an old rancher once said, "There is no wisdom to be gained in the second kick of a horse." There are some pains that are so traumatic our minds do shut off, but these are not the kinds of issues I am talking about. If you have been hurt, you will remember the offense, even after you forgive the individual.

The key to knowing whether or not you have truly forgiven is not measured by your memory, but by how much that recollection has control over you. If somebody in your life, who you see regularly, was the culprit and you have forgiven that person, it is likely the first time you see the person after you forgive them, a flood of emotions will come upon you much like those you had before you forgave the person. When those emotions arrive, simply declare your forgiveness of the person once again, and tell Satan you are not going to believe his lie because you know you have forgiven the person. The next time you see that person, the flood of emotions will not be as strong, but they will still be there. Once again, reaffirm your forgiveness, address Satan's lie, and continue about your business. By repeating this activity, you will find over time, the power of the offense will dissipate. There will come a time in your life when the offense will become a distant memory and you can walk in total freedom.

Forgiveness Doesn't Mean You Will Return to Receive the Same Treatment Again

Forgiveness does not mean you have to be someone's punching bag. The idea that forgiveness means you have to restore people to the same relationship they had with you before the offense is ludicrous at best and destructive in most cases. The idea that a mother should place her children back in the same dangerous situation simply because her husband asks for forgiveness, and she grants it, is criminal. There is absolutely nothing wrong with forgiving an individual while dialing the phone to turn that person in for child abuse.

Forgiveness is a gift, but trust must be earned. I have been married to my wife a very long time. I can say that in all of our married life, I have never gone through her phone logs to see who she has been calling. I never check her purchases to see who she might be buying gifts for. I have never questioned her about her friends or where she chooses to go. Over the 40 plus years we've been married, she has earned my trust. But, if one day, I discovered she had been cheating on me with another man, I hope I would have the ability to forgive her. I can guarantee, however, I would begin looking at her phone logs, examining her credit card receipts, and questioning where she was going and who she was going to be with each time she left the house. Her infidelity would reduce her trust level to zero. She would have to earn my trust over time, even though I had given her my forgiveness. It would be fool hearted for me to not hold her accountable, unless I enjoyed being mistreated.

I saw a wonderful example of the forgiveness/trust tension play out while pastoring. A woman came to my office door with hatred in her eyes. I can still hear her shouting, "I am going to kill him!" After helping her calm down, I asked her who she was going to kill and why was she going to kill him. She told me that she was going to kill her husband because he had inappropriately touched their adopted daughter. The daughter was not a minor, so there was no legal action she could take. I told her she was not going to kill anyone, and she admitted she felt like it, but she was not going to do so. She then looked at me, square in the eyes, and said she was going to divorce him. I explained that I was not God, and I could not tell her what to do. I also told her I didn't want her to do anything in a rash manner. I told her to go home and ask God what He would have her to do in the situation. She complied and said she would return the next day.

When she returned, she said God had told her to forgive her husband, but to take remedial action. I asked her what that was going to look like. She said her husband would have to move out of the home for at least a year, go to Christian counseling during that time, and he could have no interaction with family for at least six months. As both her and her husband's pastor, I told her we would remove him from the praise team, ask him to confess to the entire church body on the next Sunday evening, and we would never allow him to work with children or youth again. He agreed to her demands as well as to mine.

Over the next 12 months, her husband earned back the trust of both his wife and the church family. The husband was allowed back into his home and he was restored to his position on the praise team. When I transitioned out of that church, the family was still intact and serving God together in the church. I give a great deal of credit to this Christian woman who gave forgiveness and provided an opportunity for trust to be earned back.

Forgiveness Doesn't Change the Character of the Offender

I wish the story I just told ended there. A few years later, the man repeated his offense. The wife had done everything she knew to do. This time she forgave him, but filed for a divorce. She made a rational decision, rather than an emotional one. As much as I would like to tell you otherwise, our forgiveness doesn't necessarily change the offender.

A basic principle I hope you have seen is forgiveness really isn't for the person who has done the offense. It is for the person who was offended. Many people argue the culprit does not deserve to be forgiven. Some even say they will not forgive a person until the person is repentant. This may come as a revelation to you, but some people who hurt you are not sorry, and never will be. If you wait until the person asks for forgiveness, they may continue to control you for the rest of your life. If you want freedom from your pain, you may have to forgive a person who truly does not deserve to be forgiven, or even want it.

A number of years ago I heard the story of a promising young lady who had an entrepreneurial spirit. She decided she wanted to start a business. She found a house on a busy highway that she could lease to start her business. She had enough money to turn one of the rooms into a tanning station and another room into a reception area. She told all of her friends about her business and it flourished from the beginning. One day a man, who the owner had never met, came into the reception area and told her he wanted to get a tan. She went into the room where the tanning bed was to make sure everything was clean and in order for the customer. When she went back into the reception area, the man grabbed her and proceeded to rape her and beat her until she was unconscious. He left her business and drove away not knowing whether she was dead or alive.

Miraculously the young lady survived this traumatic event. The man, who attacked her, was never located. He would never pay for the crime he committed against her. It's very unlikely he would even remember her. She was probably just one in a string of attacks he committed randomly against innocent victims.

The young lady had a decision to make. Would she forgive this individual, even when the person didn't ask for her forgiveness, or would she hold on to the injustice committed against her and allow it to control her future?

Some people reading this chapter have to face the same question for themselves. Sometimes we have to give the gift of forgiveness to those who don't deserve it, and don't care if they get it. Sometimes we even have to give it to people who were no longer alive. As crazy as it sounds, some of us allow individuals to continue to control our lives from their graves. If you want to be free, don't wait for the character of the person who hurt you to change. Grant forgiveness to them now.

Forgiveness Doesn't Return Everything to Normal

Another misconception concerning forgiveness is, if we will forgive, everything will go back to the way it was before the offense occurred. I wish I could tell you that this is true, but it isn't. Evil exists in the world and sometimes evil changes the life of innocent people forever.

As a pastor, I saw many people's lives irreversibly damaged. I would have to tell them it was their responsibility to forgive. I could see the pain in their eyes as they attempted to get their life back as they once knew it. But forgiveness does not bring a cheating husband back to the family. Forgiveness does not bring a daughter back to life, after being killed by a drunk driver. Forgiveness does not refill a bank account, after a fellow Christian uses a Ponzi scheme against them. Forgiveness does not restore our lives to what they were, but forgiveness can place us on a path that will be much brighter than that intended by the person who committed the offense against us.

Conclusion

Forgiveness is the ultimate form of love because it reflects the very nature of God. It must be given unconditionally as a gift. Trust must be rebuilt with those we forgive, but the starting point is a spiritual decision to release a person from the offense they have perpetrated against us.

But it is really up to you what you do with the pain which has been inflicted on you. You can ignore it and hope the pain will go away. It won't. It will flare up at the most unexpected and inconvenient times. You can retaliate against the person and hope you will feel vindicated. You won't. But you can try these options. It is your pain, and it is your right to do whatever you wish with it. If you choose these options, you will become stuck in the depths of bitterness that will keep you from taking steps toward God.

Or you can chose to forgive. This is a tough choice, but it is the only one that will give you freedom and bring you into closer alignment with God.

So what will you choose?

Study Guide Questions

1. What does the author suggest is the most common issues that prevents Christians from maturing in Christ?

2. What characteristic is revealed in a Christian who does not practice forgiveness?

3. How many times did Jesus tell His disciples they were required to forgive?

4. What did the author say was a better alternative to retaliation?

5. What does a person's willingness to forgive reveal about their trust in Jesus?

6. According to the author, what was Jesus attempting to teach when He told His disciples to turn the other cheek, if someone slapped them?

7. What is the difference between forgiveness and trust?

8. How would you respond to someone who tells you that you should forgive and forget?

9. Why is it unwise to wait for a person to ask for forgiveness before you give it?

FIFTEEN

SPIRITUAL FORMATION THROUGH INTEGRITY

The word "integrity" is used in many different contexts. In the automobile industry, integrity is determined by the sturdiness of its frame. If a car lacks integrity, it is likely the tires will wear unevenly and the various parts will be negatively affected by the unwanted vibrations that result from misalignment. A car can get into an accident and have very little visible damage, but it will be totaled by the insurance company if the auto body shop reports the frame has been compromised. So in the automobile world, integrity speaks of a straight, solid frame that supports all of the rest of the components that sits on it.

In the world of mathematics, integrity is closely linked to the word "integer." An integer is a whole number as opposed to a fraction. An integer is complete in itself. There is no half or quarter involved. It is all or nothing. A 5 is a 5; nothing more or nothing less. You don't have to worry about rounding it up or rounding it down. You can always count on a 5 to be a 5. So in the math world, an integer is consistent and trustworthy. This is clearly a definition of a person who has integrity, as well.

In the world of architecture, integrity is determined by the foundation a structure is built on. If the architect has not drawn plans for a good foundation, or the construction workers have not followed good plans, it puts the structure in jeopardy. Sadly, history establishes this truth. On January 10, 2010, a 7.1 magnitude earthquake rocked the island nation of Haiti. Aftershocks of 5.9 and 5.5 magnitude compounded the destruction of buildings that looked solid before the earthquake occurred. I remember seeing a newly constructed hotel reduced to rubble. The Haitian government reported 300,000 people died as a result of the earthquake. Most of the deaths were attributed to the nation's lack of building codes. Though a 7.1 earthquake is huge, much of the devastation of the quake could have been minimized if the buildings, in the country, had been built on appropriate foundations. So integrity in the world of architecture is what goes on under the surface, rather than the beauty that is seen when one looks at the structure. No matter how beautiful the structure appears on the surface, if the foundation is not right, it will eventually crumble. As a carpenter, Jesus knew the rules of architecture and applied them in His sermons. He taught the importance of a firm foundation when preaching on the mountain side. He told the crowd:

> Everyone then who hears these words of mine and does them will be like a wise man who built his house on the rock. And the rain fell, and the floods came, and the winds blew and beat on that house, but it did not fall, because it had been founded on the rock. And everyone who hears these words of mine and does not do them will be like a foolish man who built his house on the sand. And the rain fell, and the floods came, and the winds blew and beat against that house, and it fell, and great was the fall of it (Matthew 7:24-27).

It is clear Jesus wanted His followers to build on a spiritual foundation that would not fail. He has the same desire for those of us who follow Him today.

God's Definitions of Integrity

It is nice to understand some of the basic definitions of integrity associated with various occupations, but ultimately for spiritual formation to take place, a person needs to understand how God defines integrity. Let's look at what the Bible says about integrity. These insights are not listed with any particular priority in mind. Each one is vitally important for us, if we wish to live a mature Christian life.

Consistent Living

As rear wheels must follow the path of the front wheels of the car, so must a person's actions follow their beliefs. God has little tolerance for individuals who say they believe one thing while living lives that contradict the declaration. Jesus, addressing the Laodiceans, explains His displeasure with them because they were living a conflicted life. He states, "I know your works: you are neither cold nor hot. Would that you were either cold or hot! So, because you are lukewarm, and neither hot nor cold, I will spit you out of my mouth" (Revelation 3:15-16).

Some people will argue Jesus was not qualifying hot as good, or cold as bad in these verses. They would argue either hot or cold was considered as acceptable given the reputation of the water supply at Laodicea, in the first century. Regardless of whether one wants to argue that both hot and cold are good options, or if one is an appropriate choice and the other is to be avoided, Jesus was clearly sharing His displeasure that the Laodiceans had not chosen one or the other. These believers were choosing neither hot nor cold and were satisfied with a lukewarm spiritual existence.

Too many Western Christians have chosen a lukewarm spiritual existence. They follow God when it meets their needs and follow their own desires when that meets their needs. A person of integrity will always follow God, even when following Him is difficult. Jesus was teaching the Laodiceans that they had to make a choice. They had to choose to follow God with all of their being, or follow their own desires, but they could not have it both ways.

I understand the desire to live with a foot on each side of the spiritual fence. Throughout my high school years, I straddled the fence spiritually. I grew up going to church from the time I was eight-years old. I loved Jesus and wanted to spend eternity with Him. But I also wanted to experience all that life offered, much of which was not reflective of God's priorities for my life.

I attempted to keep my spiritual world separate from my fleshly desires. As a result, I would attend church faithfully, and even served on the youth group's executive team, while spending nearly every Friday and Saturday night drinking alcohol with my friends. I remember many nights going to bed inebriated, but right before I went to sleep I would pray and ask God to forgive me for my sins, so I would go to heaven, if I were to die before morning. Looking back on those prayers, I now understand they were my feeble attempt at purchasing spiritual fire insurance because all I was really concerned about was staying out of the Lake of Fire my pastor always talked about. But in my heart of hearts, I can also look back on those times and realize I loved Jesus. I was conflicted between two pursuers.

I may have continued living in this conflicted manner if it had not been for a youth pastor who wanted to make an example of my life. He wanted others in the youth group to avoid living a duplicitous lifestyle. He had suspected I was living with feet on each side of the fence, but he could never prove it. This all changed after I returned from a trip to Canada with the French club from my school. I made a few missteps in my well-crafted plan to keep my secular life hidden from those involved in my sacred existence.

I grew up in a very poor family, so this trip to Québec was one of the first times I had ever stayed in a hotel. The hotel room was expensive and the towels were very nice. All of our towels at home were very thin from wear. The hotel towels were thick and soft and absorbed water readily. I figured, since the school had paid so much for the hotel room, it was logical for me to take one of these towels home with me. I packed it in my suitcase not really thinking that I had stolen from the hotel.

One evening I went for a walk and I happened onto a piano bar. I went in and sat for a while, drinking and listening to the music. I was underage and it was against school policy for a student to drink on a school trip. I got back to my room undetected. I really didn't feel I had done anything wrong, so I didn't think much about it.

A third miscalculation I made on this trip was buying Black Cat firecrackers. Firecrackers were illegal in my home State of Maine. Being able to purchase a ready supply in Canada, especially so close to the 4th of July, was a no-brainer. I made my purchase and I wrapped them up in the hotel towel so they would not get lost or stolen.

I didn't think much about any of this until I got home from the trip and the telephone rang in my home. It was the youth pastor on the line. He asked me three simple questions. First he asked, "Did you drink alcohol while you were on your school trip to Canada?" I was not one to lie, so I answered, "Yes." Second he asked, "Did you steal a towel from the hotel that you stayed in during the trip?" Once again, I answered, "yes." His third question made me ponder. He asked, "Did you commit a felony while you were on the trip to Canada?" I really didn't know what he was talking about, so I asked him to explain. He asked if I had brought fireworks illegally into the United States. That I could answer. I told him, "Yes." He then asked me to come to the youth group room at a set time when he would put me on trial before a panel of my peers.

I showed up at the appointed time and confessed to my wayward acts. I was sent upstairs to await the decision of the panel concerning my punishment. I remember sitting on the pew thinking two things. The first thing I thought was how stupid it was for the youth pastor to treat me this way. My wife, who was my girlfriend at the time, was on that panel and does not see it exactly the way I saw it, but to me it was a vindictive act by the youth pastor. But a more important thought that crossed my mind was how stupid I was for living the life that I had chosen.

That day, sitting on a pew contemplating my life, is etched in my mind. I told myself I had to make a choice. I had to start serving God fully and turn away from behaviors that were not consistent with my love for God, or I had to begin to seek sensual pleasure with all of my energy and forgo a relationship with God. A choice had to be made that day, as far as I was concerned. Over 40 years later, I'm glad to say I chose to follow God. Have I made mistakes since that day? Of course I have. But the difference is when I sin now, it breaks my heart, in the same way it breaks God's heart. My relationship with Him is no longer simply fire insurance. He is the Lord of my life!

I believe all Christians, in their journey toward spiritual maturity, must make the decision at some point to put away their fire insurance mentality and embrace the lordship of Jesus Christ. Jesus says when you live a lukewarm life, He wants to spit you out of His mouth. This is not because of a lack of love on His part. He cannot accept anything less than a person's full dedication to Him. He is not willing to share your love any more than you would be willing to share the love of someone with whom you were romantically connected.

The apostle Paul reinforces Jesus' teaching when he tells the Corinthians to put the sinful man out of the church so, perhaps one day, he would see his wicked behavior for what it really was. (See 1 Corinthians 5:1-13.) The damnable aspect of straddling a spiritual fence is you can fool yourself into thinking you are in a healthy relationship with Jesus while in reality living a life that is self-serving. This will eventually lead to eternal separation from God, if you do not make a course correction.

The first principle of integrity is that your lifestyle must reflect your stated relationship with Jesus.

Honest Living

The second principle of integrity is honest living. The Bible demonstrates that God has a great disdain for dishonesty. The rationale for this contempt, in the grand majority of situations, is that it is the powerful who use their position to engage in dishonest activities that work against the welfare of the poor. In Proverbs, we read, "Unequal weights and unequal measures are both alike an abomination to the LORD" (Proverbs 20:10).

To understand this verse, we must be aware of how economic transactions occurred during the Old Testament period. The merchant owned the set of scales that was used to measure out the amount of produce the consumer wanted to purchase. This put all of the control in the hands of the powerful. They had the ability to adjust the scales in their favor, if they so desired. With a small adjustment, the merchant could sell 15 ounces of barley, but charge the consumer for a full pound of the grain. In each transaction, the merchant would not only receive what he was due, but he would steal a small amount from the individual who relied on his service. God never reprimands a merchant for receiving what they are due, but He is sickened by those who take something they have not earned, especially at the expense of the poor.

Today, we do not allow merchants to go unchecked in regard to their scales. The government has stepped in to measure the accuracy of gasoline pumps, scales at the grocery store, and the amount of product inserted into potato chip bags. Much of the theft that occurs today takes on a different form. It may be cheating in an athletic event, by taking steroids or other performance-enhancing drugs in order to receive an edge over the competition. Or we may see it in the classroom where a student does not study for an exam, but leans over and steals answers from a student who did study. In both of these cases, the rationale often used to justify the dishonest act is that it is a victimless crime. The person who takes the drugs to perform better argues it doesn't hinder his competitor from playing well. Students who cheat feel they do not lower the score of the person who studied when they take information they did not work for.

The reason cheating is viewed as theft is because God expects people to receive what they earn, but not to garner benefits they did not work for. The apostle Paul taught if you don't work, you don't eat (2 Thessalonians 3:10). As a Christian, we should expect to receive rewards in correlation to the amount of effort we put into the task. If I choose to study, I should expect to receive a grade commensurate with the amount of effort I have put in. But, if I choose to play video games, rather than read my textbook, or go out on a date instead of studying for the exam, I should be satisfied with a grade which reflects my lack of academic effort.

Having taught at both the high school and university level, I have heard nearly all of the excuses that exist to justify cheating. But each excuse boils down to the person's belief they deserve something for nothing. Christians, who are people of integrity, will be content with what they earn, and not seek to take something that belongs to others.

Transparent Living

A third principle of biblical integrity is that our external behavior will reflect our inner spiritual condition. We spoke about hypocrisy earlier in the book, so we will not spend a great deal of time here rehashing the importance of living transparently. Suffice it to say, we must not attempt to impress those around us when we know this is not who we really are. Jesus could not have made this principle clearer to His followers when He said, "Beware of practicing your righteousness before other people in order to be seen by them, for then you will have no reward from your Father who is in heaven" (Matthew 6:1).

There is such a temptation to learn the expectations associated with Christianity and to do those things in public to impress others. This may occur because we feel we must please authority figures in our lives, or perhaps we do it to garner a relationship with people of the opposite sex who require their boyfriend or girlfriend to be a solid Christian. We must remember it really doesn't matter what other people believe about us. We must live with ourselves, and realize that God knows what is really taking place in our lives.

Blameless Living

A fourth principle of biblical integrity is blameless living. Blameless living does not mean we are perfect in all we do and say. Blameless living means it is our desire to be people of integrity and when our integrity has been compromised, we are repentant and seek to remedy any wrong that may have occurred.

One of my favorite stories in Scripture is found in Genesis 20. Abraham had moved his family to the Negev. He was afraid Abimelech, the king of Gerar, would see his wife and desire her. He reasoned Abimelech would kill him, in order to get Sarah. To protect himself, he told people in the region that Sarah was his sister. When Abimelech heard Sarah was Abraham's sister, he sent to get her so she could become one of his wives.

One night, as the king was going to sleep, perhaps even thinking about Sarah, God spoke to him in a dream. The words Abimelech heard probably caused him to sit straight up in bed. My paraphrase of what God said is, "Abimelech, I am going to kill you." God then went on to explain to him why he was going to receive such severe punishment. God informed Abimelech, he was about to sleep with another man's wife.

This is the part of the story I really like. Abimelech begins to defend himself to God by saying he didn't know he was doing anything wrong. He assured God he had not done anything to violate Sarah, up to this point. In his own words, Abimelech said, "Lord, will you kill an innocent people? Did he not himself say to me, 'She is my sister'? And she herself said, 'He is my brother.' In the integrity of my heart and the innocence of my hands I have done this" (Genesis 20:4-5).

God's response to Abimelech is classic. He assured him that He was not going to kill Abimelech. God then explained He was only trying to get his attention before he did something which would violate his integrity (Genesis 20:6).

God has not changed over time. He still gives believers fair warning when they are about to do something to compromise their spiritual integrity. God doesn't generally approach people and tell them He is going to kill them any longer. Instead, today, the Holy Spirit convicts Christians when they are about to do something displeasing to God. People of integrity will hear the conviction of the Holy Spirit and adjust their behavior, in accordance with God's will, as Abimelech did.

Abimelech could have ignored God and followed through on his sexual journey with Sarah. This pleasure would have come at a great cost to the king. Christians too can ignore the Holy Spirit and continue to do things that displease God, but to do so is very foolish. Individuals who claim Jesus is their Lord will respond positively to the Holy Spirit's warnings in their lives, if they are people of integrity.

The Benefits of Integrity

Just as a lack of integrity will result in negative spiritual consequences, living a life of spiritual integrity pays great spiritual benefits. Once again, the benefits I will list are in no special order, and all can be expected by the person who lives consistently, honestly, transparently, and blamelessly.

God is on Your Side

The first benefit of a life of integrity is we never have to worry about pleasing God. We can be confident we will have His approval because our desire is to do His will. The Psalmist understood the value of being a person of integrity. He declared that experiencing the presence of God is conditional on a person's integrity; "But you have upheld me because of my integrity, and set me in your presence forever" (Psalm 41:12).

There is a great deal of theological debate between well-meaning Christians regarding how secure a believer's salvation is. Christians don't have to worry about "once saved, always saved" or "losing our salvation," if they are people of integrity. A person of integrity does not live so close to the line of disobedience that they ever have to worry about stepping outside of God's will.

I don't know about you, but I want God to be on my side when I face life's challenges. I am willing to be on His side in order to be assured of this benefit. Living a life of integrity sometimes means saying no to immediate gratification. But the promise of God's presence, while on earth, and eternally in heaven, is worth the sacrifice and suffering I may face for serving God today. The apostle Paul explained this concept to the Romans this way, "For I consider that the sufferings of this present time are not worth comparing with the glory that is to be revealed to us" (Romans 8:18).

Children Are Blessed

Some individuals reading this book right now may not be able to fully relate to this point yet, but nevertheless, it is still a significant benefit. Parents want their children to have the best. The writer of Proverbs promises that one way we can assure our children a blessed life is to be a person of integrity, "The righteous who walks in his integrity — blessed are his children after him!" (Proverbs 20:7).

Even though you may not be married yet, or have children of your own, you were a child at one point in your life. You know what it was like to have parents who either had integrity or lacked integrity. If you had parents who had integrity, you could have confidence they would do what they said. You could be proud to be around them because they lived in the same way inside of the house as they did outside of the house. They were not perfect people. They made mistakes on occasion. But, when they did make mistakes, they were quick to repent. They were saddened by the missteps they had taken. More than likely, you have made it a goal to emulate them in your own life.

Unfortunately, some people reading this book grew up with parents who lacked integrity. You watched them as they deceived people. It did not surprise you when they put on a good front when in public, but lived a contradictory life at home. You never could count on them because their word could not be trusted. Their goal was self-satisfaction, rather than attempting to satisfy God, even though they claimed to be Christians. More than likely, you have chosen either to live a life that lacks integrity, in regard to your Christian faith, or perhaps you have walked away from your Christian faith completely. A rare few individuals, who grow up in homes not built on integrity, will choose a path of integrity for themselves. When this occurs, it breaks a cycle of destruction.

An old children's song states, "Be careful little eyes what you see, be careful little ears what you hear." The essence of the song is that God is watching and knows what you are looking at and listening to. As true as this may be, parents must remember they also have little ones (and some not so little ones) watching and listening to everything they do and say. A parent should not be surprised if the actions and word selection of their children reflects their parents' choices.

It is much easier to be a good example for our children if we choose to live with integrity. Our actions and attitudes will be a reflection of our desire to please God.

Parents must never set themselves up as a supreme being. Just as they teach their children how to live with integrity, they must also teach their children how to live when they make mistakes in their lives. Parents can teach their children a great deal about God's grace and His mercy as they live out their lives openly and transparently before their children. Children, who have parents like this, are truly blessed.

A Clear Conscience

A third blessing associated with integrity is the ability to live with a clear conscience. You never have to wonder what you have said to an individual if you have always told the truth. You would never have to worry about getting caught doing something wrong if you have not done something wrong.

I have had the privilege of working in jobs that have allowed me to travel across the United States and to many parts of the world. I have spent hundreds of nights alone in hotels with opportunities to cheat on my wife, if I chose to do so. It's very possible, if I had cheated on my wife, no one would have ever known. But, if I had done so, I would have always been looking over my shoulder. Did somebody see me who knew me that I hadn't seen? Was there a credit card receipt with telltale signs that could expose an indiscretion? Might the woman I was involved with call my wife to cause trouble? Perhaps I might talk in my sleep and reveal my sin. A real benefit of living with integrity, in regard to my marriage, is I can put my head on the pillow every night knowing there is no dark secret looming that could destroy my marriage or my ministry.

If you live a life of integrity, you will not have to worry about the IRS auditing your books. If you live a life of integrity, you will not have to worry about a teacher discovering you plagiarized on a paper. If you live a life of integrity, you will not have to worry about having your lies uncovered and the humiliation often associated with this. Many worries could be relieved, if we would simply live our lives with integrity and trust God to assist us, as we follow Him. The writer of Proverbs gives us this insight, "The integrity of the upright guides them, but the crookedness of the treacherous destroys them" (Proverbs 11:3). Choose to be guided by integrity to avoid unnecessary pain.

You Can Live with Yourself

Finally, one of the greatest benefits of living with integrity is I can live with myself. I want to be able to respect who I am. No one knows me the way I know myself. I can fool others, but I always know the true me. There are individuals who literally drive themselves insane because of the guilt and shame they hold onto while putting up a front that looks healthy. But, if I cannot live with who I am, my life will be tragic. I will disrespect myself and I will allow others to disrespect me.

Some people choose to live without integrity because they see the short-term gains they can achieve if they compromise their integrity. I have seen students choose to cheat in the classroom because they think doing so will help them stay on the athletic field or secure scholarships. I've watched pastors steal sermons from the Internet and preach them as their own because they feel this will make them seem to be more polished, with little effort on their part. I know individuals who will fudge on their income tax return in order to save a few hundred dollars and justify it because they feel the government does not spend their money in an appropriate fashion.

All of these short-term gains can have long-term negative consequences if the person is caught. But whether or not they are caught, individuals who cheat, in one fashion or another, weaken their self-perception, as well as the perception of others. The writer of Proverbs says it well, "Better is a poor person who walks in his integrity than one who is crooked in speech and is a fool" (Proverbs 19:1).

Conclusion

A significant part of our spiritual formation is making the decision to make Jesus both our Savior and our Lord. This means we will determine that His word and His desires are superior to ours. We will make the choice to serve Him fully and allow our behavior to reflect the beliefs we say we hold. When we do this, we will be honest individuals who live blameless before the Lord. Great benefits are enjoyed by those who take steps toward God in this manner.

Study Guide Questions

1. What spiritual lessons can be learned from the earthquakes in Haiti?

2. What four principles does the author address concerning integrity?

3. What principle was Jesus teaching to the Laodiceans in the book of Revelation?

4. What does the author mean when he refers to "fire insurance" in regard to salvation?

5. Why does God despise cheating?

6. What does it mean to live blamelessly?

7. What four benefits can a Christian expect if they are people of integrity?

8. How does the Holy Spirit help us maintain our integrity?

9. How do children benefit from parents who live with integrity?

10. Why do some Christians choose to live without integrity?

SIXTEEN

SPIRITUAL FORMATION THROUGH VOCATION

The term "vocation" comes from a Latin word that is translated into English as "to call." During medieval times, the idea of vocation was limited to those who were involved in church occupations. With the advent of Protestantism and the theology of the priesthood of believers, vocation became more associated with any type of work performed that is acceptable in the eyes of God. We will explore this tension in the chapter, but a generally accepted definition of vocation is "an occupation that reflects God's call in one's life."

In this chapter, we will discuss why work is important for the Christian, what the call of God on a person's life looks like, how to determine God's will in regard to vocation, and how a person's faith will impact the way he performs his vocation. When Christians fully understand the concept of vocation, and find their place as workers in God's Kingdom, they will live abundant and fruitful lives expressing their unique gifts and talents. A biblical perspective on vocation and calling should lead us to see work, not as simply an occupation that provides us with money, but as a vocation that expresses who God has uniquely created us to be.

God-The First Worker

The very first words of the Bible displays God at work. "In the beginning, God created the heavens and the earth" (Genesis 1:1). The Scripture records He continued to work for six days and then He rested from His work. (See Genesis 2:1-3.) This stoppage of work is referred to as a Sabbath rest. It will become a standard requirement for all believers who work. (See Exodus 20:8-11 and Leviticus 23:3.)

God did not stop working when Creation was completed. God continues to work in the lives of believers and in the affairs of this world. The apostle Paul states that Christ created all things and continues to hold all things together in our world (Colossians 1:15-20). The Psalmist states God never slumbers and is always aware of what is going on in the lives of His followers (Psalm 121:1-8). And we see God actively intervenes in the lives of His people when necessary (Exodus 3:7-9).

God is not passive. He is at work at all times. We see, throughout the Old Testament, God was active in setting up and taking down leaders. In the New Testament, we see Him active in orchestrating efforts to bring salvation to all nations, establishing authority within the nations, and guiding the Church. To accomplish much of His work, He has chosen to delegate His authority to humans. God has gifted humans, in a variety of ways, to accomplish His will on earth. The benediction in the letter to the Hebrews expresses this well, "Now may the God of peace who brought again from the dead our Lord Jesus, the great shepherd of the sheep, by the blood of the eternal covenant, equip you with everything good that you may do his will, working in us that which is pleasing in his sight, through Jesus Christ, to whom be glory forever and ever. Amen" (Hebrews 13:20-21).

The Bible says we were made in the image of God. (See Genesis 1:27.) He set the example for us regarding work by being intentional about His work, which is designed to benefit His creation. He expects us to be intentional about our work, as well.

Humans-Designed to Work

A common quest for all humans is to find significance. Most individuals will flounder in their quest for self-worth until they find a vocation that allows them to express themselves in the manner God designed them to accomplish. God created us to be people who can find our fulfillment through our relationship with Him and as active participants in His plan for His creation.

Work is an expression of how God made us in His own image. Once God created the first human, He placed him in the Garden and gave him work to do. The Bible records Adam going about the business of naming the animals and tending the land. (See Genesis 2:15-20.) He was satisfied with his work, but Adam discovered that he needed another human in his life.

Not everyone who engages in work has the same level of fulfillment as Adam did in the Garden. If we are honest with ourselves, there are some jobs we are asked to do that leave us feeling empty. The writer of Ecclesiastes explains why some jobs leave us feeling fulfilled, while others seem to drain the life from us. He says when we work to establish our own name, to accumulate wealth, or to achieve acceptance among our peers, our work will leave us feeling empty because in the back of our mind we know one day it will all have been for nothing. But the writer of Ecclesiastes provides the secret to fulfillment in our work. He says, if we work in conjunction with the purposes of God and seek His wisdom while doing it, we will find joy and fulfillment because what we accomplish will remain standing long after we have finished our time on earth. (See Ecclesiastes 2:17- 26.)

Since humans are made in the image of God, and since God never sleeps on the job, He knew it was going to be a challenge for humans who found a vocation they enjoyed to ever stop to rest. As a result, God built a designated rest stop that should regulate and invigorate the believer. The Sabbath is not a rule established to put prohibitions on the behavior of individuals, but as a means of helping people to understand it is okay to rest from the important tasks they had been assigned by God to do. Jesus explained it in this fashion, "The Sabbath was made for man, not man for the Sabbath" (Mark 2:27).

People, who work jobs simply to put food on the table and pay the bills they have accumulated, often spend a great deal of time looking at the clock to see how long it is until lunch or the end of the day. They often long for the weekend or for their next vacation. People who have found their true vocation will look at the clock, but instead of wishing the end of the day would come, they wish to have more time to accomplish the tasks they have before them. People, who have discovered a vocation will often have to be forced to take a vacation. Having found a vocation myself, and having at one time worked in a place simply for the paycheck, I encourage everyone to seek a vocation.

God commands people to work to the degree they are able. The apostle Paul addresses individuals who chose not to engage in work in the church at Thessalonica. He said,

> For even when we were with you, we would give you this command: If anyone is not willing to work, let him not eat. For we hear that some among you walk in idleness, not busy at work, but busybodies. Now such persons we command and encourage in the Lord Jesus Christ to do their work quietly and to earn their own living (2 Thessalonians 3:10-12).

In today's society, many people do whatever they can to get out of working. The unemployment rolls are filled with people who could get a job if they wanted to get off their couches. Christians should never avoid working and expect others to take care of them. Only those with a true disability should rely on others to meet their financial needs. It is not ideal to take a job just for the paycheck, but until you locate the vocation that will bring you fulfillment, it is your responsibility to take care of yourself and your family financially however you can. If you do not take this responsibility seriously, the apostle Paul says you are worse than an unbeliever. "But if anyone does not provide for his relatives, and especially for members of his household, he has denied the faith and is worse than an unbeliever" (1 Timothy 5:8). And who knows, perhaps you will accept a job you don't really want, but it will turn into a vocation that you love.

The believer's call to work never ends. When we get to the New Heaven and New Earth, contrary to what some believe, we will not be sitting around playing harps. The Bible says we will be at work building, planting, and harvesting. (See Isaiah 65:17-25.) I do not claim to be an expert on heaven, but the Bible indicates that just as work was a valued part of the existence of the pre-Fall human, it will be a valued part of the existence of perfected humanity in heaven.

There is no doubt humans were made to work. It must be understood that vocation does not equal a paycheck. There are many vocations, like parenting, caring for the home, volunteering at a food bank, and serving as a mentor, which allow us to have a purpose, but do not result in a paycheck. Some people will hold a job which meets their financial needs and allows them to do their vocation on the side. Nearly half of the pastors in America today work a job outside of the church in order to fulfill their vocation of serving people through the local church.

Sacred Versus Secular

As mentioned in the introduction to this chapter, the idea of sacred work versus secular work was a creation of the medieval Roman Catholic Church. The idea of the clergy, or the "called ones," was limited to those who were dedicated to spiritual activity. The priests, monks, and nuns, of the day, did very little that would be associated with the natural world. Their job was to pray, study the Scriptures, and care for the spiritual needs of individuals. This led their vocations to be seen as more spiritual than the jobs held by the laity, or the "non-called people."

The Protestant church, under the leadership of Martin Luther, rejected the artificial distinction between the called and the non-called individuals, within the body of Christ. Based on his understanding of 1 Corinthians 7:20 and 1 Peter 2:9, he argued that all believers are priests because all believers are called. By extension, he believed all types of work that gave honor to God were sacred. A person's vocation could manifest itself through nearly any occupation. Luther did not call for a disbanding of the priesthood. Instead, he argued that "the people" should join the ranks of the "called."

In the New Testament, we see at least two categories of vocations occupied by followers of Jesus. Each of these vocations were necessary for the establishment of the kingdom of God. Jesus never saw one category as being superior in worth to the other.

Those in the first category were individuals who left a previous occupation and accepted a new vocation. These individuals received their pay from a new source. We generally call these individuals Jesus' disciples. Levi the tax collector left his government job to follow Jesus (Luke 5:29). Peter and Andrew left their fishing boats to follow Jesus (Matthew 4:18-22), as did James and John (Mark 1:19-21). In total, only 12 individuals became "full-time" followers of Jesus.

The second category of believers who Jesus could count on did not make a job change. They were not with Him on a daily basis. They continued to work their non-religious jobs. These individuals would be much like a businessman today who serves on the board of a church. These individuals were always available to Jesus, whenever called upon. Their hearts were fully behind His mission. Even though they worked a "non-religious job, their vocation was expanding the kingdom of God. Some examples of people in this category include wealthy men like Joseph of Arimathea (Luke 24:50-51), Mary and Martha (Luke 10:38-42), Lazarus (John 11), Peter's mother-in-law (Mark 1:29-34), and the wealthy women, who assisted Jesus financially (Luke 8:3).

We must be careful not to elevate one type of work over another. Too often a materialistic mindset will minimize the role of the spiritual leader. I enjoy watching reruns of the television show M*A*S*H. In the show, Father Mulcahy is always battling to keep the importance of the spiritual needs of the patients in focus for the doctors. Many times his services are relegated to praying over the dead. In this program, the skills of the surgeons are valued much higher than the prayers of the priests. In our society today, this mindset is shared by many. It must not be the view of Christians who are seeking to advance the kingdom of God.

A materialistic mindset may overemphasize the value of the surgeon, but many in Evangelical and Pentecostal traditions emphasize the spiritual over the natural. These individuals pray for healings, when people are sick, but seldom stop to pray for the surgeon to use their skills effectively or researchers to discover new ways to treat the diseases they pray against. This is often a result of not seeing the significance of these types of jobs for the expansion of the Kingdom.

Both the supernatural and the natural are used by God to accomplish His purposes on earth. He needs people in all vocations and we must honor those who follow His lead into the various roles some might label as secular. The Bible clearly identifies various "secular" roles as important to fulfilling God's purposes. Builders and crafts persons were vital to the construction of the Tabernacle and Temple (Exodus 35:2-3; 1 Chronicles 28:11-12). We see administration (1 Corinthians 12:28), political leadership (Romans 13:1-7), financier (Romans 12:8), and those who show hospitality (1 Corinthians 12:28) as callings (vocations) in Scripture.

The only jobs which cannot be considered vocations are those that promote something forbidden by Scripture or incompatible with the values found there. Although not an exhaustive list, some of the jobs that fit into this category are jobs that require murder (this would not include military service or a prison official carrying out orders from the government) (Exodus 20:13), any job that would require adultery (Exodus 20:14), jobs that entail stealing or cheating someone (Exodus 20:15), jobs that encourage you to be a false witness (Exodus 20:16), and jobs designed to oppress the poor (Leviticus 25:26). Willfully choosing an occupation that works to diminish the kingdom of God or degrades His creation is considered illegitimate.

In summary, there is no difference between a sacred and a secular job. All work is honorable, as long as it brings glory to God and it advances the kingdom of God in some way.

Determining Your Call

Some people reading this may be wondering how they can find a vocation that will bring fulfillment and serve the greater cause of the kingdom of God. These are good questions and fortunately the Bible gives us insights that will help answer these questions.

All people are first and foremost called to be followers of Jesus Christ and to live as a reflection of Him. (See Romans. 1:7; 1 Corinthians 1:2, 9, 1 Cor. 1:9, 26, 2 Cor. 3:18; Ephesians 4:1; 2 Timothy 1:9; 1 Peter 1:15-16, 2:9, 1 John 3:2-3.) Jesus made the priorities of God plain, "You shall love the Lord your God with all your heart and with all your soul and with all your mind. This is the great and first commandment. And a second is like it: You shall love your neighbor as yourself. On these two commandments depend all the Law and the Prophets" (Matthew 22:37-40).

It is instructive to hear Jesus' response to individuals who wanted to know what He wanted them to do to please Him. He wasn't as interested in them doing something as He was in them believing something that would transform them; "Then they said to him, 'What must we do, to be doing the works of God?' Jesus answered them, 'This is the work of God, that you believe in him whom he has sent'" (John 6:28-29).

The apostle Paul opens many of his letters reminding his readers of the call that was placed on his life to become a Christian. In addition to this call, he had a more specific vocation as an apostle. We must remember what we do for work is secondary to our relationship to God. It is this relationship that will cause our light to shine in otherwise dark places (Matthew 5:14-16). Our calling to follow Jesus will result in outward signs of the inward transformation which occurred through our salvation. Micah helps us visualize what a "called" person looks like, "What does the LORD require of you but to do justice, and to love kindness, and to walk humbly with your God?" (Micah 6:8).

Once we have established our primary call to follow Jesus, we can begin to look at ways to determine a vocational fit for us in regard to our work. Let's see what we can discover from Scripture that will help us in this endeavor.

There are some times God will undeniably call us to a specific vocation and even tell us the specific location where He wants us to carry out that vocation. Although a very rare occurrence, the Bible does record God calling some people in this specific manner. Examples of those asked to make a specific vocational change by God include Noah (Genesis 6), Moses and Aaron (Exodus 3:4, 28:1), Samuel (1 Samuel 3:10), Jeremiah (Jeremiah 1:4-5), and Amos (Amos 7:15). We can also see God's specific direction in the life of Abraham (Genesis 11-12), Joseph (Genesis 41:50-51), Gideon (Judges 6-8), Saul (1 Samuel 9), David (1 Samuel 16), the various disciples (Mark 3:14-19), and Paul and Barnabas (Acts 13:2). God also chose Bezalel and Oholiab (Exodus 31:1-6), but this was more likely as a result of their skills they already had, rather than calling them to adopt new skills as a calling.

Although impressive, the list just given represents a very small portion of the people who lived in the nearly 3000 years covered by the text of Scripture. A vast majority of people lived their life without a clear direction regarding their vocation from God. Do not fall into the trap of thinking you cannot commit to a vocation without hearing a specific word from God.

I was one of those individuals who believed God always calls specific people, to specific vocations, to a specific place, especially when it came to missionary work. I believed if God wanted me to be a missionary, He would let me know clearly, as well as where He wanted me to go. This misunderstanding prohibited me from accomplishing what God desired for me at one point in my life.

I was at a point of transition as I finished seminary. I was seeking God's will. My desire was to teach at the Bible college level. I had the qualifications, but there were no colleges in the United States that desired my services. I knew there was a need in other countries for teachers and I was willing to go. I began to fill out the paperwork to apply to become a missionary. I gave up on this effort when I convinced myself I had not been "called" to become a missionary. I felt I was not qualified for missionary service unless God specifically spoke to me about this task.

About two years later, then serving as a pastor, I was at a missionary event and had the opportunity to talk to the director of world missions for my denomination. I told him my story and he looked sad. He explained that with my qualifications, he would have accepted my application and assigned me to a field. He told me I had a wrong view of a missionary call. He explained to me if there is a need, and a person has the qualifications to meet that need, God wants to use the person to meet that need, unless He specifically closes the door. I wish I had understood this earlier.

So what do I do if God doesn't specifically direct me to a vocation?

The first step is to stop considering a "job" as a "calling" and begin to connect the meaning of a person's "call" to how we approach a job. This will make our task of determining our vocation less difficult.

With that said, let's look at some practical steps you can take to select the right job for you that you can turn into a vocation.

My conversation with the director of world missions helped me see my options, for a fulfilling vocation, could be determined by a critical evaluation of my skills, gifts, and desires. Once I had determined these components in my life, I could then determine where to practice my vocation. Let's examine these three steps in a little more detail.

First we must assess our gifts and skills. The apostle Paul teaches that God gives believers specific spiritual gifts to advance His kingdom:

Having gifts that differ according to the grace given to us, let us use them: if prophecy, in proportion to our faith; if service, in our serving; the one who teaches, in his teaching; the one who exhorts, in his exhortation; the one who contributes, in generosity; the one who leads, with zeal; the one who does acts of mercy, with cheerfulness (Romans 12:6-8).

The Bible explains that every Christian is given gifts. It is up to them to discover the gift God has given to them through the Holy Spirit and develop them. As believers mature, they will be able to use their gifts more effectively through their vocation.

Next comes our assessment of our skills. Some people focus on their weaknesses and identify what they cannot do or they attempt to increase their abilities in these areas. It is a much better idea to identify those skills which come naturally to us. It will be obvious to us over time what we are good at doing. Some people are wired to work with computers. Others love to interact with people. Some people find it fulfilling to write words on a page. Others love to work with their hands, to fix broken machinery. Some love to smell sawdust as they shape wood into fine pieces of furniture. It is important for us to discover what comes natural to us and to attempt to find an opportunity to minister to others using our skills. We will be blessed beyond measure if we are able to find employment in an area using those skill, but if not, we must let our "day" job make our vocation possible.

Combining your skills and talents with your personal desires can create a wonderful opportunity to advance the kingdom of God. Some people have a desire to help the poor. Others desire to assist in the development of children. Some people want to make a difference through medical research. Some people want to supply food to the hungry of the world. I am sitting in a hospital room right now watching nurses minister to my wife using their vocation. Only you know the desire God has instilled within you.

Following your desires in vocation is not another way of saying that you should do what makes you happy. Your vocation is not about you being happy, but about you glorifying God and ministering to others. Sometimes you will see a need and the answer to the problem will require you to become uncomfortable in the process. The apostle Paul lived a life filled with trouble as he pursued his vocation. At the end of his journey, he expresses the fulfillment his vocation brought to his life in spite of the struggles he faced.

For I am already being poured out as a drink offering, and the time of my departure has come. I have fought the good fight, I have finished the race, I have kept the faith. Henceforth there is laid up for me the crown of righteousness, which the Lord, the righteous judge, will award to me on that day, and not only to me but also to all who have loved his appearing (2 Timothy 4:6-8).

Although your vocation is not about making you happy, when you find your vocation and fulfill it, you will find happiness.

Once you determine your vocation, you will be able to determine how you wish to express it and where you can be most effective. Begin by praying, but also do research to determine where there are needs your vocation can meet. God will reveal opportunities in a variety of ways. Once you determine the needs the only step which will remain for you, is to be obedient. Your step of faith will be met by God's hand of provision.

You do not have to look to fill needs across the globe. It is likely, there are needs in your neighborhood that could be met through your vocation. It is obvious you cannot meet every need you become aware of, but you should make an effort to meet some need. You do not need to wait for a special call from God. If a need presents itself, and you have the ability to meet it, do not resort to praying about it. God has already prepared you to meet the need, so just go ahead and do it.

As much as we would like to meet all the needs that present themselves, we must know when to say "No" to an opportunity if it will stretch us too thin. Satan uses busyness to distract us from developing our relationship with God. It is essential to leave room in our schedule to maintain spiritual vitality through spending time in the presence of God. We must also reserve time for leisure and fellowship with believers.

Not everyone is going to find the perfect job that combines their gifts, talents, and desires. If you find yourself without the perfect situation, it is important that you not wait to find a vocation that is expressed through a paid position. Discover your vocation based on your gifts, skills, and desires and minister to God and others through volunteer activities.

How Should I Approach My Vocation?

A person's attitude toward one's job can actually turn it into a vocation. The Bible provides many instructions concerning work and a proper attitude for a follower of God.

John the Baptist was baptizing the crowds, who were deciding to make a commitment to God. The people sensed there should be some sort of transition in their behavior as a result of making this commitment. They asked John what they should do to demonstrate a change in their lives. John's response was very practical. He said:

Whoever has two tunics is to share with him who has none, and whoever has food is to do likewise." Tax collectors also came to be baptized and said to him, "Teacher, what shall we do?" And he said to them, "Collect no more than you are authorized to do." Soldiers also asked him, "And we, what shall we do?" And he said to them, "Do not extort money from anyone by threats or by false accusation, and be content with your wages" (Luke 3:10-14).

John's message was clear, if you get right with God, you will treat others in a godly manner. We cannot be people of vocation without it effecting our attitude toward others.

A key to an exciting vocation is learning to delight yourself with God and His people. The Psalmist catches this concept when he says, "Delight yourself in the LORD, and he will give you the desires of your heart" (Psalm 37:4). Delighting in God produces passion that yields spiritual results.

The apostle Paul tells Christians to do whatever work they are involved in as if they were working for God. Paul tells the Christian slaves of the day they must look at their job as working for God. "Whatever you do, work heartily, as for the Lord and not for men, knowing that from the Lord you will receive the inheritance as your reward. You are serving the Lord Christ" (Colossians 3:23-24). Paul was not sanctioning slavery. He was simply helping his readers to understand that no matter the job you find yourself in, you can turn it into an occasion to bring glory to God.

Conclusion

Vocation is vital in an individual's spiritual formation. It is through vocation that a Christian actuates the command to love God and love others. The Christian should always be on the look out to minister to others using the gifts, skills, and desires God has placed in the individual's heart and hands.

We must never feel that our work is spiritually inferior to someone else's work. God placed all of us in His kingdom and uses all of us to fulfill His purposes on earth. As Christians fulfill the purposes of God, they will find themselves fulfilled as well.

Study Guide Questions

1. What does the word "vocation" mean?

2. Who was the first worker?

3. How can a person keep from having their job drain life from them?

4. How long should Christians expect to work?

5. How do Roman Catholic theology and Protestant theology differ, regarding vocation?

6. What two categories did the first century Christians fit into regarding vocation?

7. What is the primary call of all Christians?

8. What three steps can a Christian use to determine one's vocation when not specifically assigned a task by God?

9. What can you expect if you delight yourself in the Lord?

SEVENTEEN

SPIRITUAL FORMATION THROUGH COMMUNITY

We have examined various spiritual disciplines that will assist us in growing strong in Christ. We must take personal responsibility to develop our spiritual life, but true spiritual maturity should not be developed in isolation.

In the Old Testament, families were the context for spiritual development. The patriarch of the clan had the responsibility of teaching the children and assuring family members maintained the standards of the tribe. During the New Testament, the context for spiritual development transitioned from the family to the community of like-minded believers. In a sense, the church became the family for those who were rejected by their own families when they aligned themselves with Jesus.

Today, the church is still the primary community where spiritual development takes place. All of the disciplines we have studied thus far are best tested among fellow believers who, like us, are attempting to walk according to the Holy Spirit (Galatians 5:16). In this chapter, we will look at the importance of belonging to a church family and how faithfully fellowshipping with others of like faith can help us grow into the people God wants us to be.

The Purpose of the Church

The purpose of the local church is varied, but I would like to highlight two reasons the local church is essential within the kingdom of God. First, the local church is the instrument God chose to use to fulfill the Great Commission (Matthew 28:16-20). It is the local church's responsibility to both equip and send individuals into the world to usher the lost into the kingdom of God. The apostle Paul identifies the primary role of the local church leader as an equipper. He tells the Ephesians the leaders of the church will teach individual Christians to learn how to reach out to the lost and to rescue them through the power of the Holy Spirit.

> And he gave the apostles, the prophets, the evangelists, the shepherds and teachers, to equip the saints for the work of ministry, for building up the body of Christ, until we all attain to the unity of the faith and of the knowledge of the Son of God, to mature manhood, to the measure of the stature of the fullness of Christ, so that we may no longer be children, tossed to and fro by the waves and carried about by every wind of doctrine, by human cunning, by craftiness in deceitful schemes. Rather, speaking the truth in love, we are to grow up in every way into him who is the head, into Christ, from whom the whole body, joined and held together by every joint with which it is equipped, when each part is working properly, makes the body grow so that it builds itself up in love (Ephesians 4:11-16).

The second purpose of the church is to help us develop our gifts and talents to further the kingdom of God. It is among a loving spiritual family where Christians can practice various disciplines and exercise their spiritual gifts without fear of reprisal (1 Timothy 4:14). There is room for error as we grow into maturity. Just as it would be unreasonable for a baby to walk in his or her first attempt, it is unreasonable that a Christian will be accomplished in performing spiritual gifts when they first receive them. Mature Christians must not criticize younger believers as they take steps toward God.

In the remainder of this chapter, we will examine these two purposes in an attempt to help us understand the importance of being a part of a spiritual community and maximizing the benefits associated with our church family.

Fulfilling the Great Commission

Discovering Our Place in the Kingdom

A key for the Great Commission to be fulfilled is for each individual to understand his or her role in accomplishing Jesus' command. Not everyone is called to be an evangelist who will train others to share the gospel and lead by example. In the same way, God doesn't ask everyone to be a pastor or a teacher. God has designed each individual just as He wants them and has a place for each in accomplishing His will. (See 1 Corinthians 12.) It is important for each of us to find our place in the kingdom of God.

I will be forever thankful for the local church and its leaders who played a pivotal role in my life. If it had not been for a very wise mentors in my local church, I do not know where I would be today. I was floundering in regard to my future. A series of events helped to shape my life. They helped me to understand the role God wanted me to play in His kingdom.

I will never forget the day Bert Skinner took me aside and helped me to understand what I was good at doing, as well as pointing out the things God did not equip me to accomplish. He could talk to me very bluntly because he had been my Sunday school teacher and had earned my trust. More than anyone else, I knew Bert loved God and he loved me. He was a witness to what it meant to be a true follower of God. He was a person I looked up to and wanted to be like when I got older.

When Bert spoke hard words to me that day, I listened to them and valued them. He told me I was worthless with my hands, which was difficult to hear since I was working on his farm using my hands every day. He suggested I find an occupation where I would be able to use my head and my mouth. There was probably nobody else who could have said those words to me and have their words make such an impact on my life. As a matter of fact, a high school teacher, who was not a follower of Christ and who I had no real relationship with other than he was my teacher, spoke equally harsh words to me about my future. Ironically, his evaluation of me was diametrically opposite of the assessment of Bert. But there was no context that provided validity to what he was saying. As a result, I ignored his words which over time proved to be wisdom on my part.

Bert was not the only one in my Christian community who helped me to shape my future contributions to the kingdom of God. Scott Garland was there when I began to question some of the very foundational issues of Christianity. He spent quality time with me. He saw I was beginning to take steps in a direction that was not leading toward God. I was not sure I wanted to spend my life investing in the local church. I was preparing to go to a public college to study psychology. Scott challenged me to attend a Christian University for my freshman year to explore if God might want to use me in some other way. He understood the importance of investing in young people. At great cost to him personally, he purchased a round-trip airline ticket from Maine to Missouri, and sent me on my way.

The church is an institution where relationships, such as those I just described, can exist. Every young person should be able to find older Christians who will help guide them in their journey to serve in the kingdom of God. I challenge you to either find a person to help guide you or you become a person willing to invest in the life of others.

Discovering the Needs

The local church is not simply about one individual helping another individual discover their unique gifts and callings. It is also a place where we learn about the vast mission field that exists. It can become easy for believers to be so focused on the spiritual development of those who fellowship with them each week, they fail to see the larger task before them.

The local church can aid in exposing believers to the needs of the world, by inviting missionaries to share the needs in the fields where they serve. It can also be a place that highlights the needs in the local communities where they live. We will never become fully mature Christians until we become aware of the needs of others and then begin to use the gifts and talents God is developing in us to minister to those needs. We may not immediately see how we can assist others given our current position in life, but being exposed to the needs in our communities, and around the world, now will help us focus our resources to begin to meet the needs of others.

When I first arrived at the Christian university as a young adult, my motivation for being there was primarily to focus on my own development. I didn't go with a desire to help anyone else. But as I began to grow spiritually, I was exposed to the vast needs in our world. The university's daily chapel services regularly exposed me to the needs of various nations and people groups. At my university, not many students studied in fields leading to the mission field or to becoming pastors of local churches. But with increased exposure to the needs that existed in the world, many students began to see how their preparation could be used to meet the needs of children in the school systems, to heal people through the various vocations in the health field, and to help provide finances for people in need through starting businesses. In my case, I saw opportunities to serve others through the local church and eventually in the college classroom as a way to use my talents and abilities.

It was not until I actually obeyed God and began using my training, gifts, and talents in the place God assigned me, that I finally took my eyes off from myself and placed them onto the needs of others. If we stay fixated on our own spiritual development, without focusing on how what we are learning can benefit others, we will remain immature, self-serving saints missing the entire point of the spiritual maturation process. Christian communities are ideal places to prod us on to good works (Hebrews 10:24).

An Avenue for Discipleship

The local church provides various avenues for discipleship. It is in the church service that we learn great truths from Scripture through the hymns and sermons. It is in Sunday school and small groups where we are able to ask questions and discuss how to apply the principles of Scripture. The local church generally provides curriculum to assist young believers to develop their knowledge of the gospel.

If we isolate ourselves from regular involvement with fellow Christians in the local church, we will rob ourselves of the ability to watch others grow, hear the opinions of others, and join with others in dissecting the word of God. These opportunities cannot be taken advantage of by watching the latest and greatest television pastor, listening to the best crafted podcast, or reading powerful authors' books. Remote ministers can provide good insights, but they do little to truly disciple a person. Ministry from "up front" only provides one element in the discipleship process. Believers must be challenged to dig into the Bible themselves, if they ever want to move from the spiritual milk provided by others to being able to eat savory meat (or hearty vegetables for my vegan friends) on their own (1 Corinthians 3:1-3).

The clearest biblical example of discipleship within a community context occurs in the life of Timothy. Paul writes to Timothy with great feeling as he recalls the discipleship journey Timothy had been on. Paul states:

> I thank God whom I serve, as did my ancestors, with a clear conscience, as I remember you constantly in my prayers night and day. As I remember your tears, I long to see you, that I may be filled with joy. I am reminded of your sincere faith, a faith that dwelt first in your grandmother Lois and your mother Eunice and now, I am sure, dwells in you as well. For this reason I remind you to fan into flame the gift of God, which is in you through the laying on of my hands, for God gave us a spirit not of fear but of power and love and self-control (2 Timothy 1:3-7).

Paul doesn't take full credit for Timothy's spiritual growth. He understands it takes a community to disciple a person. Timothy's grandmother and mother both set an example for Timothy. Lois would have been an early believer in Jesus, given her age. She passed the faith on to her daughter. Timothy would have grown up in the church watching adult leaders who worshipped around him.

One wonders where Timothy would have been if there had been no Paul in his life to mentor and encourage him. Paul was there for Timothy at crucial times in his spiritual development. He allowed Timothy to follow him and watch him in ministry (Acts 16). It was Paul who placed Timothy in the church at Ephesus to cut his teeth in ministry (1 Timothy 1:3). And, it was Paul who commissioned Timothy to carry on the mission Paul had begun (2 Timothy 2:3; 4:1-5). As we can see from reading 1 and 2 Timothy, Paul didn't leave him to struggle on his own when he faced troubles. In 1 Timothy, Paul helped Timothy set up the organizational process of the local church. In 2 Timothy, Paul encourages his young friend as Paul faced dire problems of his own.

The local church also provides the resources necessary for those called of God to complete the tasks to which He has called them. Paul and Barnabas were called of God to reach the Gentiles. The church at Antioch prayed for Paul and Barnabas, sent them on their way, and received them back when they completed their journey (Acts 13). We may never have heard of Paul and Barnabas if a praying church had not supported them on their journey. The local church has equippers, senders, and goers. Every believer should fit into one of those categories. This is what makes the local church the ideal vehicle to fulfill the Great Commission.

Every generation of Christians will have a few individuals who will attempt to live their faith without a community of believers. These individuals may have a personal relationship with Jesus, but they are missing out on so much. One reason people choose not to go to church is they really don't want to exert the effort to address differences they have with leaders in the church, or with people in the church, who are not like them. These people may live in peace at home, but they do not experience the spiritual growth that can only come from iron sharpening iron, which takes place in a community of believers (Proverbs 27:17).

Unfortunately, many individuals, with no church family, walk away from the faith without anyone knowing, or fall into heresy without someone being able to keep them from making dangerous spiritual errors. I unashamedly assert, no matter how flawed the local church might be, it is better than living your life in spiritual isolation. If you see problems in the local church that keeps you away, it may be God who is revealing these flaws to you so you can help fix them. Adopt a fireman's mentality. Don't run from the fire, but run into it, so you can make the church the community God desires.

Conclusion

Hopefully, you have seen through this discussion the value of attending a local church. Jesus declared the church would remain until He returned to remove it from the earth (Matthew 16:17-19). If Jesus saw the church as being that valuable, then we need to hold it in the same high esteem. We know the Church is not a building. The Church is comprised of people who love God with all of their minds, hearts, and bodies, and who love others in demonstrable ways.

Christianity is not a solo event. It must be done in community if we seek to be all God has created us to be and to accomplish His will on earth. I am not saying an individual on some remote island, or in solitary confinement in a prison camp, cannot be a Christian. What I am saying is if we have the choice to fellowship with believers on a regular basis, and we forgo that opportunity, we are robbing ourselves from the best God has planned for us. Allow church attendance to assist you as you engage in the spiritual formation process. Paul taught the Galatians that spiritual formation was their own responsibility, but he based that on the fact there would be many brothers and sisters who were available to help in the process (Galatians 6:1-5).

Study Guide Questions

1. Compare the Old Testament and New Testament context for spiritual formation.

2. What are the two purposes of the local church identified by the author?

3. What does the author say is the key for the Great Commission to be fulfilled?

4. How does the local church help believers become aware of needs in the world?

5. Why is belonging to a local church more valuable to the discipleship than trying to be a "solo" Christian?

6. Briefly describe the discipleship journey of Timothy?

7. How should Christians respond if they see problems in the church?

EIGHTEEN

THE LOCAL CHURCH: A LABORATORY FOR SPIRITUAL FORMATION

As we bring this section of the book to a close, I would like to review some of the spiritual disciplines we have examined thus far, and see how participation in the local church can help us reach our goals of spiritual maturity.

Make Commitments

We learned water baptism is not a perfunctory event. Water baptism is the signal an individual has chosen to love God and love others as a part of the Christian community. When a person makes a commitment to Jesus through water baptism, it is logical for the person to join a local church. This will demonstrate the person's ongoing commitment to the vision of the church and to the welfare of their fellow believers.

There is a growing tendency for people to not make long-term commitments to a local church. The reason people tend to jump from church to church is because they have adopted the consumer mentality that is prevalent in our materialistic society. Often, we treat churches the same way we treat fast food restaurants. If something changes about the food at McDonald's, we stop going there and buy our hamburgers at Burger King. Instead of attempting to address the problem, we run to the next option that is available to us.

My illustration is flawed because I have no opportunity to change the quality of the food at McDonald's because I have no ownership in the restaurant. My relationship with the restaurant is transactional. I give them money and they give me food. If my relationship with the local church is transactional then it reveals I have not made a personal commitment to its success. If I adopt a transactional mindset, then it is logical for me to leave a church when I am no longer getting what I feel I am paying for.

Not making a commitment to a local church is reasonable, if the individual has recently moved from one community to another. It is reasonable for individuals to visit various churches when they first arrive in a community. But once individuals have identified a church body they believe God has sent them to, they should make a commitment to that body for the remainder of the time they are in that community. There are rare exceptions to this rule. If heresy arises in the church and it is not dealt with properly by the leadership, it is wise to walk away from the church. Short of this, there is very little reason for a person to disassociate from a church body to which God has lead them.

What I hope you can see is our commitment to a local church must be based on how we can serve the needs of believers in that spiritual community. The pastor of the local church should never have to worry about us walking away from the congregation simply because our preferences are not being catered to.

Practice Bible Study

Many people only open their Bibles when they go to church. This is because they either do not see the practicality of the word of God in their own lives, or they are intimidated by Scripture. Church attendance can act as a means to encourage individuals to read their Bibles throughout the week. Church attendance can provide incentive to study the Bible, through small group Bible studies and Sunday school classes.

Church attendance will enhance our appreciation for Bible study. Attending a church where a pastor spends quality time preparing the sermon will demonstrate the product of effective Bible study. A well-crafted sermon will explain the passage and bring the biblical text to life. The sermon will help you make application of the Bible passage to your life. Individual Bible study is wonderful, but it is important to have others examine your conclusions and give you feedback as to the accuracy of your findings. Peter taught that Scripture should be interpreted within a community of believers to prevent the possibility of heresy (2 Peter 1:20).

Prioritize Prayer

Prayer is one of the most talked about elements of the Christian faith, but often one of the least employed disciplines. It is easy to go through a day and become so busy we don't even think about God, let alone pray. Attending church provides us, at a minimum, a regular prioritization of the importance of prayer. Few churches go through an entire church service without someone praying. These prayers as reminders we should carry out prayer in our own life on a regular basis.

One of the best places to learn to pray is among fellow believers in a local church. Listening to others pray often provides a framework to help individuals learn how to pray for themselves. The local church provides a variety of settings where prayers are offered. If individuals attend small groups or Sunday school, they will hear individuals leading prayer for the needs of others. In these settings, it also provides the new believer with opportunities to lead a prayer in a safe environment. The encouragement the new believer receives can propel them to take more risks in praying in other settings.

Another benefit of being a part of a church family is hearing the testimonies of answered prayers of others who have faced similar situations as you. These testimonies should give you confidence prayer works and encouragement to take your needs to God in prayer. As individuals begin to share their testimonies, you will often hear how God changed the heart of the person praying and how that person was used by God to be a part of the answer to the prayer. When this occurs, you are reminded of the part God wants you to play in ministry to others.

Engage Worship

Where else in the world do people set aside 20 to 45 minutes each week to sing songs that focus on God? Church is a unique experience because its primary purpose is to direct our minds towards the holiness of God. Obviously the 45 minutes or so we spend singing songs to God at church is not the full array of worship necessary in a believer's life, but it is an illustration of how our attention should be directed toward God throughout the week.

We are blessed today with Christian radio stations and online options that encourage worship through music. Unfortunately, listening to music on the radio can often serve as entertainment, rather than focusing our attention on the greatness of God. Entertainment fills our needs. Worship takes our attention off from us and centers it on God. We can avoid substituting entertainment for worship if we associate the songs we hear on the radio with a worship experience we had in church when the same songs were sung. There is something about the atmosphere of a church service which enhances the worship experience. When we join together with fellow believers, with a singular purpose of worshiping God, there is a heightened awareness of Him. Attending church with a community of believers will enhance our individual worship throughout the week.

Live Authentically

The world says that it values authenticity, but few are willing to take the risk to live an authentic life. Individuals who are honest about their feelings and faults are often cannibalized by those who they associate with in the world. As a result, many people live behind a mask. They feel forced to live a lie. This incongruence often eats them up on the inside. This leads to shame and insecurity because they are afraid somebody will find out who they really are. Christians should not have to live with this fear.

The beauty of being a believer, and belonging to a community of like-minded believers, is we do not have to live to impress others. We do not even have to impress God. He is already impressed with us because He made us to be the people we are. When we surround ourselves with fellow believers, they should encouraged us to learn to live with integrity. Our unique qualities are needed for the local church to fully function (1 Corinthians 12). The church is not a place to pretend.

If the church you attend is a place where you feel you must put on a façade, it is not a church that is following the mandates of Jesus, in this area. I encourage you to help transform your church community into a place that is accepting of others. Never lie to yourself, or to anyone else for that matter. God wants us to be fully sold out to Him and to live our lives from the inside out. The church should be a place where we can work through our struggles as we learn to trust fellow believers to assist us with our struggles.

Love Others

The premise of this book is that Jesus desires that we have two priorities; to love God and to love others. Loving God is the easiest part of Jesus' commandment. Loving others can become difficult when the people around us are hateful. Jesus understood this fully because he was hated by many individuals in His life on earth. Jesus was not speaking without experience when he said the real test of Christianity is how we love those who treat us poorly (Matthew 5:43-48).

Exercise Forgiveness

It is likely that you have at least one person in your life who has treated you unfairly. Sometimes the way you have been treated goes well beyond unfair and crosses the line into brutality. But it doesn't matter the degree to which you were offended by the person, the Bible still calls us to love, both those who treat us well and those who don't deserve our love. The local church is a place to confront those who have hurt us and to love them through it. This requires us to exercise forgiveness.

I would like to be able to say everyone in the church will treat you well. The truth is the church is made up of broken people. To coin a phrase from an important book, "hurt people hurt people." When we are among fellow believers, we expect individuals to treat us well because they claim to be followers of Christ. When they hurt us, it makes the sting hurt just a little bit more.

Many letters in the Bible were written to churches being torn by broken relationships. Repeatedly, there is a call to unity. It is the desire of God for Christians to live in harmony (Romans 12:16). The local church is the arena God has designed for Christians to work out their differences. The church is a place where we are encouraged to see people the way God sees them. We begin to understand how God forgave us when we were undeserving. We may never be able to understand why people did what they did to us, but we are able to live with our differences because we have a common Savior. Paul challenged Christians to work out all of their differences, so they could be good witnesses of the gospel to the world (1 Corinthians 6:1-11). Christians must practice principles of conflict resolution, see life from the other person's perspective, and live in a community where everyone does not necessarily see eye to eye.

Serve Others

Attempting to live a Christian life without the benefit of a church family will often result in devoted Christians sitting on their couches, reading their Bibles, thinking about spiritual things, but doing very little to serve others. This kind of existence will result in a religious person who looks much more like a Pharisee than Jesus.

There are many places to perform acts of service in the world today, but there is no place that has as many avenues for service to others, as the local church. There is an array of opportunities to serve fellow brothers and sisters within the church. But a church, which reflects the priorities of Christ, will also provide service to the local community in which it resides, as well as service around the world.

Each week church members are presented with the needs that exist in our world and the opportunities to meet those needs. A church that focuses entirely on their own needs seldom grows because the people become myopic. But a church that teaches its members to serve others, equips them to do so, and presents opportunities for them to carry out these acts of service, will grow numerically, as the people within the church grow spiritually.

Embrace Submission

The key to successfully living, in any family, is a willingness to submit one to another. No sibling has ever gone through his/her entire life without having an argument. We all want to have our own way (James 4:1-12). A skillful parent figures out a way to allow their children to feel like they are winners, even when they don't get their way in a particular situation. No healthy family allows the same child to always get his/her way.

The local church is a great place for us to learn to submit one to another. The worship team is not always going to get their own way in a healthy church. Neither are the Christian education leaders. Sometimes a person is going to have to serve in the nursery, even though they don't want to do so. And not everyone is going to always have the worship music they prefer. A church family should be a place where we learn to get our own way on occasion, but allow others to have their own way on other occasions.

Ultimately, being a part of the family of God helps us to learn how to submit to Jesus. All of us want to have the most power in a situation. This will lead to struggles to set the agenda and determine the priorities for the local church. Often, this will result in conflicts between a pastor and a board member. But being part of the church family helps us to realize that it's neither the pastor's nor the board member's view that really matters in a situation. The only opinion that matters is the opinion of Jesus. We must remember, He is the head of the Church. In order for us to learn submission to Jesus, we must prioritize spending time with Him, to determine what His will is in a particular situation. This determination is best accomplished through a community of believers who are unified in their attempt to accomplish Jesus' will through their local church.

Be Generous

One of the most evident ways of displaying the image of Christ in our lives is through our generosity. God showed His generosity to us by sending us His Son as a sacrifice for our sins (Romans 5:8). Generosity has many expressions which can occur both inside of the church, as well as to those who have yet to follow Jesus. Attending a local church reminds us to be generous each time the offering plate is passed.

Some people become offended at the church because it appears church leaders only care about money. Some churches go overboard in their appeal for money, but that does not negate the importance of the weekly offering. The offering reminds us of our need to be generous with the resources God has provided to us, but it also should remind us of the generosity of God toward us. As praying in church should remind us that we ought to be praying at home, giving in the weekly offering at church should remind us of the importance of being generous to family members and others who are in need around us.

Research has demonstrated going to church increases a person's generosity. A recent survey shows Evangelical Christians give an average of $1450 per year to charitable causes, such as church, compared to $600 per year for the average non-religious person. Another study shows that 57% of Christians that attend church each week are "givers" whereas 56% of those who only attend occasionally are "keepers." This survey labeled a giver as someone who showed generosity in all aspects of their lives. The keepers looked to keep what they had and desired to have additional resources given to them. If you want to reflect the generosity of God in your life, make it a practice to attend church on a regular basis.

Foster Gratefulness

One of the most important elements of a church service is Holy Communion. Communion, by its very nature, must take place within a church setting. Although there are cases where Communion can be given in a setting outside the church, such as a hospital room or on the battlefield, these are anomalies, rather than the rule. The purpose of practicing Communion on a regular basis is twofold. First, it is an opportunity for us to examine our relationships with fellow believers. But a second purpose equally important is to remind us of the great gift Jesus gave to us at Calvary and three days later at the empty tomb. This is a time of celebration where we have the opportunity to stop, reflect, and then give thanks to God.

Practicing Communion should also remind us of all the other great gifts God has provided for us. Scripture teaches all good gifts come from above (James 1:17). We possess nothing that did not originate with God. Ungrateful individuals will look at what they possess and declare it is the result of their hard work and ingenuity. It is understandable for the atheist to make these declarations. It is illogical for someone who says they believe in God to take His gifts for granted. The reason many Christians don't offer thanks isn't because they think God is stingy. They tend to neglect gratefulness because they do not pause long enough to reflect on all the ways God has blessed them.

As I write today, I am sitting on a balcony, overlooking a beautiful golf course, at a resort in Idaho. I could be ungrateful because I am taking precious vacation time to write this book, instead of spending time on the course. Instead of being frustrated, I have chosen to reflect on the wonderful gifts God has given to me. Among those gifts is the voice recognition software I purchased. I am blessed to not have to type every word on a keyboard. He's provided me with a computer that will store my documents, so they don't get misplaced. As I look around my surroundings, I thank God for the trees and the beautiful grass covering the golf course. And how can I neglect being grateful for the eyes He gave me which allow me to see so many wonderful images? But perhaps my greatest degree of gratefulness comes from the fact He has provided me with a mind that can process my thoughts and the images I behold.

When was the last time that you just paused to express gratitude to God? Perhaps it was the last time you took Holy Communion at your church. If this is the case, I encourage you to use Holy Communion to jumpstart your gratitude to propel you towards a deeper appreciation of God and the gifts He has given to you. Communion is a wonderful way to take steps toward God.

Conclusion

The local church is a great setting to develop your spiritual life. Being surrounded by a loving family provides you with the opportunity to make mistakes without fear of reprisal. Find spiritual mentors who will assist you, challenge you, and hold you accountable.

An added benefit to making a commitment to the local church is that it teaches you to have commitments to other important institutions in your life, such as marriage. The divorce rate in Western civilization is appalling, but unfortunately it is as high among those who attend church as it is among those who do not attend church. More and more Christians are choosing to live together, rather than making a commitment to marriage. Those who have learned commitment to brothers and sisters within the body of Christ, regardless of their personal preferences, will be more likely to sustain a lifetime commitment of marriage. God says He hates divorce (Malachi 2:16). He says this because He values commitment. Jesus illustrates the importance of living a life of honoring one's commitments when He says, "Let what you say be simply 'Yes' or 'No'" (Matthew 5:37).

If you have not found a local church to attend, it is vital that you do in order to keep moving forward in your spiritual development.

Study Guide Questions

1. What does the author mean when he says the local church is a laboratory for spiritual development?

2. How does church attendance enhance the practice of Bible study?

3. How does church attendance help us to live confidently and authentically?

4. How does the weekly offering promote generosity?

5. In what way does participation in Holy Communion jumpstart our gratefulness?

6. How does church membership improve the possibility of a lifetime commitment to a marriage partner?

UNIT FOUR

SEEING LIFE THROUGH A BIBLICAL LENS

NINETEEN

DEFINING A CHRISTIAN WORLDVIEW

Effective spiritual formation should produce changed behavior, but changed behavior is ultimately conditional on the way a person thinks. The apostle Paul taught a great deal about the impact the thinking process has on personal behavior. A centerpiece of Pauline theology, found in the letter to the Romans, declares:

> I appeal to you therefore, brothers, by the mercies of God, to present your bodies as a living sacrifice, holy and acceptable to God, which is your spiritual worship. Do not be conformed to this world, but be transformed by the renewal of your mind, that by testing you may discern what is the will of God, what is good and acceptable and perfect (Romans 12:1-2).

Paul's emphasis on the importance of the intellect on determining a person's behavior can also be seen when he tells people to "consider" in order to achieve a proper attitude (Romans 8:18); to "think about these things" to maintain a proper spiritual perspective (Philippians 4:8); to "reason" in order to gain understanding (Acts 17:17); and to "remember" information, such as the fact of the resurrection, which will change the way a person lives (1 Corinthians 15:1).

If what we think determines our behavior, it is important to evaluate what causes us to think the way we do. Our perspective on life determines how we think. We view and interpret information through unique lenses formed by our experiences, the culture we live in, the philosophies we embrace, and religious beliefs we hold. The circumstances that shape the way we see and understands life produces our worldview or "epistemology."

Our Worldview and the Church

Everyone has a worldview whether they know it or not. A person's worldview affects nearly all aspects of his/her life. We don't often think about a person's worldview effecting food choices, but it does. I learned this a few years ago. My wife and I were on our first cruise. While enjoying the pool area, I decided to get into the large hot tub. I settled down beside a man and his wife. We quickly struck up a conversation. I discovered he worked for a tortilla chip manufacturer that sold chips, both in Mexico and in Texas. I asked him if he sold the same line of chips in both locations. He shared with me that the chips he sold in Mexico were significantly different than the chips he sold in Texas, even though they carried the same name and logo. He explained that the Mexican consumer has a different preference than the people in Texas. The Mexicans perceived a chip should taste one way, while Texans perceived it should taste another way. Instead of trying to change a person's view in regard to the flavor and texture of a chip, they simply created two different recipes for two different people groups.

I often inquire, of my students, if they prefer authentic Mexican food or Mexican food from a place like Taco Bell. Most of them laugh, and quickly say they prefer authentic Mexican food. I shock them when I tell them I would much rather eat food from Taco Bell. After I make this confession, many others in the room are brave enough to say they would rather eat food from Taco Bell, as well. I then go on to explain that Taco Bell is successful in the United States because it is inexpensive, but also because they have captured the preference of the American audience. In other words, they have Americanized Mexican food and turned it into something most Americans actually prefer to the original.

The way we view Christianity is shaped by our preferences more often than we would like to admit. Very few churches in the United States, and in the Western world for that matter, truly reflect the priorities of the Early Church. The Church, in the first century, was a community made up of people who needed each other, cared for each other, and ministered to one another. Today's Western Church tends to be more consumer oriented and self-centered. This may sound judgmental, but if we will honestly examine the music we sing, the sermons we hear, and the frequency with which people change churches when something doesn't go the way they desire it to go, we may discover I am closer to the truth than what we may want to admit.

The Basis of a Christian Worldview

There are many types of worldviews. Our focus will be limited to the distinguishing factors between a secular worldview and Christian thought. Secularists do not see the Bible or God as having a significant role in establishing priorities for their lives. According to secularists, if God does exist, He lives at church where they may occasionally go visit Him. Christians build their worldview on the opposite presupposition. Christians believe God holds ultimate authority over every aspect of their life. They believe His will is clearly communicated through the Bible. Secularists see themselves as the center of their universe. They believe they hold ultimate authority over their lives. Christians do not have this view because when they chose to follow Jesus, they also chose to give Him authority over their eternal destiny, as well as, their day-to-day practices.

Secularists are aided in the propagation of their faith each day through the media, both broadcast and social, as progressive thinking pulls individuals away from a biblical foundation. School systems are designed to negate Christian thought by totally eliminating Christian values from the educational curriculum. When Christian concepts are mentioned, they are degraded by many teachers. Textbooks are chosen that champion secular philosophies. It is not surprising that many young adults, who grew up in the church, are more secularized than they are Christianized due to the quantity of information that is force-fed to them through secular institutions.

The church has not helped the situation. In recent years, it has abandoned systematic teaching of the Scriptures to young people through Sunday school and have relied on large gatherings with little chance for interaction, questions, or application of Scripture. Because the student is not been given a chance to examine both sides of issues in public school, and the only place they hear about God is in a large group church setting, the result is many Christians who say they serve God have adopted a secular worldview.

Our Worldview and Our Spiritual Formation

Christians must assess their own worldview to understand, more fully, why they act as they do and to determine if changes need to be made to become aligned more closely with God's desires for their lives. Many Christians, who claim to live according to a biblical worldview, have never examined what the Bible says about important topics. Instead, they simply absorb what others say, or make uninformed decisions about life. It is very possible for a Christian to hold two conflicting beliefs concerning an issue without recognizing the spiritual implications of this dichotomy. Too many Christians engage in non-biblical practices while claiming to believe the Bible is the standard for their faith and conduct. Often, they do not recognize the incongruence because they have not stopped to examine what the Bible says about important topics such as how they spend money, engage in relationships, and embrace political movements. Many of these Christians operate from a non-biblical worldview without realizing it. They engage in sacred activities on Sunday and then embrace a secular worldview throughout the week. It is as if they believe if their spirit is okay with God, then they can make decisions regarding the rest of their life devoid of spiritual considerations.

It is important for Christians to examine the basis of their worldview so they will be able to understand their behavior. The first step is for Christians to not only read their Bibles, but also to study the major doctrines found there. When this occurs, Christians will be better able to see how the biblical vantage point is different than the philosophies being purported by those around them. If they do not determine what the Bible teaches concerning topics, such as the use of power, sex, and money, they will allow what they hear on television or see on social media to shape their worldview. The result will be behavior which more closely reflects a non-biblical worldview than the biblical worldview Christians claim they embrace.

Over time, the replacement of a non-biblical worldview, among Christians, for a biblical worldview, has resulted in a weakened church, as evidenced by increased immorality and lack of ethics among its members. Many people, who attend church on a regular basis, look little different than their non-Christian counterparts. Christian employees steal time from their employees by calling in sick when they are not and help themselves to office supplies for personal use in violation of the clear teaching of Scripture regarding the way a Christian should behave in the workplace. The amount of pornography used by those who sit in the pew will reveal the believer sees sex quite differently than what is outline in Scripture. A review of the debt load of many Christians reveal a worldview devoid of biblical principles.

The local church is made up of people who bring their worldview with them when they come to church. Due to the makeup of some churches, they look more like a social club than an expression of the kingdom of God. Examples of this can be seen by how the church has changed its views on things such as premarital sex, divorce, consumerism, and the way we address the needs of the poor.

Scope of This Unit

A person's worldview affects all aspects of life, but no book is going to be able to deal with every element that a worldview touches in a person's life. There are three areas that seem to come to the surface when we hear the sad report of a Christian going off the rails. These areas are the abuse of power, the participation in sexual immorality, or the misuse of finances. Many examples of prominent ministers could be listed who have fallen in one of these areas. The list of Christians in non-religious settings who have fallen as a result of a compromised worldview might be even longer.

It is my assumption that most, if not all, people have weaknesses in one of these three areas. Few have weaknesses in all three. The enemy of our soul will play on a person's weakness, as he did with the original couple. We give Satan an easy win when we don't even know what an appropriate use of power, sex, or money is according to Scripture.

Few Christians set out to destroy themselves and their families. The purpose of this unit is to help Christians to take a serious look at the influences that shape their worldview in the areas of power, sex, and money, and to examine the biblical approach to each on.

Conclusion

Christians should understand what God desires and live accordingly in all areas of their life at all times. The Bible teaches the way people think is the way they will behave (Proverbs 23:7). So let's begin to examine what you believe about the important areas of power, sex, and money.

Study Guide Questions

1. What is changed behavior conditional on?

2. What determines how a person thinks?

3. What role do secularists think God should play in a person's priorities?

4. How are secularists aided in the propagation of their faith?

5. How can Christians avoid living a duplicitous life?

6. What three areas tend to disqualify Christians from Christian service most often?

TWENTY

UNDERSTANDING POWER

Power; everyone wants it; everyone has it. You might think this is an overstatement. You might be the person who doesn't want the responsibility that comes along with power, but I would guess, down deep, you want to have some control over your life. Others might want power, but they feel that they don't have any. The truth is you do have power. You have power over the businesses in your community who make decisions based on your purchasing habits. You have power over younger people through your example. You have power to choose how you will live your life.

The struggles some people have with power are rooted in a basic insecurity in their lives. They feel out of control, so they attempt to control everyone and everything. This quest is often frustrated by those who do not cooperate with them and do things their own way. They set standards and expect others to follow those standards, often getting angry when others don't live up to them. Even though it may look like they are trying to turn people into miniature versions of themselves, they really are not trying to control others. They are simply trying to gain control over their own lives.

In this chapter, we will look at how power has been used in various institutions, the types of power Christians have at their disposal, and how to increase one's influence in order to be able to make a greater contribution to God's kingdom.

Distribution of Power

As Christians, we know all power comes from God, but how power should be distributed at the human level is a matter of debate. There are many approaches to power distribution, but I will limit myself in this section to a "top down" approach, a "cooperative" approach, and a generic "hybrid" approach. Understanding the differences, in the way institutions distribute power, will help you understand how your church, your place of employment, and even how your family functions. Hopefully, this information will assist you in choosing a style of leadership that will service you, as you serve others, through the power you possess.

Top-Down Leadership

The Roman Catholic Church believes primarily in a "top-down" approach to power. This top-down understanding of power plays into their belief that there is a distinction between the "clergy" (ordained ministers) and the "laity" (people). The Roman Catholic Church believes God speaks through the leadership of the Church to the people. The Pope is seen as sitting in the seat of the apostle Peter who, the Roman Catholic Church believes, is the foundation of the Church. They base this on Jesus' declaration that it would be on Peter (the rock) that Jesus would build the Church (Matthew 16:18). As a result, the Pope is seen as holding the most spiritual authority on earth. He has the right to issue decrees *ex cathedra* (with the full authority of the office), but generally decrees are issued by the "magisterium," or teaching authority, of the Church, which consists of the Pope and the bishops. During Medieval times, the people (laity), were restricted from reading Scripture on their own, if they could read, and were seen as incapable of hearing directly from God. They received their instructions from the top and were expected to follow obediently. This has changed, to a degree, since Vatican II, but the belief in the Apostolic Succession, which gives the Pope his authority, remains intact, as well as a hierarchical form of power distribution.

Top-down leadership is not limited to the Roman Catholic Church. Most modern militaries function with a top down authority structure. Just as the Roman Catholic Church has a two-tier structure, most militaries are broken into two classes of people; the officers and the enlisted personnel. Generals, in the army, hold the most power and authority, other than the president of the United States. They are commissioned to give orders to those below them in the chain of command. Only, on the rarest occasion, will an enlisted soldier hold a conversation with a high ranking officer. No matter how high you get in the enlisted ranks, you are always lower than the lowest officer. Much like the gap that exists between the clergy and the laity in the Roman Catholic Church, there is a distinction between the officers and enlisted in all branches of the military. Anyone, who has been in the military, fully understands the chain of command associated with the top down approach to leadership.

The top-down approach has been the primary leadership style in the United States for much of its existence. Although nothing to be proud of, the plantation system used in the early days in parts of the country, were built on a top-down leadership style. Schools in the early days of our country were developed on a two-tier platform. The role of the "head master" and the "student" was clearly delineated. The teacher held the authority and the student was to learn what the teacher taught and to obey his/her every demand. Our governmental system was established for the wellbeing of the citizenry, but it is clear those "in power" make the rules and those who disregard those rules pay a penalty for their insubordination.

If you examine major corporations in America in the early 20th century, you would discover almost all businesses functioned with a top-down approach to power. Henry Ford established his automobile empire using a top-down approach. The owner hired managers, who they communicated with directly. The managers would communicate with supervisors. Supervisors would communicate with the workers. The workers would do the job they had been assigned, the way they were told to do it. If the worker chose to do the task in another fashion, the worker was in jeopardy of losing his job. The workers had no direct contact with the owner. If the worker had a better idea, they would have to share it with their supervisor and hope he would take it to the next level of leadership. It was the top-down distribution of power in the workplace that precipitated the establishment of labor unions. Originally, these unions were formed to give a voice to the laborers of the organization who felt they were not being heard by management.

You may have grown up in a home that used a top-down approach to leadership. Dad was the head of the house and made all of the decisions. He shared the rules with your mom, who was expected to carry them out through the children while he was at work. The children were expected to obey without question. It would be unwise, for the child, to second guess the directive or to talk back because the punishment could be very severe. If you lived in a top-down home, you probably heard a variation of this phrase, "As long as you put your feet under my table, you will do what I ask you to do with no back talk."

Please understand, I am not criticizing the top-down leadership. As long it is used for the well-being of the people the leader serves, it is a good form of power distribution. Top-down leaders, who care for those under them, are often labeled "benevolent dictators." A Major in the military may not allow a private to talk directly to him, but if he has the best interest of the troops he leads in his heart, he will make decisions that benefit the soldiers. If a supervisor cares about the workers, he will see himself as an advocate for their needs. If a dad loves his family, he will not use his power to abuse them, but to assist them to grow up in a healthy home. It can be reassuring to live under the authority of a benevolent dictator.

For years, members of the Roman Catholic Church have trusted their leadership. They willfully submit to a top-down authority structure because they feel it has served their needs. On occasion, we will see an abuse of power within the Roman Catholic Church, but generally this is limited to a few individuals, who succumb to the temptation to use power in a self-serving manner. Generally, these individuals are reprimanded and confidence is restored within the organization.

There are obvious problems which can surface with the top-down leadership style. It concentrates the power among very few individuals. It does not provide a way for information and good ideas to make it from the rank and file to the top level, without several filters. It can also create "haves" and "have-nots" in an organization.

Cooperative Leadership

There were many issues, in the Roman Catholic Church, which the Reformers protested against. As mentioned previously, one of these was the artificial distinction between the clergy and the laity. People, like Martin Luther, read the New Testament and discovered that all Christians have a calling and should be considered "priests." The early Reformers did not call for the removal of an "official" clergy, but they felt there should not be separate rules for a "spiritual group" and a "not so spiritual group." Luther put his belief on display by being married, which had been off limits to him as a Roman Catholic priest.

The early Reformer's removal of a spiritual distinction between the clergy and laity lead to a complete removal of the distinction from an organizational stand point with the advent of the Anabaptist movement. These individuals adopted an elders system of leadership. A person's leadership position in the church was determined by his spiritual maturity. The church members identified spiritually mature leaders who brought specific talents to the leadership table. In this cooperative structure of leadership, one elder may be a "preaching" elder, and another may be an elder with expertise in finances. One elder was not considered as more spiritual than another. In some traditions, the preaching/teaching responsibility of the church rotates among the elders.

In more recent years, we have seen the cooperative approach to power result in a congregational form of government in many churches. In congregational governments, outside leadership has no control over the local congregation. Most of these churches select and ordain their own pastor. The pastor works with and for the congregation. The decisions are made by the people, even if the pastor helps to set the agenda. In a congregational based church, every member has a "voice" and a "vote" in regulatory issues of the local church.

The modern American educational system has embraced the idea of a cooperative use of power. The top-down system of a teacher telling students what they should learn, when they should learn it, and how they should learn information has been replaced by individual student plans. Student need and development is of supreme importance to the modern teacher. Some students flourish in one area, while another may excel in a totally different arena. Students are allowed to maximize their potential, but they also receive individual attention in areas where they have deficiencies. Learning to read, write and do arithmetic has been replaced with listening to the needs and desires of the student. Students and parents get to speak into the learning process. Some people long for the top-down approach in education to return, but it will take a cultural change for that to occur. This is not to say there are no top-down schools that still exist, but they are becoming a dying breed.

Many businesses that embraced a top-down approach have gone out of business or have had to make significant adjustments. With globalization and ready access to the Internet, people have felt empowered. Most young adults are no longer satisfied to work in a job where they have no input to the system. They do not see themselves as junior officers, making their way to the top of the organizational chart, after serving the company for a good portion of their lives. They want to make a difference immediately, so many young adults have abandoned the top down organizations and have embraced either cooperative leadership environments or entrepreneurialism.

In cooperative leadership, people are valued for who they are, rather than for the number of items they produce. Teams are developed which bring together people from a variety of areas of expertise, including those with the hands-on experience of actually constructing the product. When the product makes its way out the door of the factory, everyone feels ownership and pride in what is produced. This type of cooperative leadership has become the norm in businesses today.

A family that uses cooperative power allows the children to have as much say in a decision that affects them, as the mother and father. The mom and dad may still be the provider of information that limits the children's decision, and they may reserve the right to adjust the decision for the well-being of all involved, but the children feel they have had a say in the matter. In these families, vacations are arranged based on the desires of all of the members. When considering curfews, the children have the opportunity to make their case and to ask for a compromise. These children are consulted when the family is considering a move. Although the wishes of the children may not determine the final decision, they feel like they have been heard and respected as a valued member of the family. This kind of leadership produces good results, if both parents are on board with allowing their children to have a significant influence in the shape of the family.

It may sound like I am advocating for the cooperative approach to leadership. It is my preferred style, but I am under no delusion it is without problems. A top-down approach to leadership is much more efficient than a cooperative style. In a top-down approach, the boss tells you what to do and you do it. The job gets done, and you can move on to something else. A cooperative approach to power takes much more time and places more responsibility on more people. You have to work together, and respect each other. In a cooperative approach, no one gets his/her way all the time. In a cooperative approach to power, a single person can hold up the progress of the group. Just as trust is essential in the top-down approach, the trustworthiness of the leader must be intact for positive leadership to take place in a cooperative approach to power, as well. For cooperative leadership to work in the local church, we must believe all Christians can hear from God and we must be willing to trust one another to use their power in the best interest of all.

Hybrid Approaches

A hybrid approach takes the best qualities of two items, joins them together, and creates a new item. I will present a couple of examples of a hybrid approach to power distribution. I will leave it to you to be the judge if these hybrid approaches to the use of power are actually superior.

In the church, one hybrid approach is having a pastoral staff that primarily deals with the spiritual aspects of a congregation and an elder board that provides input and assistance when requested by the pastoral staff. As with any hybrid, you have to be careful. Some churches that use this approach introduce a two-tier leadership structure unintentionally. Even though they would argue they embrace the priesthood of believer theology, they communicate to the individuals in the congregation the credentialed ministers are more spiritual than the elders who sit in the pew and receive their teaching. The positive of this hybrid approach is that individuals in the church are encouraged to grow in their walk with Jesus, with the assistance of a professionally trained mentor. Those, who do not feel a distinct "call" to vocational ministry, are given an opportunity to serve people through the gifts the Holy Spirit has given to them.

A hybrid approach to families may use both the top-down approach and the cooperative approach, not by meshing them, but by using one approach and then the other. Allowing a two-year-old to call the shots for the family is unwise. Young children benefit greatly from the loving guidance of a parent. To have rules established that the child can count on gives them a feeling of confidence and security. But there comes a time, and the parent will have to determine this, a parent can seek increasing amounts of input from the child regarding family life. Allowing a teen to help set curfew is one example of this. Much teenage rebellion can be avoided if parents discover a way to transition from a top-down model to a cooperative model of power distribution, so when the child reaches the age of adulthood, they are ready to move out of the house filled with confidence that they can make good decisions. A word of caution is warranted. It is never good to switch back and forth between a top-down and a cooperative approach with children. This uncertainty will cause instability within your child. You will also encounter behavior problems because the child will seem rebellious when they think it is cooperative time and you are enforcing a top-down approach to leadership. Consistency is always the best option in the distribution of power.

The great thing about hybrid approaches is you cannot limit their expressions. I have just given you a couple of examples to allow you to consider other ways to use the power God has given to you.

Types of Leadership

There have been thousands of book written on the topic of leadership. My purpose is not to explore all the types of leadership in the world today. In this chapter, I want to look at three general types of power most people will encounter in their lives. In the next chapter, I will explore three additional types that have direct correlation to the kingdom of God. This chapter will focus on positional power, attained power, and spiritual power.

Positional Power

Positional power is the authority you are given when you accept a leadership position. Positional power is important, but it is only a beginning. If you do not use your positional power wisely, you will not have any power before you know it.

I remember my second year of teaching high school students in California. My classroom was next to the classroom to a teacher entering his first year of teaching. I made friends with him and gave him some of the same advice, I got the year before which helped me survive. He either didn't listen or just couldn't understand.

He started the year fine. Students gave him the same respect any other teacher received at the school. As is typical with students, they tested him to see what he was made of.

Unfortunately, they discovered he was weak. He attempted to assert his power as a teacher, but every day I heard laughter and ridicule coming from the classroom next door. I could have gone in and rescued him, but that would not have helped him to establish his authority. I knew his life as a teacher was not going to last long when I saw all of his students sneak out of the classroom while his back was turned to write on the chalkboard. I felt terrible when I saw him outside looking desperately for where his class had disappeared.

In my current role, I hear too many stories of students who are hired at a church and believe they have the power to make significant changes immediately upon accepting a new position. They see the mess the group is in when they arrive, and they begin to make changes. Most find their ideas are not welcome, but they insist people respond to their new vision for the group. Many are forced to look for new employment after serving for less than a year, because they failed to establish respect. This problem is not limited to church workers. Anyone accepting a new role has very limited authority and should not assume a title equals unlimited power.

Attained Power

Attained authority is authority, or power, you earn over time. Let's look at how attained power works.

Let's say you take a job and the positional power you have provides five coins which you can spend on any decision you would like to make. It is important how you use your "decision coins." Your decision coins will make you or break you in your organization. You will earn more coins when you make good decisions, and you will lose coins when you make bad decisions. If you choose to just keep your coins in your pocket, nothing will get accomplished, and eventually your coins and your authority will be taken from you and given to another person (Matthew 25:28).

Let's play out a couple of "coin" scenarios. We will start with a negative example. You are a youth pastor in Texas. You decide to move the primary youth service to Friday night. The youth and leaders, in the church, tell you it is not a good idea because football is big on Friday nights in Texas. You think your charisma will compel students to attend "your" Friday night service, so you do it anyway. All of your students now have to choose between going to youth group and going to the high school football game. Even after trying to guilt them into come to church to worship God over going to be entertained, the youth group attendance drops from 50 to 5 students. This was a pretty costly decision. You spent the majority of your coins for nothing, other than to attempt to prove you were right. This leaves you with very little influence. If you are smart, you will look for a few small wins to regain some credibility. If you are not wise, you will squander the rest of your influence and soon you will be looking for a new job.

Now let's look at a real life positive example of how coins can be used. A pastor and his family came to a strong church. He and his wife were given the standard five coins upon arrival. The pastor's wife was a very energetic and strong woman. Over the first ten years of her time at the church, she took on the role of Christian education director for adults because discipleship and evangelism was her passion. She made some decisions to change the discipleship program which were well received. She earned more coins as a result of the good decisions she had made. She used those additional decision coins to start a large women's conference. This was a financial risk to the church and to her decision coin account. What if no one came? What would happen if the ladies of the church felt she was overstepping her authority? The conference was a huge success. She earned many more coins. She used those coins to challenge the church to practice Lent for the first time. She asked people in the church to give up something they enjoyed for 40 days. She didn't ask them to give up something big. She asked the people to set aside $2.50 a day for 40 days to help eradicate poverty in the congregation. The first year, the church responded by giving nearly $80,000. This was seen as a great success. She earned even more decision coins. She wasn't finished. One day, she stood up in front of the congregation and told them about the struggles single pregnant women were experiencing. She told the congregation they did a good job of preaching against abortion, and even walking in marches against abortion, but now it was time to step up and help those moms who were convinced to keep their babies. She decided to spend a lot of her accumulated coins by presenting a crazy idea to the congregation. She asked for $2 million to buy a mansion that was on the market, which the church could convert into a home to train young women in marketable skills and care for them as the awaited their babies. And guess what, that day the people rallied behind her vision and committed to give her the money. The "Mansion" has been a great success. This woman has more coins to spend today than projects to spend them on because she has earned the right to ask. People know she is not going to propose something she has not determined to be the will of God.

This is what 20-plus years of good decision-making can produce. I can't imagine how the people at the church would have responded if the pastor's wife had asked for the $2 million dollars her first Sunday at the church. They probably would have asked the pastor's family to repack their moving van. Earning the right to make big decisions takes time. Unfortunately, people tend to be impatient. Many leaders leave a situation before they have had time to make a difference. Use your power wisely so you can help others improve their lives.

209 | P a g e

Spiritual Power

Spiritual power is attained through a relationship with Jesus Christ. You gain the title of "Christian" when you accept Jesus as your Savior. But you attain spiritual power by making good decisions in response to the prompting of the Holy Spirit. As you learn to walk in obedience, you will have more power to positively impact the lives of others. Remember, this is a process and all God asks is that you continue to take steps toward Him.

Let's look at the measures by which spiritual power is assessed. First, spiritual power is based in love. The Bible is clear that the priorities of God are to love Him and to love others. The closer you are to God, the more you will love others. If you are not in love with Jesus, and the people He died for, you need to attain more spiritual power in your life (1 John 4:7).

So how do I get the power to love others? Jesus told the disciples to wait until the Holy Spirit came upon them so they could receive the power needed to love people as He loved them. If you have not received this power, as mentioned in chapter 3, it is available to you. (See Acts 1:8 and Acts 2:4)

Those with spiritual power will live in obedience. In the Old Testament, the themes of "trust" and "obey" are pervasive. If we have spiritual power, we will have learned to trust God fully. When we trust Him, we will be willing to do whatever He asks, even when it doesn't make sense to us. We will not fear, even if it means entering a lion's den or being cast into a fiery furnace. We may die as a result of God's commands, but we can be assured we will come out of the situation alive in His eternal presence.

Next, you can assess your spiritual power by your humility. We have discussed humility earlier in the book, but let me remind you humility is not weakness. Humility is viewing yourself the way God views you, and viewing others as God sees them. Humility says, if God wishes to lower me to raise another, I am okay. If He chooses to raise me, I am fine with that as well. Humility is a result of understanding who I am in relationship to God.

Those with spiritual power will have a countenance of joy. This doesn't mean you are giddy and happy when things go wrong in your life, but it does mean you will experience joy because you are confident Jesus will never leave you or walk away from you during your trial. Joy is an inward condition that reflects our ultimate trust in God.

Those with spiritual power will serve others. I love the quote from Martin Luther regarding service. He stated, "A Christian is a perfectly free lord of all, subject to none. A Christian is a perfectly dutiful servant of all, subject to all." Luther understood Christians do not have to do anything to earn their salvation. There are no rules and regulations thrust on Christians that, when fulfilled, deem them acceptable in the eyes of God. But as a Christian grows in their spiritual power, they will want to serve the needs of others. There is nothing too lowly for a Christian to engage. Just as Jesus washed the feet of His disciples, a person with spiritual power will take up a towel and wash the dirty feet of others. (See John 13:1-17.)

Conclusion

Power manifests itself in a variety of ways. Whether you choose to use top-down authority or a more cooperative style, make sure to have the welfare of the people you serve as your highest priority. Be patient in growing your influence. Don't give up when you seem to have little authority. While growing your influence through wise decisions, cultivate your spiritual power through developing your relationship with Jesus. Don't waste the power God has invested in you. He gave you power to use as you accomplish your role in the expansion of the kingdom of God. In the next chapter, practical ways to use your attained spiritual power will be presented.

Study Guide Questions

1. What is the root problem for those who struggle with attempting to control other people?

2. Explain what is meant by a "top-down" use of power?

3. Explain what is meant by a "cooperative" use of power?

4. Explain the Roman Catholic Church's distribution of power?

5. Explain the Anabaptist view of the distribution of power in a local church?

6. What is a "hybrid" approach to power?

7. Explain how education has changed from a top-down style of leadership to a cooperative style of leadership?

8. What is positional power and explain its limitations?

9. What is attained power and how does a person achieve this type of power?

10. Provide three examples of spiritual power and explain how each is used?

TWENTY ONE

USING POWER TO ADVANCE GOD'S KINGDOM

Super heroes were an important part of my life as a kid. I loved to watch the 1960s television version of Batman and Superman. I am probably showing my age when I also admit I enjoyed the Green Hornet, as well as the early version of the Incredible Hulk. Today's young people have a much wider array of super heroes to enjoy. Some of the ones I used to watch are nearly unrecognizable today because the plot of the stories have turned so dark.

As long as plays and motion pictures have existed, there has always been a clash between the protagonist (the hero) and the antagonist (the villain). The common characteristic of antagonists is they use their power to increase their assets and position, regardless of who gets hurt in the process. The common characteristic of protagonists is they are willing to make personal sacrifices for the good of others. In most of these clashes, good and evil battle it out toe-to-toe, and at times, it looks like evil is going to triumph. But in the end, good almost always comes out as the ultimate victor.

Whether the writers of these stories realize it or not, they are simply retelling the story of the biblical account of the clash between God and Satan. The truth they are reinforcing is, that no matter how bad the situation looks in our cities and in the world, evil will not prevail. God will be the ultimate victor. Christians have aligned themselves on the right side of the conflict.

Until the end of time, there will be evil in the world. As Christians, it is our responsibility to use the power that we have to combat evil and to bring God's goodness into situations where we have influence. Unfortunately, some people, who call themselves Christians, use power to enhance their lives, rather than to enrich the lives of others.

In this chapter, we will discover ways we can maximize the power God has given to us. God has called us to be super heroes to rescue those who are in spiritual peril.

The Use of Power

God is the ultimate power that exists. When He made humans in His image, He chose to share His power with them. He gave Adam and Eve dominion over the planet and over the animals (Genesis 1:27-28).

When sin entered the world, the act of dominion became more difficult for the original couple. Sin took a well-ordered world and threw it into chaos. The Bible is filled with stories of people who attempted to reclaim order in their lives by establishing their own standards which reflected their fallen condition. Cain attempted to regain control by killing his brother Abel (Genesis 4:8). The people during Noah's time attempted to establish a standard different from God's in regard to relationships (Genesis 6:1-8). The people at the Tower of Babel sought to reach God through their own efforts (Genesis 11:1-9). The people of Israel attempted to take control of the situation, when they felt God and Moses had abandoned them, by forming and worshipping the golden calf (Exodus 32:1-6), the Israelites did what was right, in their own eyes, during the time of the Judges (Judges 17:6), and King Saul rejected the commands of God when he thought he was losing control of a situation (1 Samuel 13:7-10). I could go on with biblical examples of people who attempted to gain control through their own wisdom, when life seemed out of control for them, which resulted in disaster.

God gave us an opportunity to share His power, but He did not give us the right to supersede His authority. A biblical use of power must advance the cause of Christ and bring value to the people that we lead.

History is filled with leaders who used power in a destructive manner. Herod killed all the male children under two years of age in an attempt to secure his throne (Matthew 2:16). Hitler killed nearly 11 million people, in an attempt to conceal his own lineage, and establish himself as the supreme ruler in the world. The Khmer Rouge regime tortured and killed over a million of their Cambodian brothers and sisters in an attempt to retard the development of the nation.

Fortunately, there are wonderful examples of people using their power in a positive manner. The first and foremost example of a positive use of power is Jesus. He gave His life so others could live. Other examples, from more recent times, include President Washington who led an army to free the new land when he could have retired to his estate in comfort. William Wilberforce and Abraham Lincoln exerted their influence to see slavery abolished in England and America, respectively, at great cost to themselves. Winston Churchill and Franklin Roosevelt used their power and influence to stop the senseless genocide of the Third Reich. And any list of individuals who used their influence to help others would be incomplete without mentioning Martin Luther King Jr. He did more for civil rights in the United States than any other person through peaceful protests and personal sacrifice. These are just a few of the heroes who have made a positive impact through the use of personal power.

As Christians, we must first recognize the power God has given to us and purpose to use it to assist others. We must avoid being greedy with our power. When we use our power primarily to advance our agenda, or to make our lives more comfortable, we will fail to advance the cause of Christ. A key, to being able to use our power to help others, is learning to trust God with our future. When we do, it will allow us to focus on the needs of others.

Assessing Our Use of Power

Many people never assess how they are using the power God has given to them. It may surprise some people to discover they are doing pretty well with the power they have been assigned. It may come as a shock to other people to discover they are using their power in ways which are displeasing to God. And finally, there will be some people who will walk away from this chapter recognizing they have been entrapped by the power of others. These people need to be set free from theses oppressive acts.

Let's take a look at different types of power that will help us assess where we are in regard to power.

Perceptive Power

Have you ever been to the zoo? If so, you probably think you have seen a lion, a tiger, and a bear (Oh, my!). I am afraid to tell you; you are mistaken. You saw something that looked like a lion, a tiger, and a bear, but all you really saw was a shell of a lion, a tiger, and a bear. See, no self-respecting lion would lay around a cage all day waiting for someone to come out and throw it a dead chicken. A real lion would be prancing across the African plain looking for its own prey. It would roar letting all the other animals know he was the king of the jungle. A real lion is fierce. He would not tolerate people invading his space. I am sorry to tell you, the lion you saw at the zoo is a domesticated version of the lion God created. A real lion has perceptive power.

Perceptive power allows a person to see themselves the way God sees them. It permits them to act in accordance with God's intended purpose when He created them. Perceptive power allows individuals to recognize the resources God has infused them with. Once they perceive these resources in themselves, they will be able to operate at their full potential.

Perceptive power allows us to see the possibilities that God has planned for us. It recognizes God made each one of us in a unique fashion, and wants to use us in a unique manner. Think about it. Everyone reading this book has a unique set of finger prints. Not only that, but each of us have unique retinas. And each of us have been given unique DNA profiles. Have you ever thought why God would create each of us uniquely, if He wanted us to be clones of one another? He doesn't. It is an insult to God's creative powers when we try to be like someone else. People, with perceptive power, will not allow someone to domesticate them. We must make the bold move of acknowledging the power God has given to us, and live in freedom, outside of the cage of domestication.

People, with perceptive power, have the confidence to live outside of the norms established by the crowds. Perceptive people really don't care if they are accepted by others. They know they are accepted by God. This doesn't mean they live as a narcissist. Just the opposite is true. People, with perceptive power, are so confident in their relationship with Jesus, they can focus their attention on the needs of others.

A person, who has perceptive power, can be used by God to minister to those who are lost or broken in some fashion. They have no fear because perfect love (a relationship with Jesus) casts out all fear (Psalm 34:4; 1 John 4:18). We do not have to worry about anything, because a healthy reliance on God will remove worry from our lives (1 Peter 5:7). We will not be concerned about the power of Satan in our lives because perceptive power recognizes greater is He that is within us, than he that is in the world (1 John 4:4). Those, with perceptive power, are able to see clearly and walk toward God confidently.

Oppressive Power

Oppressive power is the influence used by the zoo keeper which keep the animals under control. He trains the animals to become dependent on him and to respond to him in a way that will entertain the crowds. It is the zoo keeper's goal to use the animals as a means of income. The zoo keeper cares more about his welfare than the welfare of the animals inside the cages.

Those who use oppressive power are self-serving. They desire to use others to make their lives more pleasant. They really don't care about God and His design for our lives. They desire for us to become their servants.

Satan is the author of oppressive power. The Bible says Satan exists to steal, kill, and destroy, while Jesus comes to give life (John 10:10). Satan accomplishes his task by entrapping a person, much like the zoo keeper entraps the lion in a cage at the zoo. His tools are lies, guilt, shame, and intimidation.

Oppressive power comes in many forms. The most obvious form is displayed by oppressive regimes which use the people they lead to gain what they desire. People like Hitler, Mussolini, Pot, and Lenin fall into this category. No one, who is objective, would deny the fact these people were offspring of Satan.

But oppressive power can be seen in less obvious ways. A father, who forces his son to be an athlete when God created the young boy to be a dancer, is using oppressive power. A mother, who makes her daughter go to dance lessons when she wants to play football, is using oppressive power. Many parents attempt to live a life they wished they had lived through their children. They think they are doing the child a favor, but really they are using the child to make their own lives better. Parents should discover how God created their children and then help them reach their God given potential. God has given each of us a unique life to live. People, who exercise oppressive power, attempt to make people fit into a mold, in their image, rather than allowing the person to develop the image of God within them.

I am always accused of giving dating advice to my students, and here I go again. I believe it is essential that you not allow a boyfriend or a girlfriend use oppressive power against you. Let me explain. Oppressive power does not allow room for spontaneity. Those who oppress want to have control, at all times. So, if you are dating someone who is uncomfortable with you being the unique person God has created you to be, run away as fast as you can. If your boyfriend doesn't like the way you break out in giggles when you are nervous, he is not the right person for you. If your girlfriend is always complaining about how you dress or comb your hair, walk away while you still can. People who try to control you in little ways while you are dating will only try to control you more after you are married.

People who use oppressive power are not satisfied unless they can shape you into what they have determined is beneficial to them. They do not want you to be controlled by your own decisions, or even the leading of the Holy Spirit. Just as Satan thought he knew more than God, those who oppress others believe their standards are supreme. If you subject yourself to living with an oppressor, you will feel the image of God within you shrink, until one day it shrivels, and you feel dead inside. Avoid being a puppet on an oppressor's hand.

Those who exercise oppressive power treat people as objects. We see this in all dictatorships, whether they be a head of state, or the head of a household. You know what oppressive power looks like if you have ever worked a job where the boss doesn't care about you or your needs because the job has to be done. They make it clear, if you decide to stay home with a sick child, they will fire you and replace you with another object (employee). It is truly wonderful to work for a boss who takes the time to know you and actually cares about your needs. It is true the job needs to get done, but most of us will do a better job when we are treated with dignity and respect.

If you are reading this and you discover you are an oppressor, it is time for you to change teams. You are reflecting the values of Satan much more than the values of God. Life is not all about you and your desires. I know it is hard to let go of the control you think you have. Probably, it is a reflection of your lack of trust in God. Perhaps you have been hurt in some way, and you cannot trust anyone but yourself. If you are honest, you must admit always having to be in control is hard. You worry and fear the future. Your body reveals the stress you are under through headaches and tension. It is hard to hold the world on your shoulders. Actually it is impossible. This is why your world feels out of control no matter how hard you attempt to hold it together. It won't get any better, as long as you attempt to do God's job. May I encourage you to repent and let God take control of your life, as well as the life of those with whom you associate? God made you to be the perfect you. Allow others to be the perfect "them" that He made them to be.

Redemptive Power

Satan does not want you to be perceptive. He will do whatever it takes to blind you to the truth that you can have perceptive power. Oppressed people have a very hard time seeing a better future. They need someone to take them by the hand and show them the way.

A few years ago, the Super Bowl came to the Dallas area. As with all Super Bowls, hundreds of sex trafficked women were brought to the city to service visitors. One group of women were housed in a cheap hotel, not far from the more expensive hotels where they would be forced to sell themselves. The trip from one hotel to the next was about four blocks. The women walked those four blocks unsupervised by their captor. A reporter, who was doing a story on human trafficking, asked the girls why they didn't run away, rather than keep going to do something they did not want to do. Their answer was informative. They explained they didn't see freedom as an option, and they didn't know how to live in freedom, if they chose to walk away. They had been domesticated.

People, who have been oppressed by Satan, and entrapped in sin, often do not know how to get free. Oppressed people cannot become perceptive people unless someone who is perceptive shows them the way, and helps them grow in their freedom through spiritual formation. People, with perceptive power, are the only ones who can show oppressed people the way to freedom. We must help them understand the power of sin no longer holds any power over them. When Jesus died and rose again, His sacrificial act covered every sin that has been committed, is currently being committed, and will ever be committed (Hebrews 10:12; 1 John 1:7). We either believe this is the truth, or we are left alone to deal with the consequences of our sins. The only thing separating a Christian from a non-Christian is the willingness to believe this truth and to act according to it.

I like to look at it this way. If you go to a circus, you will see an 11,000 pound elephant controlled by a small metal peg connected to a collar around its leg which is attached by a metal chain. Everyone knows this powerful elephant could get away with little effort; everyone except the elephant. When the elephant was a 220 pound baby, the circus handler placed a metal collar around the baby's leg and attached it to a similar post by a chain. When the baby elephant tried to get away, it couldn't. At some point, the elephant pulled hard and the metal collar cut into the elephant's leg. Each time the elephant pulled, it felt pain as the cut was irritated. It learned to avoid pain, by not trying to get away. The 11,000 pound elephant remembers the pain and no longer even tries to get away, even though it could.

People who are oppressed feel like the elephant. They have tried, time and time again, to be free from the chains of their particular vice, but they have remained trapped. When they accept Jesus into their lives, the chains are broken, but they do not realize they can simply walk away from their addiction, if they would take a step toward God.

Jesus helps reinforce the fact that all the chains of sin have been broken through a very short, but powerful parable. Jesus tells a story of a strong man who is guarding his possessions. The robber comes into the house and ties up the strong man and then proceeds to take the possessions belonging to the man. In this parable, Jesus is the robber and the strong man is Satan. Jesus is explaining He has done everything needed to rescue those who have been under the influence of Satan. Everyone can be set free, if they will simply walk into the waiting arms of Jesus (Mark 3:27).

The only people who can rescue the oppressed are people who have achieved perceptive power. In the Old Testament, we hear God ask the question, "Who will stand in the gap for me?" (Ezekiel 22:30). I believe He is asking the same question today.

Jesus set the example for perceptive people who are willing to stand in the gap. Jesus was in heaven and looked at the earth. It was filled with people who were entrapped by the wiles of Satan. Jesus took the ultimate step of love and courage by leaving His place in glory to come to our place (Philippians 2:5-11). Once He came, the eyes of some were opened, as He showed them the path to freedom. A few hundred people walked this path of freedom, as a result of Jesus' act of heroism. But then it was time for Him to return to heaven. He commissioned the few, who had found perceptive power, to find others who were oppressed and to share the way to freedom (Acts 1:6-11). They accepted the challenge. Thousands began to see their potential through Christ. These thousands took on the challenge of Jesus. Some were persecuted for their efforts, but it did not stop them. Within the first hundred years after Jesus' death, people were finding freedom throughout the known world. We are a fruit of this process. Now it is our turn to take up the challenge to stand in the gap to become heroes who recue people from the oppressor.

There are many, both in local churches and those outside, who need someone to take them by the hand and help them walk toward freedom. This is not a job reserved for the religious class. It is true pastors have a major role in helping people to find freedom. In addition, social workers have a great opportunity to help people discover a better way to live. Financial planners can use their perceptive power to help those in financial need to discover a path to freedom. Police officers see the darkest side of humanity which provides them great opportunity to offer hope to the hopeless. These are but a few examples of how Christians can stand in the gap for those who believe they are still entrapped by sin. Allow the commission of Jesus to be yours: "The Spirit of the Lord is upon me, because he has anointed me to proclaim good news to the poor. He has sent me to proclaim liberty to the captives and recovering of sight to the blind, to set at liberty those who are oppressed, to proclaim the year of the Lord's favor" (Luke 4:18, 19).

The only hope for our nation, and our world, is for people with perceptive power to accept the challenge to go into the dark places of this world and bring hope to those who feel hopeless. This might come at a great personal cost. Many people who have taken the challenge to rescue others have given their lives. William Wilberforce, Martin Luther King Jr., Abraham Lincoln, and Jesus all gave their lives in their effort to set people free. A perceptive person does not walk away from this challenge. They understand the crucial nature of their heroic assignment. They accept the challenge of the Great Commission of Jesus to go into all the world and set people free, no matter the cost. (See Philippians 1:21.)

Perhaps you are caught in the trap of the oppressor. If you recognize deception has ensnared you, I encourage you to seek help from someone who has found freedom. The first step is recognizing your condition. Once that is done, I challenge you to rattle the chains of sin that hold you, and discover that you can walk away through the power of Jesus.

It is likely, when Satan has discovered that you have escaped his prison, he will try to get you back. One tactic he will use is to accuse you of your past. He will make you feel condemned, if you allow him to do so. Remember what the apostle Paul told the Romans, when they faced this type of accusation:

> There is therefore now no condemnation for those who are in Christ Jesus. For the law of the Spirit of life has set you free in Christ Jesus from the law of sin and death. For God has done what the law, weakened by the flesh, could not do. By sending his own Son in the likeness of sinful flesh and for sin, he condemned sin in the flesh, in order that the righteous requirement of the law might be fulfilled in us, who walk not according to the flesh but according to the Spirit (Romans 8:1-4).

Don't listen to the accusations of Satan. Once you have found freedom, do not allow yourself to be drawn back into the entrapment of sin. Paul encourages you, "For freedom Christ has set us free; stand firm therefore, and do not submit again to a yoke of slavery." (Galatians 5:1) If you have accepted Jesus as your Savior and placed your trust in His death and resurrection, you are already free (John 8:36). Live in that freedom!

Conclusion

The Spirit of the Lord resides in every Christian. The logical extension of this is that every Christian should naturally have perceptive power. Jesus removed the scales of sin from our eyes at salvation, so we could see the truth (1 Corinthians 2:6-16). We must open our eyes to the freedom available to us and live in it. When we do, we will want others to experience this same freedom. Be a perceptive Christian who uses redemptive power to expand the kingdom of God. When you do, you will be fulfilling the Great Commandment to love God and love others.

Power can be used for good or for evil. Chose to use your power to defend those who have little power. We need spiritual super heroes who will fight on behalf of the hurting. Are you willing to don your cape and do battle for those who are in spiritual peril?

Study Guide Questions

1. How are antagonists and protagonists in movies a reflection of the biblical narrative?

2. For use of power to be considered biblical, what must the power produce?

3. Who were three people or groups identified, in this chapter, who exercised positive biblical power?

4. Why does the author say the lions you see at the zoo are not real lions?

5. Describe perceptive power as given in this chapter.

6. Describe oppressive power as given in this chapter.

7. Describe redemptive power as given in this chapter.

8. Describe the redemptive power process, which Jesus set in motion, and continues today.

9. What should a Christian do who is caught in a trap of oppression?

10. What category of power do you currently exhibit in your life?

TWENTY TWO

EXPLORING VIEWS OF SEX

One cannot watch television long without witnessing the sexual saturation of Western civilization. What was once confined to the back rooms of adult oriented stores, or to the seedy movie theaters, is now openly talked about in popular television programs made available through broadcast media which any child can consume. Sexual immorality has not only become acceptable behavior in society; it has become an expectation.

A recent survey of North American adolescents and young adults reveals a great deal about what they think about sex. The survey shared the young peoples' thoughts about birth control, sexually transmitted diseases, and frequency of sex. One third of the young people surveyed had been pressured to have sex. Young males felt pressure to have sex at a higher rate than their female counterparts. When asked about virginity, 60% of those surveyed said virginity is a nice concept but they thought no one really remains a virgin until marriage. Of those surveyed, nearly 10% said they had their first consensual sexual intercourse when they were 13 years-old or younger. Christians would hope the sexual experience of Christian young adults would be different. Unfortunately, candid conversations with students in the know about sexual activity among students on a Christian university campus would indicate otherwise.

One reason for sexual immorality among young adults, who claim to know Christ, is a lack of a clear and strong voice concerning sexual matters on the part of parents and churches. A recent informal Christian university class survey revealed how few Christian young adults receive information, about sex, from spiritual authorities in their lives. Of the 62 students in one of my classrooms, only three said their church had ever addressed the subject of sex and only eight of the 62 (13%) said their parent(s) had talked to them about sex from a biblical perspective. If this low percentage is reflective of Christian homes, which have a clear message they could share about sex, one can only imagine the percentage of teens and young adults who have healthy conversations about sex in homes with no biblical influence.

Christian young people must be exposed to the various worldviews regarding sex and determine what they believe and why they believe it, if we have hope to see a difference in the behavior of Christians and that of those who do not have a relationship with Jesus. The church and Christian parent must not be silent on the subject. Hopefully, the few pages of this book dedicated to the topic of sex will provide a basic framework for understanding what God desires regarding sexual behavior.

Secular View of Sex

Sex sells! This slogan drives marketing executives, entertainment moguls, and Internet websites. According to the website, Webroot.com, every second 28,258 users are watching pornography on the Internet. In that same second, $3075.64 is being spent on pornography on the Internet. Sex is big business for those who seek to oppress others, for their own personal benefit.

Secularized sex, as displayed on the pages of pornography and the various types of projection screens available today, seldom display sex as a means of building a healthy relationship between marriage partners. Instead, sexual exploits, served up for public consumption, focus on the animalistic fulfillment of personal lust. This view of sex is dangerous in many ways. One danger of the secular worldview of sex involves the lack of value individuals place on this sacred act.

A secular worldview of sex can be summarized as "Me first." Individuals are expected to score personal wins through sexual conquest. Young males often report their conquests to their friends with no regard to the feelings, or reputation, of the girl they conquered. These reports, whether true or not, make the individual look more powerful among his friends and leaves those, who did not "get some," feel less of a man.

A "Me first" view of sex changes the focus of sex from an act of love, which seeks the best for another, to an act that is selfish in nature. A person who has a primary view of sex as an act that brings himself pleasure will have no problem walking away from the relationship, once the pleasure is no longer satisfying. Sadly, the divorce rates in the Western world reflects the secular philosophy of sex has won the day in many homes.

Another danger a secular worldview presents concerns the way a person views his or her partner. When lust replaces love, as the motivation for sex, it loses its meaning. Lust seeks to possess something for one's personal pleasure. The object of the lust is not taken into consideration. A person can lust after a new automobile. They can lust after a promotion. Or, they can lust over a member of the opposite sex. In each of these cases, the object of the lust is just that, an object. This is one reason why viewing pornography is such a damnable activity. It teaches the person that sexual desires can be fulfilled with no consideration for the person who they are using for his/her pleasure. Lust turns the other person into an object, a thing, a non-person.

Many who embrace a secular worldview of sex narrow their definition of love to the act of sexual intercourse. Sexual intercourse is only a small aspect of a person's sexuality. By definition, "intercourse" is communication. "Sexual" intercourse is communication with the person you love, through sexual expression. Each time a person has sexual intercourse, they are communicating something. A secular worldview of sexual intercourse communicates "I am selfish" or "I will use you to fulfill my needs; if you receive pleasure, I am glad, but that is not my primary concern."

A secular worldview of sex does not take long-term commitment into the equation. Few, who embrace a secular view of sex, would argue a lifetime commitment is required for a person to engage in sexual intercourse. And why would they since they consider themselves as little more than an animal, and few of the other animals in the world demand commitment to enjoy sexual pleasure. The risk of a lifetime of less-than-fulfilling sex awaits those who embrace a selfish attitude toward sex.

Still another danger of embracing a self-centered, self-pleasing approach to sex, is a lack of true intimacy. Intimacy results from knowing someone deeply. In a dating relationship, a couple stops getting to know one another as soon as sexual intercourse begins. No longer does the couple spend time in conversation, enjoying common pursuits, or even spending time with mutual friends. Instead, almost every moment they are together is focused on getting alone and pursuing sexual pleasure. When they are done having sex, they often end up arguing or planning their next exploit. True intimacy is forfeited for carnal pleasure. Sexual intercourse before marriage is a path to separation, rather than union. The earlier in the relationship that the sexual intercourse begins, the less likely the relationship will reap positive fruit. A secular worldview of sex is a short cut for those who simply do not want to expend the energy to build a meaningful relationship.

Those who do not know Jesus personally cannot be blamed for embracing a self-centered view of sex. An appropriate view of sex depends on an understanding of the union of God and His creation. Since the fall of humanity, in the Garden of Eden, the best non-Christians can experience, regarding sex, is a substitute made in their own image (See Romans 1:18-32.). The non-Christian has not experienced the unity those who have united with Christ experience. The ultimate tragedy occurs when Christians, who have experienced that union, fall for the tricks of the enemy and settle for less than God has planned for them.

A Skewed Christian View of Sex

I attend many marriage ceremonies of Christian young adults. I often find myself standing and talking to students as we socialize at the reception waiting for the bridal party to arrive. It is not unusual to have a student ask, "How can they do this?" I have been around long enough to know what they are asking, but I always make them form their question. They clarify by asking, "How can they go from seeing sex as bad all of their lives, and now embrace it as something that is good and enjoy it tonight?" Their question reveals a flaw in their basic theology of sex. But, how do so many Christian young adults arrive at this faulty thinking?

Most of us were taught, either implicitly or explicitly, that sex is bad, dirty and a subject never to be discussed in public. As a child, if we exposed our sexual parts in public we were scolded and told to get dressed. If we said something that was remotely sexual in nature, our parents quickly hushed us. They may have not told us our sexuality was wrong, but their attitudes communicated it. This often left us confused. It created a barrier that prevented us from approaching our parents when we had questions about our bodies or about sex. Often these children learn about sex from those who pervert sex in some manner. Why wouldn't a child begin to think that sex was somehow bad? And why would this not carry over into adulthood if no one was willing to share a biblical perspective with the person.

Sex in the First Century

Members of the Early Church did not live in isolation. As much as they may have wished all the members of their congregation would remain sexually pure, this was nearly impossible because of the influence of the society in which they lived. Although the Greco-Roman law mandated monogamy, Greco-Roman men were allowed to have sexual encounters with multiple partners, with no negative consequence. The sexual practices of the first century were not much different than we see today in Western culture.

Pagan religions also influenced the Early Church. Sacred prostitution, in the pagan temples, was commonplace. These were not prostitutes in the classical sense; rather they were worshippers who felt they could regain their virginity by engaging in sexual relations with God. Women would go to the temple, disrobe, and wait for an agent of God to have intercourse with them. Many of the converts to the Early Church were participants in Temple prostitution in cities like Corinth. This practice drew an outcry and reaction from the Church leaders. It was natural for people to begin to think sex was evil when they heard the Church speak against specific sexual practices.

The primary philosophy of the secular culture, during the time of the Early Church, was dualism. Dualism taught the world is broken into two spheres, good and evil or flesh and spirit. Dualistic philosophers believed everything seen as material (flesh) was inherently evil and considered everything spiritual as good. Dualism resulted in two extreme reactions. The first was asceticism. Asceticism restricted all sexual activity, even among married persons, because it was fleshly and thus it was evil. The second extreme argued that since all a person should care about is the spirit of a person, what they did with their body was of no consequence. As a result, dualism lead them to believe there were no restrictions on their sexual activities.

The culture, pagan religions, and philosophy of the day forced the Early Church to come to grips with their culture regarding sexuality. Paul's teachings on sex, as limited as they are, prohibited promiscuity and championed marital sex. (See 1 Corinthians 7.)

The Development of a Theology of Sex

Where did our parents arrive at the conclusion that sex is bad or "nasty"? Unfortunately, to find the answer to that question, one must look to the pulpits of the Christian Church. Again, one must ask, "How could those entrusted with the Word of God arrive at conclusions that seem so far from the clear teachings of the Bible?" To arrive at that answer, a person must examine the teachings of the Ante-Nicene Fathers.

Using their understanding of Paul and his writings, the Church Fathers trumpeted the virtues of asceticism, condemning illicit sex, and later carried this attitude over to the practice of sex in marriage. The Church Fathers' stance on sex, which developed over the next few decades, was reactionary rather than exegetical in nature.

A review of the progression of thought that took place over the years by various Church Fathers will help people understand why many in the church today view sex as a "necessary evil" at best and definitely a topic not to be discussed in proper company.

An elevated view of celibacy manifested itself as early as the time of Ignatius. His motivation was not primarily moral. He was concerned about the imminent return of Christ.

Ignatius was not against sex in marriage. He encouraged those who married to engage in sexual intercourse. Ignatius' contribution to the discussion of sex has more to do with the increased acceptance of celibacy as a viable option for believers.

The writings of the Shepherd of Hermas were the first to assign a value to the celibate life. The Church leaders made a distinct shift in their thinking at this point. Leaders began to view celibacy as spiritually superior to the married life, while still accepting marriage as a viable option for the weaker members of the Church.

Irenaeus' contribution to this issue centers on the fall of man. In his work, *Against Heresies*, Irenaeus contrasts Eve's disobedience, through her submission to evil, with the obedience of the Virgin Mary, through her submission to God. Irenaeus' teachings initiated the view that women are the transmitters of sin, and he believed the primary vehicle of this transmission was sexual intercourse. He continued his thought by arguing for the perpetual virginity of Mary, who delivered our source of salvation. Mary's choice to remain celibate (as believed by Irenaeus), even though married, elevated her well above Eve who succumbed to evil's temptation.

Tertullian contributed more to the formation of Ante-Nicene thought concerning sex and marriage than any other person. Tertullian's personal background greatly influenced his theology. Tertullian was an adulterer before he accepted Jesus as his Savior. Although he was forgiven, he continued to feel guilty for his past behavior. He did not distinguish extramarital sex from marital sex, since both acts were performed in like manner. As a result, Tertullian argued all sexual intercourse, in marriage or outside of marriage, was evil.

Tertullian was one of the first to verbalize the idea that women were the vehicle of the transmission of sin. This affected his view of marriage because of the impossibility of separating a woman's moral status and her marital status. In his treatise, *On the Dress of Women*, Tertullian told his female audience they should look as unappealing as possible to not attract the eyes of men. He also told them they should walk with their heads down in shame in recognition of the sin initiated by their ancestor (Eve).

Tertullian held a low view of marriage, but because it was God's invention, he could not condemn it. He did not fully condemn sexual intercourse in marriage because he saw no other way to procreate. He did teach, however, if a couple had sexual intercourse, they should perform the act as quickly as possible and find no pleasure in it. Tertullian clearly taught sex was a necessary evil that a truly spiritual person would learn to endure to procreate.

Origen did not write much about sex and marriage, but what he did write had a major impact on early thought. His views centered primarily on Eve's sin. Origen's theory of the Fall centered on the serpent's seduction of Eve. He believed the serpent physically infected her. This encounter was of an illicit nature that produced shame. He equated all sexual intercourse as "wantonness." As a consequence, Origen argued that all sexual activity was inherently wrong and was the basis of all actual sin.

Origen believed sex in marriage was a perversion of God's original plan. Origen believed sexual intercourse did not occur until after the fall of humanity. He felt if Eve had not succumbed to the serpent, procreation would have occurred through a "mystical angelic manner." Origen felt so strongly about the idea of sex being the basis of sin that he castrated himself before being ordained. The writings of Gregory of Nyssa suggest Origen felt man did not have sex organs before the Fall.

The theology of the Ante-Nicene Fathers played a major role in the teachings of Augustine, who worked these thoughts into a well-defined theology. To understand Augustine's views of sex, you must understand his pre-conversion life.

Augustine was anything but a saint when he was a youth. A review of his young life reveals Augustine's sexual exploits rivaled that of a young Hugh Hefner. As with Tertullian, Augustine's past caused him to build a reactionary theology of sex, rather than a biblical theology. In the *City of God*, he refers to all sexual intercourse as shameful.

It was not until the birth of the Protestant movement, and especially the teaching of the Puritans, that a celebrative view of sex reemerged among leaders of the church.

A Balanced View of Sex

The traditional view of the first century Church, regarding sex, does not resemble the theology of "necessary" sex taught by many of those who came after them in next few centuries. The first century Church held to the traditional Jewish view of sex. They viewed sexual intercourse in marriage as a celebration to God. Clement of Rome and Polycarp, early second century Church leaders, reflect the teaching of the apostles. They viewed marriage as good and encouraged its continuance. Sexual intercourse was seen as a blessing, both for pleasure and procreation. These two early leaders expressed concern regarding marriage's limiting effect on ministry, but overall they had a positive outlook on the subject. Celibacy was seen as an acceptable alternative, but not the ideal.

As discussed previously, there was a theological shift concerning the value of sex in marriage, over the next few centuries, based on the leaders' reaction to the condition of their world. However, even during this period, there were leaders such as Clement of Alexandria that took issue with his theological peers.

The Reformation reopened the door to the subject of the appropriate role of marriage and sexual intercourse. Many Reformers rejected the supremacy of celibacy and chose to marry. The first substantial discussion of the proper role of sex in marriage occurred among the Puritans. Puritans called for companionship within marriage and a healthy sex life as a vital part of that companionship.

The Bible supports the Puritan's assertions concerning sexual intercourse in marriage. Sexual intercourse was a key component in God's creative plan. "God created us male and female (Genesis 1:27). He chose to make us sexual beings. He ordained marriage between a man and a woman (Genesis 2:24). God designed the sexual experience to hold a husband and wife together as they express their lifetime commitment through this special event.

God established the marriage covenant as the first human institution and the first rule of that institution was for the man and the woman to engage in sexual intercourse. God commanded the couple to "Multiple and fill the earth and subdue it" (Genesis 1:28). Unless Origen was correct concerning the pre-Fall physiology of man, this command required the act of sex and God called it "very good" (Genesis 1:31).

The Bible is not squeamish when it speaks about sexual relationships. People have attempted to rationalize away the graphic sexual content contained in the Song of Solomon by allegorizing the text to reflect God's love for His people. An honest reading of the text does not allow this. The Song of Solomon clearly presents the passion of two people anticipating a robust sexual experience within a life-long relationship.

Conclusion

A biblical world-view of the act of sex and sexuality reflects God's ultimate love for humanity in the Garden of Eden. God-ordained sex provides a vehicle for communication like none other between a husband and wife. It creates a unity providing security and trust. It fosters the development of a healthy relationship with no need for shame. It results in mutual respect. It is built on the same commitment that Jesus has made to all of those who follow Him, "Never will I leave you; never will I forsake you" (Hebrews 13:5).

Let's return to the wedding reception. How do Christians see sex as evil one moment and wonderful the next? I like to explain it this way. If I bought my 8 year-old grandson a brand new Corvette and gave it to him, it would be a good gift. If he attempted to drive it, at 8 years-old, he would damage it. His misuse of the good gift would hurt him. He might associate all cars as evil, but it would not be the car that was evil, it would be his misuse of the vehicle that caused him pain. If he had waited to drive the car until he learned to drive and obtained a license, he would fully benefit from the good gift that I had given to him. The same is true with sex. The gift always was good and always will be. It will be beneficial if used as designed by the Giver. Satan wants us to skew our understanding of sex because he knows the positive power inherent in this wonderful gift of God. If he can't get us to abuse the gift, he will try to get us to avoid it.

The responsible Christian leader must address their own worldview of sex and help others to determine why they feel the way they do, about sex, if any hope exists to see sexual purity regain prominence in the Christian community. Our task is to wrestle the dagger out of hell's hand and cut the cords of immorality that bind us. Sex is a wonderful gift given to us by God. In the next chapter, we will see what a healthy view of sex looks like from God's perspective.

Study Guide Questions

1. How can the secular view of sex be summed up?

2. What is a key danger of watching pornography?

3. What does the author say occurs when a person lusts?

4. What is "intercourse"?

5. What was the result of dualism in the Early Church regarding sex?

6. Explain Tertullian's view on sex.

7. How did the first century Church view sex?

8. How did the Reformers view sex and marriage?

9. What does the Song of Solomon (Songs) teach about sex?

10. How did the author respond to the questioning raised by students at the wedding reception?

TWENTY THREE

SEX THE WAY GOD INTENDED

The Bible clearly teaches sex is a good gift from God. Unfortunately, every good gift offered by God can be distorted by Satan. God designed sex and marriage to illustrate the union God has with His followers. It is the primary communication tool God chose for a husband and wife to share their love and commitment to one another. Each time the married couple have sex, they affirm that they will never leave one another or forsake one another for any reason; "until death do us part." Sex, which is biblical, will reflect the regulations God has placed upon it. Satan's ploy is to encourage humans to violate God's regulations and to cheapen this wonderful gift from God. He desires the very act God designed to unify a married couple to pull them apart.

God placed four boundaries around sex to protect us. I like to call the four walls "God's sex box." These walls are similar to the walls that protected Adam and Eve inside the Garden of Eden. If the two original humans had been satisfied to stay inside God's boundaries, they would have been able to enjoy all of the blessings God intended for them. In like manner, if humans will stay inside the "sex box" God has designed, they too can experience sex the way God intended.

Unfortunately, people seldom are satisfied to stay inside any of the boundaries God sets for them. They believe if they do it their own way, it will somehow be more satisfying. No one would deny individuals who engage in illicit sexual activities enjoy themselves. But enjoyment is not the ultimate goal of sex. Even though people enjoy illicit sex, it seldom leaves a person feeling fulfilled. Satan attempts to convince Christians that following God and His plan will result in them forfeiting sexual pleasure. Satan tells them God doesn't really want them happy. This is the same tactic he used on Eve in the Garden. Nothing could be further from the truth!

A lack of contentment with what God offers is the basis of all sin. God has offered humanity great sex within the marriage relationship, but for many it is not enough. The apostle Paul identifies the perversions that arise from a lack of contentment with marriage and the gift of sex. The lack of contentment, with God and His gifts, ultimately leads to immorality.

> Therefore God gave them up in the lusts of their hearts to impurity, to the dishonoring of their bodies among themselves, because they exchanged the truth about God for a lie and worshiped and served the creature rather than the Creator, who is blessed forever! Amen.
>
> For this reason God gave them up to dishonorable passions. For their women exchanged natural relations for those that are contrary to nature; and the men likewise gave up natural relations with women and were consumed with passion for one another, men committing shameless acts with men and receiving in themselves the due penalty for their error.
>
> And since they did not see fit to acknowledge God, God gave them up to a debased mind to do what ought not to be done. They were filled with all manner of unrighteousness, evil, covetousness, malice. They are full of envy, murder, strife, deceit, maliciousness. They are gossips, slanderers, haters of God, insolent, haughty, boastful, inventors of evil, disobedient to parents, foolish, faithless, heartless, ruthless. Though they know God's righteous decree that those who practice such things deserve to die, they not only do them but give approval to those who practice them. (Romans 1:24-32.)

So what are the boundaries that God has placed around His special gift of sex?

Between Two Humans

The first boundary God set to protect sex is the requirement that sex be between two humans. God informed the Israelites, a human must never have sex with an animal: "Whoever lies with an animal shall be put to death" (Exodus 22:19). Most people, especially Christians, have no problem keeping this protective boundary in place. I have yet to meet one of my students who goes to the local zoo to pick up his/her date on a Friday night.

Bestiality was practiced in the ancient near east during biblical times. Examples can be seen among the Babylonians and the Egyptians. Bestiality was practiced in Babylonia, especially during the Spring Fertility Rites. Ancient Egyptians portrayed bestiality on tomb walls and used themes of bestiality in their mythology.

In modern times, bestiality is rare, but not unknown. As of this writing, only 40 states have laws that outlaw bestiality. The results of a research project completed in 1974 stated that 4.9% of men and 1.9% of women have engaged in sex with an animal at least once. Given the current sexual climate, it would not be surprising if these numbers have risen.

The fact some people resort to bestiality reveals how desperately they want to be independent from God. Pure sexual satisfaction cannot be the motivation when choosing sex with an animal over having sex with another human. This behavior is clearly rebellious toward God. God understood the potential for evil in those He created. This is why He had to declare His will regarding sexual interaction between the species.

Between Members of the Opposite Sex

Sex with a member of the opposite sex forms the second side of the protective box. God created a man and a woman with interconnecting genitals and immediately told them to be fruitful and multiply (Genesis 1:28). In the next chapter of Genesis, Moses, the recorder of Genesis, uses Adam and Eve' relationship to explain God's plan for marriage. "Therefore a man shall leave his father and his mother and hold fast to his wife, and they shall become one flesh. And the man and his wife were both naked and were not ashamed" (Genesis 2:24-25). The theme of "oneness" encompasses all aspects of their relationship, including the sexual union.

Many have wondered why Moses would mention leaving ones mother and father when Adam and Eve didn't have a mother or a father. The only reason Moses would have mentioned a mother and father is he was describing a marital union people would have recognized during the time of his writing. It was Moses' assumption that marriage would be between a man and a woman. There is no indication in Scripture that God ever sanctions same-gender sexual relations.

Less than two-generations ago, the idea of a homosexual relationship was considered odd. The term "queer" was associated with those involve in homosexual relationships because of its unusual nature. Today, if individuals do not accept a homosexual relationship as equal to a heterosexual relationship, they are the "odd" ones. They are considered bigoted. Homosexuality has become normalized in our society. Many states have accepted homosexual marriage as equal to a traditional marriage. Those in homosexual unions are no longer "queer," in Western culture.

Homosexual relationships are not new. In Roman culture, in the first century, homosexual unions (men with men) were an accepted part of the culture. Although accepted in the culture of the first century, neither the Jewish leaders nor the Christian leaders saw it as an acceptable relational option.

Some would like to point to David and Jonathan's relationship in the Old Testament as a "homosexual" relationship. No serious student of the Old Testament would come to this conclusion. Even a casual reading of the text, most often pointed to by those who would like to rewrite the biblical narrative, reveals a sexual relationship between these two friends was not assumed by the author:

David finished talking to Saul. After that, Jonathan became David's closest friend. He loved David as much as he loved himself. (From that day on Saul kept David as his servant and didn't let him go back to his family.) So Jonathan made a pledge of mutual loyalty with David because he loved him as much as he loved himself (1Samuel 18:1-3).

Rather than a homosexual relationship, David and Jonathan's relationship was more akin to Jesus' statement about true love: "Greater love has no one than this, that someone lay down his life for his friends" (John 15:13).

Today homosexuality has not only been embraced as a positive alternative to a heterosexual relationship in society in general, it has been accepted as an acceptable option in some segments of the Christian Church. Denominations that endorse homosexual marriages argue that it is not fair to prohibit a person from having a lifetime of love simply because they were born with a desire for the same sex. The philosophy of these denominational leaders is that love supersedes the Law, therefore, we must ere on the side of a loving act rather than hold to a harsh biblical position that makes people feel condemned.

There is great danger with this type of a philosophy. The danger is not in attempting to show love to people. The danger is the adoption of a postmodern hermeneutic of Scripture. This philosophy allows the reader of Scripture to determine how much of the Bible is still authoritative and to reject any part that is not acceptable to the current culture.

The consequences of this way of viewing the Bible raised its head this week in the national news. An evangelical preacher opened in prayer at the dedication of a new U.S. embassy. Many progressive politicians and members of left-leaning news outlets objected to the pastor being asked to pray at the event. They accused him of being a hate-monger because he unashamedly proclaims, from his pulpit, if you do not believe in the death and resurrection of Jesus, you will spend eternity in Hell. These individuals did not debate the teaching of the Scriptures on this matter. They simply declared the portions of Bible that support his proclamation should be eliminated, or at least ignored. To do otherwise would be narrow minded and unkind to others who embrace a different faith tradition. This same line of reasoning can be used concerning any topic in the Bible which is not acceptable to a person, including homosexuality. A postmodern interpretation of the Bible renders the Bible powerless. Without the authority of Scripture, Christianity can be shaped into the image of humans, rather than humans being formed and shaped into the image of God.

The authority of Scripture must not be watered down by the opinions of humans. Homosexuality will not produce a sexual union of the quality God intended when He gave us the wonderful gift of sex.

On a side note, Christians should not abuse or condemn a person because of homosexual behavior. The problem is not the behavior, but the belief system behind the behavior. Those who choose to replace God's standards, for their own, need expressions of God's love, just as anyone else who has been deceived by Satan. It is not homosexuality that will not keep a person out of heaven. It is a lack of faith in the death and resurrection of Jesus. We must not hate the homosexual. Instead, we must show them true love, which is available through a relationship with Jesus.

Between Covenantal Partners

The third protective boundary regarding our sexual activity requires followers of God to unite sexually (if they choose to marry) with another covenant person. A covenant person is someone of the same faith tradition. In the Old Testament, this meant an Israelite was required to marry another Israelite. Moses laid out the rules concerning covenantal relationships:

Observe what I command you this day. Behold, I will drive out before you the Amorites, the Canaanites, the Hittites, the Perizzites, the Hivites, and the Jebusites. Take care, lest you make a covenant with the inhabitants of the land to which you go, lest it become a snare in your midst. You shall tear down their altars and break their pillars and cut down their Asherim (for you shall worship no other god, for the LORD, whose name is Jealous, is a jealous God), lest you make a covenant with the inhabitants of the land, and when they whore after their gods and sacrifice to their gods and you are invited, you eat of his sacrifice, and you take of their daughters for your sons, and their daughters whore after their gods and make your sons whore after their gods. (Exodus 34:11-16.)

The rationale behind God's covenantal restriction regarding marriage was quite simple. A person must serve God, and Him alone. The problem with an Israelite man marrying a Canaanite woman was the woman would want to have a child at some point. The woman, who served the Canaanite gods, would want to offer a sacrifice to Baal to ensure a pregnancy. The Israelite man would, more than likely, agree to this to increase the size of his family. Through a mixed-marriage, the Israelite man would be sucked into polytheism without giving it much thought. God knew this would be the case, so to protect the Israelites from the temptation to serve other gods, He forbid mixed marriages. A quick review of Israelite history proved God's declaration was accurate. The thing that continued to separate the Jewish people from their God stemmed from polytheism fostered through disobedience to the command to limit themselves to covenantal marriages.

A person might read this and ask how this principle applies to Christian relationships today. It is clear that we no longer offer sacrifices before we have sex with our spouse. And isn't this just an Old Testament law that was fulfilled through the death and resurrection of Jesus?

Fortunately, the New Testament does not keep us guessing regarding this very important subject. Paul explains the importance of covenantal relationships when writing to the Corinthian church:

Do not be yoked together with unbelievers. For what do righteousness and wickedness have in common? Or what fellowship can light have with darkness? What harmony is there between Christ and Belial? Or what does a believer have in common with an unbeliever? What agreement is there between the temple of God and idols? For we are the temple of the living God (2 Corinthians 6:14-16).

Paul's rationale against spiritually mixed relationships is the same as that argued by Moses. If two people are going to live in harmony, they should be serving the same God. How can two people be loyal to their spiritual convictions, to their relationship, and to themselves if they can't even agree on the God they serve?

Another side note is needed here. For many years, people have attempted to use the "unequally yoked" passage to forbid mixed racial marriages. There is no indication that Paul was saying a Christian Gentile could not marry a Christian Jew. These two groups would have been the furthest apart in regard to "race" in the first century. If Paul was trying to keep the races separated, he could have said so. His focus was attempting to help Christians remain fully committed to God. The best way to do this, in regard to marriage, is for a committed believer to limit his/her choice to another committed follower of Jesus when considering marriage.

Some Christians will justify dating and marrying a non-Christian because they are convinced this will be the avenue God uses to convert the person. These individuals may even be able to point out an example or two where a mixed spiritual marriage resulted in the non-Christian accepting Jesus as his/her Savior. A couple of exceptions to a rule laid out in Scripture does not justify a person to ignore God's word. If a person were to evaluate all mixed spiritual marriages, one would discover the wisdom of a believer following God's commandment. Few individuals who have ignore this command testify of a fulfilling marriage. Many end in disaster. Unfortunately, in an attempt to hold a marriage together, some Christians compromise their faith, and walk away from the church. Pragmatic examples of successful spiritually mixed marriages must never be used in an attempt to negate the authority of Scripture.

If two non-believers get married and, after marriage, one of the partners accepts Jesus as Savior, this does not mean the new Christian needs to divorce or separate from the non-believer. We are fortunate the apostle Paul had the foresight to anticipate this scenario. Once again, writing to the Corinthian church, Paul counsels the new believer to stay in the marital relationship they were in when they first believed. Paul anticipates the non-believer in the relationship may not want to remain with his/her spouse, but the decision to stay in the marriage or step away from it is the option of the non-believing spouse. The Bible teaches, if the non-believer wants to leave, the new believer should set him/her free. The new believer is then free to marry a believer, if they so choose. (See 1 Corinthians 7:12-24.)

Staying within the boundary of covenantal marriage was not really much of a problem until more recent days. The Roman Catholic Church has held that no marriage is sanctioned unless it is performed by the Church. To be able to get married by the Church, both people were required to be members of the Roman Catholic Church. This policy safeguarded the sanctity of marriage and ensured that only two Christians could get married. With the advent of Protestantism, the perimeters of the Church were widened, but the insistence on a church wedding between two Christians was maintained.

The Roman Catholic Church has maintained its standards regarding marriage. There are many expressions of the Protestant Church and many adjustments to requirements for marriage. Some Protestant churches still restrict marriage to two Christians, while others have opened their doors for pastors to perform marriages for "whomever may come." This latter view has led to many couples seeking to get married in the church, not for the spiritual commitment the building represents, but because of the décor of the building and the potential for beautiful wedding pictures.

The assumption of a covenantal relationship is no longer the norm in the United States. What has changed?

For years, the Church and its ministers controlled the institution of marriage. It wasn't until 1913 that the Federal government, of the United States, declared marriage as a part of the law which they oversaw. With that move, the government began to take ownership of marriage.

For many years, the Church and the government coexisted in regard to marriage. This is no longer the case. Now the government owns the institution of marriage. The government identifies who is able to perform a wedding (many categories of officiants have no religious connection; i.e. judges, captains of ships; justice of the peace; and in Colorado, the couple can do their own wedding), keeps record of the marriages, oversees the dissolution of a marriage, and determines who is qualified to be married. The most obvious example of how the Church has been removed from the equation regarding marriage is the recent laws sanctioning same-sex marriages. This decision was made without the voice of church leaders being seriously considered.

Christian ministers can personally limit their services to individuals who are Christians, but when they perform any wedding today, they solemnize the union by the authority given to them by the State where they perform the wedding, rather than by the authority that resides in the Church. One prominent Christian writer suggests there should be two types of weddings performed in the United States; one the government oversees and has authority over and one the Church oversees and has authority over. If this were to ever occur, marriage might regain significance among those who embrace the Christian faith.

So should a Christian even care about the covenantal element of marriage today? By all means! Marriage was God's idea. He designed it for a specific purpose. It is God's illustration of His relationship with His people. Paul explains:

Husbands, love your wives, as Christ loved the church and gave himself up for her, that he might sanctify her, having cleansed her by the washing of water with the word, so that he might present the church to himself in splendor, without spot or wrinkle or any such thing, that she might be holy and without blemish. In the same way husbands should love their wives as their own bodies. He who loves his wife loves himself. For no one ever hated his own flesh, but nourishes and cherishes it, just as Christ does the church, because we are members of his body. "Therefore a man shall leave his father and mother and hold fast to his wife, and the two shall become one flesh." This mystery is profound, and I am saying that it refers to Christ and the church (Ephesians 5:25-32.)

Of course Satan is going to attempt to strip this meaningful depiction of its evangelistic meaning. He does not want people seeing the potential of a meaningful relationship with God, and he doesn't want people to see the potential that marriage holds if they will submit to God and His standards. Unfortunately, the Church has slept while agents of Satan wrestled this extremely important institution away from the Church. Today, marriage in America is a governmental transaction on par with obtaining a driver's license. It is the Church's responsibility to reclaim the covenantal nature of marriage and allow the world to once again see God's unfailing love for humanity, through the loving commitment of two followers of Christ.

Between Life-Long Partners

The final side of the "sex box" demands that sexual intercourse only occur between two people who have made a life-long commitment; with a spouse. The apostle Paul describes a healthy and happy sexual relationship between a man and his wife:

The husband should give to his wife her conjugal rights, and likewise the wife to her husband. For the wife does not have authority over her own body, but the husband does. Likewise the husband does not have authority over his own body, but the wife does. Do not deprive one another, except perhaps by agreement for a limited time, that you may devote yourselves to prayer; but then come together again, so that Satan may not tempt you because of your lack of self-control (1 Corinthians 7:3-5).

Sex is to be conducted within the safety of the marriage commitment. It is to be one man with one woman. It is to be mutually satisfying and mutually consensual. It is not to be forced, but also not to be manipulative. And it is to be a commitment that lasts from the day of consummation to the day when one of the couple dies. "A wife is bound to her husband as long as he lives. But if her husband dies, she is free to be married to whom she wishes, only in the Lord" (1 Corinthians 7:39).

Some may argue that marriage today looks different than it did in biblical times. This is true. As stated previously, the state has gotten involved in marriage today. It has become just a piece of paper for some people. But one thing that has not changed is God's intention for marriage. Throughout biblical times, it was assumed that a marriage would last a lifetime. In the Old Testament, people took this so seriously that when a man wanted to end a marriage, the only option he had was to bash his wife's head against a wall to kill her. In this way, he could maintain the "letter of the Law." Moses saw this perversion of thinking and introduced divorce to the community to protect the life of the woman, but divorce was never God's intent.

In the book of Malachi, God clearly declares his attitude towards divorce. He says:

"This is another thing you do: you cover the altar of the LORD with tears, with weeping and with groaning, because He no longer regards the offering or accepts it with favor from your hand. Yet you say, 'For what reason?' Because the LORD has been a witness between you and the wife of your youth, against whom you have dealt treacherously, though she is your companion and your wife by covenant. But not one has done so who has a remnant of the Spirit. And what did that one do while he was seeking a godly offspring? Take heed then to your spirit, and let no one deal treacherously against the wife of your youth. For I hate divorce," says the LORD, the God of Israel, "and him who covers his garment with wrong," says the LORD of hosts. "So take heed to your spirit, that you do not deal treacherously" (Malachi 2:13-16, NASB).

The reason God hates divorce is because it dissolves a commitment that was intended for a lifetime. Divorce is a form of a lie. When individuals get married, they are promising to care for one another even when life's circumstances change.

Perhaps a more significant reason God hates divorce is because a lack of commitment to one another, by followers of God, calls into question the person's commitment to God. If a person can walk away from a person they loved when circumstances change, then they will be prone to do the same thing when the person's relationship with God is no longer satisfying. Most divorces occur either because of the lack of faithfulness or a failure to communicate. These are the same reasons some Christians walk away from their relationship with God. God hates it when individuals choose to separate themselves from Him in order to embrace pleasures which they see as having greater value than their commitment to Him.

God has made a commitment to us to never leave us or forsake us. He expects believers to live up to their promise that they made to Him when they accepted Jesus as their Savior.

Jesus explained His view of marriage and divorce:

And Pharisees came up to him and tested him by asking, "Is it lawful to divorce one's wife for any cause?" He answered, "Have you not read that he who created them from the beginning made them male and female, and said, 'Therefore a man shall leave his father and his mother and hold fast to his wife, and the two shall become one flesh'? So they are no longer two but one flesh. What therefore God has joined together, let not man separate." They said to him, "Why then did Moses command one to give a certificate of divorce and to send her away?" He said to them, "Because of your hardness of heart Moses allowed you to divorce your wives, but from the beginning it was not so. And I say to you: whoever divorces his wife, except for sexual immorality, and marries another, commits adultery" (Matthew 19:3-9).

When Christians divorce their spouses, they are communicating they are not willing to work on their marriage and they do not believe the power of God can heal any strain that may exist. It is true that Jesus provided cover for divorce in the case of marital infidelity (Matthew 19:9), but even in that case, as we saw in the chapter on forgiveness, the preferable choice is to forgive and to reestablish trust. This will demonstrate the forgiveness of God to those who fail in their commitments to Him.

Few people enter marriage anticipating the marriage will end. Every couple, I have watched get married, promise they will love and care for one another until death separates them. This lifetime commitment is a requirement for sex to be within the guidelines established by God.

Earlier, I mentioned that Christians today, who stand against homosexuality, are called bigots. Today, Christians, who stand against premarital sex, are called fools. If you watch any movie or television program, the plot assumes the characters in the show will have sex with someone at least by the third date. And the idea that you would wait until you got married to have sex is archaic to a secular mindset. The philosophy promoted by Hollywood is reinforced in the public schools. The majority of schools, which address sexual relations, will show a video on sexually transmitted diseases, suggest that students refrain from having sexual intercourse before marriage, but since they assume students will not be able to control themselves, they tell the students how to avoid pregnancy through the use of contraceptives.

Many people, both young and old, have been convinced by the arguments made by secular forces. To suggest to many young adults today, even those in the church, that being a virgin when they get married is God's ideal for a couple, makes you seem irrelevant. How far we have gotten from the clear teachings of Scripture!

The next chapter of this book is designed to help you see why God designed His "sex box." Of utmost importance to Paul is that sex would be held in the high esteem God intended when He created this wonderful act of love. Hopefully, you will discover principles that will help you stand strong when your friends call you a fool for not giving yourself away sexually before you are ready to make a commitment to a person for a life time.

Conclusion

Marriages is one of the most effective ways God has to demonstrate His love and commitment to humans. He was careful to protect it by setting boundaries.

Satan's design is to destroy a human's relationship with God, no matter the cost. He is slowly and consistently creating an environment that causes individuals to question the goodness and wisdom of God. Over the years, we have seen society, under his influence, tear down each of the protective walls God has constructed around the sexual act.

First, Satan suggested that we devalue the covenantal aspect of marriage and we have agreed to do so. Second, he belittled the importance of a lifetime commitment as a prerequisite to participation in sexual intercourse. Sex is no longer seen as a sacred act between a husband and wife. It is now seen, by most in society, as a recreational activity designed simply for momentary pleasure to be performed with anyone who is willing. Third, he promoted same gender sex as equal to the union between a man and woman. Sadly, even some in the Church have embraced this lie in an attempt to demonstrate love and acceptance. Finally, Satan is in the process of convincing those who are openly rebellious against God to promote sex outside of the human experience. Bestiality is already practiced by some, and over time, will find a greater acceptance in society. With modern technology, it is not inconceivable that people will attempt to replace the gift God designed to join two humans with sexual activities with robots and other inanimate objects. There is no end to the rebellion some humans will go to in an attempt to be free from the boundaries placed on them by a loving God.

Nothing that Satan can offer will ever be as good as the gift of sex that God gave us, when used as He designed it. Sex is not an added benefit to a relationship. Sex is the glue that holds a marriage together. Each time a husband and wife have sexual intercourse, they are communicating that they will never leave one another or forsake one another. This assurance provides confidence for the couple when times get tough. Sexual intercourse is also a physical reminder of the assurance they have in God's commitment to their relationship.

I have just presented you with the way to have the best sex ever. Hold firm to the boundaries God has set for the wonderful gift of sex and you will experience a lifetime of satisfying, fulfilling, and God-honoring sexual expression.

Study Guide Questions

1. How does God view sex?

2. Why is marriage and the sexual union between a man and woman important to God?

3. What are the four sides of the "sex box" discussed in this chapter?

4. Why is homosexuality outside of God's will for Christians?

5. How would you respond to a person who said that David and Jonathan had a homosexual relationship?

6. Why does God insist that a believer not marry a non-believer?

7. How would you respond to a person who attempts to justify sex outside of marriage by arguing that in the Old Testament there was no official marriage between one man and one woman?

8. Why did Moses allow for divorce among the Israelites?

9. According to the Bible, when should a marriage between two believers end?

10. How has Satan systematically attempted to minimize the value of marriage?

TWENTY FOUR

COMBATTING SEXUAL SIN

Each semester, I ask my students if they ever had a serious conversation with a Christian adult about sex. In most classes, I have less than 20% of the students respond in the affirmative. As we have seen in a previous chapter, many Christian parents don't know how to talk about sex, or they don't want to because they feel they shouldn't talk about a "dirty" subject with their children. Hopefully this chapter will help you, if you are a part of the 80% who have not had a chance to talk to somebody about sex. You can also use this material when you have children of your own.

A question I get asked every semester is, "How far is too far?" regarding sexual expression outside of marriage. Knowing this, I get ahead of the issue by asking my students this question. Their responses often reveal a lack of serious consideration of the subject, which is not surprising considering their lack of spiritual guidance in this important area. This is very dangerous because most people are not thinking clearly when hormones are flowing, and the opportunity for fornication presents itself. It is vital that we determine appropriate limits before we get into a sexually charged situation.

Some people would argue the question, "How far is too far?" is the wrong question for people to ask regarding sexual behavior. I would agree, but it is a great way to begin discussing sex with a group of students. I wish I didn't have to address sexual immorality (fornication) at all, but it is one of the most powerful ways Satan uses to destroy the testimony of Christians. He knows, if a Christian yields to the temptation to engage in illicit sexual behavior, he can bring shame to the believer and embarrassment to the kingdom of God. Learning what God expects in regard to sexual behavior is essential for the believer.

What is Fornication?

We must first define the term "fornication." The Greek word for "fornication" is *porneia*. Fornication is any sexual activity outside of "God's sex box," which was described in the previous chapter. It is also not limited to sexual engagement with another person. Probably you have heard the term "pornography." This word is made up of two Greek words *porneia* – "fornication" and *grapho* – "to write." So pornography is fornication in written form. Today that would include photos, videos, romance novels, and any other media used to promote immoral sexual thoughts and actions.

The city of Corinth was a hotbed for *porneia*. The culture was sexually saturated. When a person came to Jesus, they recognized that the sexual norms they were accustomed to were inappropriate for a Christian. They began to think differently about sex, but they were confused regarding acceptable Christian behavior due to the dualistic philosophy in their culture.

Accepting dualistic thinking resulted in new believers either rejecting all pleasurable physical activities or they felt free to use their bodies without restraint. Paul addresses the first extreme in 1 Corinthians 7, where he endorses sex within marriage. He uses 1 Corinthians 6:10-20 to address the second extreme. It is this passage of Scripture that I want to address in this chapter. If you have a Bible nearby, I invite you to turn to this passage of Scripture, as I unpack this important text.

Freedom Isn't a License

Paul begins by addressing the misunderstanding of some in the church that freedom in Christ allows believers to do whatever they wish with their bodies. He quotes a slogan that some of the Corinthians were using to justify their misconduct and then offers correction to their thinking. "'All things are lawful for me,' but not all things are helpful. 'All things are lawful for me,' but I will not be dominated by anything'" (1 Corinthians 6:12). Paul clearly explains that just because a thing may be technically acceptable, it is not always the best choice.

He goes on to declare a Christian should not do anything that enslaves them. I am often asked how a person knows if they have become enslaved by something. My standard response is a person can know if they are enslaved by something, if the person cannot live without it. If you cannot live without it, you should probably live without it. This applies to anything. It can be food, drink, and even physical relationships. If Jesus asks us not to do something, yet we insist on doing it anyway, there is a good chance that the action has enslaved you.

As a Christian, you must only be controlled by the Holy Spirit. Christians must not have two masters. Jesus told us that we cannot serve both money and God. In the same way, we cannot serve both sex and God. When a person accepts Jesus as Savior, the person hands the controls of his/her life to Him. If you insist on participating in fornication, even when you know it is a clear violation of God's desire for your life, you are enslaved to your sexual appetite.

Your Body Is for the Lord

"'Food is meant for the stomach and the stomach for food'"—and God will destroy both one and the other. The body is not meant for sexual immorality, but for the Lord, and the Lord for the body" (1 Corinthians 6:13).

God created human bodies in His image, with the intent they would properly reflect Him to the world (Genesis 1:27). This requires the body to be used in a manner that reflects spiritual wholeness (or holiness) in an unashamed manner. The Psalmist exclaimed, "I praise you, for I am fearfully and wonderfully made. Wonderful are your works; my soul knows it very well" (Psalm 139:14). Every aspect of our bodies were made with the intent to glorify God. This includes the parts of our bodies used to have sexual intercourse. Christians should only use these parts, like any other part of their body, in ways that please God and give Him glory. As we have seen, in the previous chapter, He has given us the boundaries of sexual expression that brings Him glory.

You Are United with God

The next part of Paul's teaching vividly presents the key reason God protects the sexual relationship. The Christian's body is a part of Christ. Paul explains, "And God raised the Lord and will also raise us up by his power. Do you not know that your bodies are members of Christ?" (1 Corinthians 6:14-15a).

When a person accepts Jesus as Savior, he/she becomes one with Him and He dwells in that person. There is never a time when a Christian can set Jesus aside, lock Him out of the room, or hide actions from Him. When a person has sexual intercourse, Jesus is present to witness it. If the Christian is engaged in an immoral sexual act, Jesus is present for the shameful transgression, and it brings Him displeasure. Therefore, to engage in sex outside of the protective sex box, God has presented to His followers, exposes Christ to an unholy union.

If sexual intercourse occurs in marriage, the Holy Spirit celebrates the activity. Some Christian married couples are very uncomfortable with the idea that the Holy Spirit is in the bedroom witnessing their sexual activity. This discomfort reveals their struggle with the celebrative nature of biblical sex. The only reason they would be uncomfortable with the Holy Spirit in their bedroom is if they believed sex is "nasty," or at least "not spiritual." Let me encourage you to rejoice with your spouse when you are engaged in sexual intercourse as a Christian married couple. The Holy Spirit is!

Fornication's Effect on Jesus

If there was any reason for a Christian to say, "No" to fornication of any kind, it is because of what it does to Jesus. Since Jesus dwells in us and is a part of us, when we participate in fornication, we are forcing Jesus to participate in this activity. Paul can't even fathom this. "Do you not know that your bodies are members of Christ? Shall I then take the members of Christ and make them members of a prostitute? Never! Or do you not know that he who is joined to a prostitute becomes one body with her? For, as it is written, 'The two will become one flesh'" (1 Corinthians 6:15-16).

Paul cautions when a person has sexual relations they unite with their sexual partner. Regardless of the attempts to wipe the experiences from one's mind, it will be impossible to eradicate it fully. How much better would a person's sex life be if they never had to think about a person they had sex with, other than their husband or wife? Too many marriages suffer from unfair comparisons of a spouse's performance in bed, to previous partners or a pornography "star." This can be avoided if Christians would avoid fornication.

But Paul indicates that the union goes beyond the man and the woman having sex. If a Christian is involved, Jesus has been united with the unsanctioned person as well when the sex act occurs. To force a person to participate in a sexual act against his/her will is rape. It is not too far of a reach to argue this is what we do to Jesus when we force Him into an unwanted sexual experience.

Before you argue this would make Jesus a part of a sinful act and diminish His deity, please understand, rape is not a sexual activity. A woman who is raped does not lose her virginity. She has not been party to a sexual activity. She has been assaulted. Instead of a club, the man uses his penis to assault her. The physical damage may not be as evident as being hit by a baseball bat, but as much, if not more, damage has occurred. The point is that unwanted participation in immorality does not make the unwilling partner guilty of the immorality.

The question I must ask Christians, who participate in fornication, is how they could treat someone who they say they love in this manner. No one would ever forcibly rape a person they loved. It is possible a person might take advantage of someone he is dating, if all he saw the person as was a source of self-pleasure. Unfortunately, it is true some ungrateful Christians follow God solely for what they can get from Him. These selfish individuals probably find "raping" Jesus as acceptable, as long as their lustful pleasures are being served. This type of activity must never be a part of a person's life who is attempting to grow in their relationship with Jesus and desiring to bring Him glory.

Value Your Union with Jesus

Those who have a desire to grow in their spiritual well-being will understand and appreciate the union which took place when they became one with Jesus at salvation. Paul describes this union, "But he who is joined to the Lord becomes one spirit with him" (1 Corinthians 6:17). This is not a union of convenience; it is a covenant of unfailing love. Just as a husband and a wife, who are truly in love, will not compromise their relationship through sexual infidelity, a Christian who loves Jesus will not risk compromising their relationship through participating in fornication.

I love my wife and I love my children. There is no way that I am going to jeopardize my relationship with the people I love for a selfish act that may bring me pleasure. My love for my family and the value I place on them does not allow me to make a potentially disastrous decision. It bewilders me to think about how Christians can make reckless choices which place their relationship with Jesus in jeopardy in exchange for sensual pleasure.

How to Respond to Sexual Temptation

So what should a Christian do when they are tempted to fornicate?

Flee Sexual Immorality

Paul's instructions are so simple and straightforward no one could miss their meaning, but thousands of Christians damage their spiritual and human relationships each year because they ignore them. When confronted with the temptation to engage in fornication, Paul says, "Flee from sexual immorality" (1 Corinthians 6:18a).

Running away from a bully, who can easily defeat you, is not being a coward. Staying and attempting to battle the enemy on your own, when you know you are weak, is not a sign of wisdom. It is being stupid. The same is true when you think you are strong enough to withstand the power of temptation. If you put yourself in compromising situations, you will eventually fall to the temptation because sex is a highly desirable, although immoral, activity.

It is not wise for a person with a problem with alcohol to hang out in bars. It is not wise for a person with a weight problem to frequent a donut shop. And it is not wise for a person who struggles with pornography to have a computer with internet access in an area of their home where no one can see what they are viewing. It is just dumb. It is also dumb to think you can say "No" to sexual immorality, if you are spending alone time with a person who is willing to allow you to do things that arouse them sexually.

I have to admit; I love fire. I enjoy building a fire in my fire pit on the first cool evening of the fall. I sit a safe distance from it as it emits its flames. Gradually, I get a little closer to the flames because I have gotten used to the heat where I am sitting. The closer I get to the fire, the warmer it feels and the more fascinated I get with how the wood ignites. Before long, my feet are on the edge of the pit. Small sparks hit my clothing, but I brush them away. A time or two, I got too close and actually got burned. As I ran cold water over my blistered skin, all I could think of was how foolish I had been to ignore all of the warnings I had been given to back away from the flames. If I had just backed away earlier, I could have saved a lot of pain. The same is true for fornication. Everyone who gets burned through sexual misconduct had many warning signs they ignored.

It is important to remember sexual expression can become intimate well before it becomes erotic. Most sexual affairs start with innocent exchanges that lead to a bond which is emotional. Once the emotional bond has developed, it is hard to recognize the danger that lurks. Many people caught in sexual affairs state they didn't see it coming. All the signs were there, but they chose to ignore them because they thought they were strong enough to resist their physical urges. It is extremely unwise to develop emotional ties with someone other than your own spouse or someone you are committed to marry. It is important to be careful how you share your inner most feelings with your fiancé before marriage, as well. Emotions open the heart to physical desires.

Paul indicates hanging around when sexual temptation entices you is dangerous. Thousands of Christians, who have yielded to temptation, have the scars to demonstrate the wisdom in Paul's words to "run away!" Avoid the scars by heeding Paul's instructions to keep far away from sexual sin.

Recognize the Seriousness of Fornication

Paul goes on to explain why fornication is such a big deal. A person can be a glutton, but the only dire consequence will be a bad heart, weak knees, and an early grave. It is not good to be unhealthy, but it is not on the same level as sexual sin. Paul states: "Every other sin a person commits is outside the body, but the sexually immoral person sins against his own body" (1 Corinthians 6:18b).

We live in a culture that nearly worships the body. Young adults will spend hours in the gym honing their various muscle groups. They are careful what foods they select to put in their bodies. They show great wisdom and care for their bodies because they know it is the only one they will ever get, and they might think a fit body will be attractive to people of the opposite sex. It seems strange to me, many of these very same people give little thought to their spiritual well-being regarding their sexual choices. According to the apostle Paul, they have their priorities backward.

Sexual immorality is different from other sins because it affects a person's view of self and the person's view of the Creator. The Christian's sexual experience, and expression, is based on the spiritual reality made possible through a committed relationship with Jesus. God uses sexual intercourse, within marriage, as a metaphor for His intimate relationship with His followers. Terms such as the "Bride of Christ" (Ephesians 5:22-23; 2 Corinthians 11:2) and verses that define the relationship He has with followers as a "mystery like that between a husband and wife" (Ephesians 5:31-32) become much less meaningful if immoral actions cheapen a person's view of sex.

Remember Your Contractual Agreement

Paul then moves his discourse against fornication to the contractual agreement we have made with the Holy Spirit when we accepted Jesus as Savior. He states that Christians have given ownership of their bodies to the Holy Spirit. "Or do you not know that your body is a temple of the Holy Spirit within you, whom you have from God? You are not your own, for you were bought with a price (1 Corinthians 6:19-20a).

As the exclusive owner of your body, the Holy Spirit has the authority to dictate who can take up residence in your body. As we saw earlier, when a person has sex with another person, they become united. The two share one another's body. If the Holy Spirit is not comfortable with this, then it must be seen as unacceptable behavior.

Let me illustrate it this way. If I owned a one bedroom home, just off campus, and advertised it for rent, I could sign a lease with a couple. After signing the contract, I could then, find another couple and sign a lease with them on the same property. And perhaps I could find a third couple and sign a contract with them. This plan would work well until the day all three couples brought their furniture and clothes to move in. If this occurred, it is doubtful all three couples would be happy to honor the contract and move into the one bedroom house. There probably would be a lot of shouting, and undoubtedly all three couples would tear up the contract and walk away from their commitment to me. No one would blame them for their decision.

In the same fashion, if we signed a contract with the Holy Spirit to allow Him to have exclusive residence in our lives, we should not be surprised if He chooses to walk away from His commitment to us, if we allow others to take up residence in our lives without His permission. Some may argue once we are saved we are always saved. It is true God will never love us any less, but He is not obligated to sanction our lifestyle decisions, if we are willfully opposed to His desires. The apostle John teaches that those who live in willful disobedience to God are fooling themselves if they think they are actually children of God (1 John 3:9-10).

For those who still are not convinced fornication is unacceptable behavior for a Christian, consider how you would feel if the person you loved, and to whom you had committed your life, brought another person into your bedroom. Consider your feelings if the two of them began having sexual relations in front of you. I know if I ever did that to my wife, she would have cause to walk away from our relationship. Why would I think the Holy Spirit would accept this type of behavior? When Christians participate in any form of fornication, they are revealing their true level of commitment to God and their level of love for Him.

Give God Glory

After laying out his rationale against fornication, Paul expresses his desire for all Christians regarding their sexual activities: "So glorify God in your body" (1 Corinthians 6:20b).

Few Christians have a problem with submitting their souls to God because there is little cost today for believing in the resurrection of Jesus. People may even be able to submit their minds to the theories associated with Christianity. They are able to say all of the right things and even quote Scripture verses. But the real test of your Christianity is your attitude toward God and what you do with your body in response to His authority in your life. If we truly love God with all of our hearts, our behavior will reflect His priorities. For the Corinthians, this meant saying "No" to all forms of fornication. It should be no different for Christians today.

When I Mess Up

Now that we have established that fornication is unacceptable for the Christian, there are a number of questions that must be answered. The intent of this chapter is not to make someone who has already engaged in fornication to feel guilty. My purpose is to establish the standard God has set in the Bible. I want to offer encouragement for those who have maintained their sexual purity to continue to do so. And, I want to offer hope to those who have made poor choices in this area of their life.

What if I Am Currently Involved in Fornication?

If you have already given in to sex outside of marriage, engaged in pornography, or been involved in habitual sexual fantasy, there is hope. The hope is not that you will stop engaging in fornication because this is not the real issue. Most people engage in fornication because they are broken in some way, and they need to find healing. Many individuals that I talk to, who participate in some form of fornication, do so because they feel a lack in some aspect of their lives. Often, I will hear stories from young ladies who engaged in fornication because they felt they needed to experience closeness with a male figure. They never could attract the attention of their fathers. They would do anything to get a man to pay attention to them. Sex was just the price they paid to be the center of some man's universe. They mistakenly thought they could achieve that through sexual involvement, only to be left even more broken when the guy got what he wanted and then walked away. Other young ladies tell of sexual abuse at a young age. They feel shame concerning their sexuality. It is a natural extension, of that feeling of shame, to consent to sexual relationships with a boyfriend or perhaps even multiple partners. The young men I have talked to who engage in various forms of fornication, will often point to insecurity. Somehow they got the impressions they didn't measure up as a man. Perhaps they were bullied at some point. They may even feel belittled by family members. So they attempt to prove their manhood through a conquest of a girl they are dating, or through pornography. Not all sexual encounters are a result of brokenness, but most healthy Christian teenagers have an easier time of saying "No" to fornication when opportunities present themselves.

If you have brokenness in your life, it is not an excuse to engage in fornication, but it may give a reason for the desire that drives you. Most individuals, who are broken, use sex as a medication, but unfortunately it only gives temporary relief from the pain they are feeling. If you are engaging in sex because of a pain that you have in your life, it is vital that you find help through Christian counseling so you can pinpoint the cause of your pain and begin to work through the issues. You will never be able to conquer your sexual immorality until you find healing through the power of the Holy Spirit. Don't allow your life to be controlled by destructive behavior. Get help as soon as possible.

God is willing to forgive you for sexual sins as much as any other sin you may engage in. There may be consequences to decisions you made that are irreversible, such as a pregnancy, an abortion, or a STD, but God is willing to forgive and forget your past and allow you to start over. If you truly repent, and determine to remain pure, God will only see your purity because of His mercy and grace. You may have to reestablish your reputation among friends, but God will see you as a totally forgiven son or daughter.

Will a Virgin Want Me, if I Have Had Premarital Sex?

This is a very good question. First, please do not tell everyone you go out with about your sexual history. It really is none of their business, at this point in the relationship. If you get to the point where you are very serious about getting married, it is only fair for you to share your sexual past, as well as any other baggage you may be carrying. Do not give graphic details of your encounters. Simply share the fact you made a poor choice previously and God has forgiven you.

Once you do this, the real decision about the future of the relationship is up to the person who has been faithful to God with their sexual decisions. If the virgin has worked hard to delay his/her sexual gratification until marriage, and he/she has decided to only marry a virgin, it is that person's right to lovingly tell you that you are not the right person for him/her because of the standards the person had set for themselves. If this occurs, you have no reason to be upset with the individual. You were the one who made the decision to have premarital sex. You may say it was before you experienced salvation, so the person is unfair to hold a previous sin against you. There is nothing unfair about a person maintaining his/her values. If the person who is a virgin has established a standard that he/she will not compromise, honor the response and move on.

If the person who is a virgin decides he/she loves you so much that the individual can overlook your past mistakes, the person has every right to adjust his/her standards. If the person does make the decision to forgive you, the person must make the commitment to never bring up your sexual past again. If the person shows this level of mercy, it is a good indication the person cherishes you and values your relationship.

What if My Girlfriend/Boyfriend and I Are Having Sex? Can We Ask God to Forgive Us and then Live Holy?

This is a tough one. I can assure you, if the two of you ask for forgiveness, God will do so. The tough part is living a holy life after you have been forgiven. The reason I say this is because once you cross a sexual boundary, it is tough to rebuild the fence and stay on the safe side of the new boundary. The establishment of a healthy relationship generally stops when the sex begins in immoral relationships. No two people, involved in adultery, are trying to develop a relationship. It is all about the passion. The same is true in a dating relationship. Once you start having sexual intercourse, you will think of little else when you are together. You really don't even want to talk when you get together. The immoral couple believe the sooner they get into bed, the better.

Because of the nature of an immoral sexual relationship, it is very hard to continue dating a person you have had sex with, if you want to stay sexually pure. Will power is not enough to keep you chaste. Praying together will often lead to feelings of intimacy which is a very dangerous emotion, if you are used to having sexual relations.

My recommendation is, if you are serious about establishing a healthy relationship, consider separating for 6 months or so. After this cooling down period, start dating again, but set firm boundaries. Use the time apart to deepen your relationship with Jesus. Some people suggest that I am foolish to recommend this because the couple might separate and never get back together again, causing undo pain. I suggest a life-long relationship built on willful disobedience to the principles of God will result in deeper pain.

Is Involvement in Fornication Really a Big Deal?

If sex was simply an animalistic or mechanical reproductive act, it would not be a big deal. Dogs and cats don't do a lot of thinking when it comes to sex. Animals go through mating cycles and really don't care who they hook up with. So many movies and television programs promote animalistic behavior as an acceptable option for people today. It is no wonder, sex has lost value in our society when it has been lowered to this level.

Sex isn't a big deal for those who are outside the community of God. As much as they care about the person they are having sex with, they will only enjoy the "shell" of the fruit of sex. They may live in committed relationships, but they do not have the ability to understand or experience the full flavor of the fruit because that can only be experienced by those who understand the unity that exists between a Christ and His followers. This does not mean that non-Christians cannot experience the physical pleasures associated with sex, but they cannot experience the spiritual dimension of sexual intercourse.

Sex really is a big deal because God made it to be a big deal. It is more than a physical transaction that provides momentary pleasure. A biblical world-view of the act of sex and sexuality reflects God's ultimate love for humanity which He displayed in the Garden of Eden.

Sex should be the purist form of communication. Just as Adam and Eve had clear and open communication with God, a husband and a wife should have clear and open communication of their love through sexual expression. Unfortunately, when people engage in fornication, they communicate selfishness and a love of physical pleasure rather than the well-being of the other person.

God made sex to demonstrate the unity between himself and His creation. When a husband and his wife engage in sexual intercourse, they cannot be any closer physically. Hopefully, this physical unity carries over into their spiritual life. Sex outside of the "box" is a charade because two bodies are intertwined, but there is no true unity. In our society, it is not uncommon for one-night stands or individuals having multiple partners. Instead of two people becoming one, those who practice fornication, leave little parts of themselves, sexually, all over the countryside.

Before the Fall, Adam and Eve could walk in the Garden naked and not be ashamed. It is interesting that the first thing Adam and Eve did after they violated their relationship with God was to cover the parts of their bodies used for sexual intimacy. God never intended sex, or even our sexual body parts, to be shameful. The beauty of sex, within a Christian marriage, is there is never any shame in regard to what goes on in their bedroom. Married couples are supposed to have sex and they can both hold their heads high the next morning after engaging in sexual intercourse. In our society, the media and entertainment world have attempted to take shame out of illicit sex to make people feel better about themselves when they violate God's standards. It doesn't work, unless they have become so hardened in their hearts toward God that they have no conscience.

God also created sex to be used in an environment of mutual respect. In a Christian marriage, the man respects the woman by keeping their relationship confidential. He treats his wife as the most important person in the world. And the woman respects the man by showing him honor and resists the temptation to belittle him in any way. The man will never degrade his wife and will seek to meet her needs sexually. The woman will show respect to her husband by not using sex as a tool to manipulate him. Mutual respect is seldom seen in those who practice fornication, since they are engaged in a disrespectful act.

And finally, God designed sexual encounters between a man and wife to be a reflection of their commitment to one another "until death do they part," just as He has made that level of commitment to us. Those who practice fornication are communicating their lack of commitment, by choosing to engage in various sexual exploits, without the benefit of marriage.

Conclusion

There is little that communicates the love of God for humanity more than a marriage between a man and a woman. Satan will do anything he can to destroy marriages. We saw, in a previous chapter, the systematic approach he has used to injure the institution of marriage. In this chapter, I hope you have seen the tactic he takes with individuals to blind them to God's intent for the sexual relationship. If you listen to Satan, you will minimize your view of sex, and worse, you will minimize your view of God.

Heed the words of the apostle Paul and avoid the pitfalls fornication brings. Satan wants to cheapen the best that God has for you. If you have already yielded to Satan's tactics, repent and rebuild your relationship according to God's standards. Honor God with your whole being; body, mind, and spirit.

Study Guide Question

1. What is "*porneia*"?

2. How does dualistic thought affect a person's view of his or her body?

3. Explain why Paul says, "All things are lawful for me."

4. Where is the Holy Spirit when a Christian engages in fornication?

5. How does a Christian's engagement in fornication affect Jesus?

6. How can a Christian show value for their relationship with Jesus?

7. What does Paul tell Christians to do when they face sexual temptation?

8. What is the spiritual danger of fornication?

9. What contractual obligation does the Holy Spirit have towards Christians who purposely involve themselves in fornication?

10. What does Paul tell Christians to do with their body?

11. What hope is there for a person who has already engaged in fornication?

TWENTY FIVE

UNDERSTANDING YOUR VIEW OF MONEY

As members of a society that places a high value on money and possessions, Christians must understand what the Bible says about money and apply these principles to their lives. To fail to do so will potentially isolate them from the Savior, rather than draw them to Him. Money plays a key role in spiritual development. This chapter will compare secular and biblical views of money and how those views impact decisions regarding one's finances.

Secular Worldviews

Secular worldviews of money tend to fall into two major categories. The first of these categories is materialism and the second is the opposite extreme known as asceticism.

Materialism

Materialism is a self-centered approach to finances. Materialism asserts that money provides an avenue for self-fulfillment. Materialism encourages people to get whatever they can, regardless of the discomfort it may cause to others. Materialism exists both in capitalistic societies and socialistic societies. In capitalistic societies, people are told to seek after material possessions at all costs. An old bumper sticker sums up the philosophy well, "He who dies with the most toys wins!" In socialistic societies, the philosophy is that all people should be treated equally and have equal goods. The government is tasked with assuring that everyone is treated in a fair manner, but this seldom occurs in socialistic societies. In most socialistic societies, those who are in governmental positions garner all of the wealth of the country and the masses live in poverty. Both capitalism and socialism are expressions of the secular worldview known as materialism.

The underpinnings of materialism is that the only thing real is the material. If we cannot touch it, see it, or smell it, it has no value. There is no place for God in a materialistic world. God calls for individuals to find their fulfillment in Him. Materialism argues, if there is a God, He is irrelevant to the realities humans face on a daily basis. Materialism says humans determine their own happiness and success and this is measured by what they achieve and accumulate.

Most Christians would not openly admit to embracing the philosophy of materialism, but observing their use of money and fixation on what it can buy, often reveals they have adopted materialism without being aware of it.

There are two specific ways I have observed materialism creeping into the Christian's mindset. The first is the way we accumulate wealth for personal gain without much thought about the conditions of others. Many Christians are so focused on taking care of themselves, they lose focus on generosity towards others. There is no doubt the Bible teaches that we must take care of our own families (See 1 Timothy 5:8), but when we spend all of our resources on ourselves, we fail to obey the clear message of Scripture to take care of poor, especially, when they are a part of the kingdom of God. The apostle John explains it this way, "But if anyone has the world's goods and sees his brother in need, yet closes his heart against him, how does God's love abide in him? Little children, let us not love in word or talk but in deed and in truth" (1 John 3:17-18).

Jesus told a parable that helps us to see His perspective of a balance between taking care of our needs and taking care of the needs of others. In the parable, Jesus describes a farmer who is about to receive his harvest. The farmer is anticipating a plentiful crop, but his barn was not empty from the previous year's harvest. As a result, he decided he was going to build a bigger barn, so he could be a good steward of the crop God had given to him. I imagine, as Jesus' listeners heard Him tell the story, they were impressed with the forethought and stewardship this farmer displayed. How shocked they must have been when they heard Jesus utter these words, "But God said to him, 'Fool! This night your soul is required of you, and the things you have prepared, whose will they be?' So is the one who lays up treasure for himself and is not rich toward God" (Luke 12:20-21).

The point of the story is this man had invested his life in gaining material blessings. He had so much wealth, he had to build a bigger barn. But in a moment, everything he had work for was meaningless. He lost his life and had nothing in eternity to show for it. This is the plight of the person who is materialistic. Instead of being generous with the possessions they have, they hoard them and find pride in the accumulation of great wealth.

Christians must never spend everything they have on themselves. To do so reinforces the materialistic concept that teaches if you work hard and earn your money, you deserve to live in luxury. Materialism creates very hard hearts toward the poor. I am not arguing for socialism or laziness. I am arguing against the notion that we are the source of our blessings, and we can use them without regard to God's desires.

People who are materialistic cringe when the offering plate goes by, when someone rings a bell outside of a store at Christmas time, or when a homeless person asks for money for a cup of coffee or some food. Being materialistic does not necessarily mean a person has a lot of possessions or money. It simply means they are unwilling to let go of the things they do possess.

I am very aware of this type of thinking because for many years I fell into the trap of materialism. My materialism shown like a neon sign one night, a few years back. I would never have admitted my materialistic mindset until that night. I was speaking at a conference. After the evening session, I went out to eat with seven of the other speakers. As we sat in the back of the restaurant decompressing from the evening ministry, a woman walked up to our table and handed each of us a slip of paper. We looked at each other when we read what was written. I'm not quoting exactly, but the essence of the message was, "I am deaf and mute and cannot hold a job. Could you please give me two dollars?" As I read those words I could feel the anger rise up inside of me. I thought to myself, *Who is this woman and why is she interrupting my meal! Why does she think she has the right to beg in the middle of a restaurant? And where is the manager who is allowing this to happen? Can't a guy eat in peace?*

About that time the minister to my right whispered to each of us, "Give me your slips." I was sure he felt the same indignation I was experiencing. I wanted him to wad the slips into a ball and throw them at her, or at least throw them away. But instead, he carefully folded the slips of paper inside a crisp $20 bill. He gently tapped the woman on the shoulder and gave her what she had asked for, plus more.

If I had been angry before, now I was ready to blow my stack. I nearly shouted at him, "What are you doing? She will just bug somebody else! You are encouraging her bad behavior!"

His response was gentle, but convicting. He told me he did not know if she really needed the money. He assured me that if she was scamming us, he was confident God could replace his twenty dollars. But the next words he spoke stabbed my heart like a dagger. He said, "If she actually needs this money, because she is indeed poor, I do not want to stand before God some day and have Him say to me, 'when I was hungry you did not feed Me.'"

(See Matthew 25:41-46.) At that moment I felt as small as an ant, but my eyes had been opened as wide as an owl's. I have never held money as tightly again. Do I continue to struggle with materialism? Yes I do, but I've made significant progress. Much like addicts do not get over their drug addiction in a moment of time, recognizing my materialistic worldview was the first step in my recovery process.

Some acts of generosity can actually be rooted in greed and materialism. On the surface, these acts appear benevolent, but a deeper evaluation reveals the motivation is to gain recognition. Some people give resources to gain a form of immortality.

I am aware of one extremely wealthy individual who didn't have children. As he was moving toward the later years of his life, he began to give away much of his wealth. People and organizations were happy to receive his gifts, but he made one condition on all of his contributions; his name had to be prominently displayed on anything that he donated. He built numerous buildings, for the local university, which all bare his name. He erected a statue of himself in a portion of town which had benefited the most from his giving. Until these objects disintegrate, or are torn down, he will not be forgotten in that city. I cannot judge his motivation for giving, but from an outside observer's perspective, it seems obvious he was attempting purchase a lasting legacy. Gifts that provide a benefit to the giver are not really gifts, thus not truly acts of generosity. Nonetheless, for a person functioning with a materialistic worldview, this man's behavior makes sense.

There's a difference between people who give in order to get recognition, and the person who gives out of a true spirit of generosity. Jesus explained it this way, "But when you give to the needy, do not let your left hand know what your right hand is doing, so that your giving may be in secret. And your Father who sees in secret will reward you" (Matthew 6:3-4). For a truly generous person, God's recognition is enough.

The second way I have seen materialism manifest itself among Christians, without them being aware of the degree that it has entrapped them, is the way they treat other human beings. Being in a university setting, there are natural levels established based on job title, educational background, and years of service. I love to challenge my students by asking them who they show more respect to; the janitor who cleans the toilets at our school or the professor who stands behind the lectern? Even though they would like to say they see both individuals as equal, most of them have to admit they show the professors more respect than they do the janitors, the cafeteria workers, or even the secretarial staff at school. I then take it one step further and ask who they would respect more; a professor or the president of the University. Once again, they had to admit they would find time spent with the president more valuable than time spent with a professor. Then I ask the question, "Why do you see the president, or a professor, as more valuable than the laborers at the school?" The answer always comes back to the educational level a professor has obtained or the position the president has achieved.

The Bible is clear there is no distinction in God's eyes in regard to the value of individuals. He created us all. He loves us all. He died for us all. And He has assigned tasks to us all, based on the gifts and talents He has given to us. There are different roles that people play, and it is true there are responsibilities and benefits that come with the various roles, but people's roles do not increase their value in the eyes of God. (See 1 Corinthians 12). Too many Christians assign value based on achievement rather than on our common humanity. The apostle James chastised Christians who expressed a materialistic view which resulted in ranking people based on accomplishments. He stated,

> My brothers, show no partiality as you hold the faith in our Lord Jesus Christ, the Lord of glory. For if a man wearing a gold ring and fine clothing comes into your assembly, and a poor man in shabby clothing also comes in, and if you pay attention to the one who wears the fine clothing and say, "You sit here in a good place," while you say to the poor man, "You stand over there," or, "Sit down at my feet," have you not then made distinctions among yourselves and become judges with evil thoughts? (James 2:1-4).

Materialism seeks to divide us. The gospel seeks to unite us. Materialism says your value will raise if you earn a college degree. The gospel says you earn a college degree so you can be more effective in ministering to the needs of others. Materialism says you rise in the ranks of power, in an organization, so you can get what you want. The gospel says you rise in the ranks of power, in an organization, so you can help others who have little hope of achieving power. Materialism says you gain fame so you can have the adoration of others. The gospel says you gain fame so you can direct others to Christ. Money, possessions, positions, and educational degrees are not the problem. The problem is a philosophy that argues all I achieve should benefit me rather than be used to fulfill the Christian's purpose in life which is to love God and to love others.

Materialism is nothing new. Examples of materialism can be found among the Christian leaders of the first century and even among Jesus' own disciples. Judas became indignant when Mary poured perfume on Jesus' feet. He claimed his motivation for anger was because the money could have been better used to feed the poor. The Bible narrator inserts an explanation of Judas' real reason for anger. The narrator explains, "He said this, not because he cared about the poor, but because he was a thief, and having charge of the moneybag he used to help himself to what was put into it" (John 12:6). Materialism ran rampant among the preachers of the first century. Paul recognized this tendency and refused to take a salary, even though it was his right to do so. Ironically, his desire to avoid the trap of materialism worked against him in the eyes of the Corinthian church. Some, in the church, felt that he was not as valuable as the preachers who enriched themselves off the people. He had to sternly correct this error in their thinking. (See 2 Corinthians 11:1-15.)

The story of the deaths of Ananias and Sapphira record the account of a husband and wife who were consumed by materialism (Acts 5:1-11). This story butts up against the story of a very generous person; Barnabas (Acts 4:36-37). The positioning of these two stories force the reader to evaluate if they are a generous person, or if they are greedy. The consequences of each posture is not masked in the text.

The ultimate form of Christian materialism is the idea that God exists to meet our needs. It is true God blesses us, loves us, and provides for us. But He provides at His own initiative. God is under no obligation to take care of us. We are not His reason for being. Too many Christians become angry when God does not give them exactly what they want, when they want it, and to the degree to which they want it. We saw some of this thinking explained in the chapter on faith, but here I want to address the root issue; it is materialistic thinking.

People who have a materialistic view of God view Him as a distributor of products. They will negotiate with Him much like they would any other merchant. If they don't get the best deal from Him, they look elsewhere. These people may go to church, but only when it benefits them. They give in the offering, as long as the blessing they receive in return is of greater value.

Some of the greediest Christians I know are not accumulating great monetary wealth. They are hoarding spiritual nuggets to feed their souls, rather than funneling the gifts God has given to them to those who are truly in need. Jesus is not pleased with this mentality. He taught, "Those who are well have no need of a physician, but those who are sick. I have not come to call the righteous but sinners to repentance." (Luke 5:31-32). Christians should be careful not to hoard all of the important spiritual resources, when so many are in real need outside the walls of the church.

Scripture clearly disapproves of selfish living. Jesus instructed His followers to serve God and to serve others. In order to accomplish these goals, one must take the focus off self and place it on others. Anytime one person's pleasure costs another person's dignity or well-being, it is unacceptable to God.

Asceticism

A common reaction, to the repulsion some people feel toward materialism, is to forgo all possessions other than the bare essentials. This approach to money and possessions is called asceticism.

A classic example of asceticism, in recent history, is the Occupy Wall Street Movement which was launched on September 17, 2011. This movement argued it was unjust that 1% of American people possessed the vast majority of the resources, in the United States. People in the Occupy Wall Street movement gathered in downtown New York to protest. They attempted to prove their point by camping out on the streets and living on a bare minimum. The essence of their argument was that possessing great wealth was evil. They argued that instead of these Wall Street tycoons lavishing material luxuries upon themselves and their families, the wealthy should live on very little, and give the rest to those in need around the world.

We see signs of asceticism throughout our culture today. The minimalist's mentality, so often associated with asceticism, argues Americans should reduce oil consumption because others on the planet need these resources. The mantra of the ascetic is that wealthy Americans should drive less miles, in smaller cars, charged by electricity, which is produced by windmills, or solar panels. They argue that they are trying to save the planet, which may be the motivation of some, but a deeper reason many adopt these positions is because innately they believe it is evil to possess something that they do not absolutely need.

Just as the church has fallen prey to materialism on occasion, they have also fallen prey to asceticism. Some church boards refuse to give a pastor a good salary package because they feel it is not a good use of church funds. Many Christians will argue a pastor should not live a luxurious life because it would send the wrong message to non-Christians. What they mean by this is, if a pastor has a nice car, a nice house, and wears nice clothes, it will look like he has bought into materialism. So their answer to this perception is to keep the family humble. It is interesting, the same people, who do not want to pay the pastor a livable salary, will go to their jobs and fight for salary packages which will allow their families to live in the luxury which they want to restrict from their pastor.

The Roman Catholic Church has played a major role in the adoption of the ascetic mindset. The Roman Catholic Church has a two-tier system; the priest and the people (often referred to as the clergy and the laity). The priest is held to a different standard than the people because he is seen as more spiritual. Because the priest is spiritual, he should not care about the material world. In the Roman Catholic Church, the priest is given a meager salary, a parsonage to live in, and a limited clothing allotment. Most priests take a vow of poverty. Roman Catholics patrons are generous with the local church, but the majority of the money they give goes to constructing beautiful buildings, that glorified God, and to outreach efforts such as schools and orphanages.

Asceticism is not a new concept. During the lifetime of Jesus, individuals separated themselves from common society forsaking material possessions in a quest to get closer to God. Consider the life of John the Baptist. He lived in the wilderness, ate locust and honey, wore clothes made of camel hair and was considered spiritual enough to baptize people with little resistance from the religious leaders (Matthew 3:4). If Jesus endorsed the ascetic life, He would have lived it like His cousin John. Jesus lived among the people and enjoyed life, as a normal member of His society. He knew how to party (Luke 5:33; John 2:1-12) and He knew how to pray (Luke 9:28). Jesus did not reject material possessions as inherently evil. He had enough money that His band of followers required the appointment of a treasurer who kept track of the money bag.

Those who truly embrace asceticism restrict a person's ability to be generous. Some of the greatest accomplishments for good, in our world, have been funded by individuals who have gained great wealth. In the United States, we have seen the owners of the Hobby Lobby chain of stores give millions of dollars to educational institutions and other nonprofit organizations. The owner of Microsoft has funded many endeavors that have benefited humanity. And many anonymous donors give out of their own wealth with no desire for recognition.

Just a few years ago, a family showed up on the university campus where I teach. The development office knew the family was coming to fund a scholarship, but we didn't know how much they were going to provide. By the time they left that day, they had given our students $2 million in scholarship money. In addition, they spontaneously provided another $5 million towards a building that they were told about that day. Since then, this anonymous family has given millions more, but they could not have given so generously if they had chosen to live an ascetic lifestyle.

Materialism argues that possessions are good and their accumulation are the scale on which a person's worth should be judged. Asceticism argues possessions are evil and the truly spiritual person will reject them. Both of these extremes neglect the fact God created all things, and He is the giver of all good gifts. James tells us, "Every good gift and every perfect gift is from above, coming down from the Father of lights, with whom there is no variation or shadow due to change" (James 1:17). It is wrong to take credit for gifts which God provided, but it is equally as wrong to say the gifts God provides are evil. The extremes resulting from dualism restrict some Christians from being able to enjoy what God has provided and lead others to live a self-reliant life.

God blesses us so we can bless others. Beware of those who say you should be ashamed because you have money in the bank. But also beware of those who try to make you feel giving away that money, to those in need, is foolishness. Christians must never be sucked into believing their value is determined by what they have, or what they have accomplished. The value of a Christian's life is determined by God; the giver of life.

Biblical Worldview

Believers should embrace a balanced worldview regarding money which leads to a life of simplicity. Simplicity requires believers to live within their means. So what does simplicity look like practically? Let's look at six principles concerning the simple life which will help you to live in financial freedom. The inspiration for some of these thoughts were derived from Richard Foster's *Celebration of Discipline*.

First, a simple life is not determined by the amount of money you have. A few years ago, there was a television show called "The Simple Life." Two children, of famous and wealthy parents, were taken to a setting each week which was outside of their comfort zone. These women, who were used to carrying their dogs around in their purses, were forced to do tasks such as slopping the pigs on a farm. The viewer came away from watching those shows feeling there was a distinct difference between the haves and have-nots in our society. Unfortunately the title of the show gave us a misconception of what the simple life really is. You can have a simple life and be a billionaire. You can have a simple life and live on minimum wage. The simple life is not determined by the amount of money you have, but by the attitude you have in regard to your possessions.

Second, simple living is a life where we possess things rather than things possessing us. You can tell if something possesses you if you can't live without it. A rule of the simple life is, "If you think you can't live without something, you should probably live without that thing." If your attitude and perspective on life is controlled by what you have or don't have, then those items have control over you. The only thing that should have control over you, as a Christian, is the Holy Spirit. If you cannot walk away from a material object or a bank account, if Jesus asks you to do so, those possessions have too much power in your life.

The New Testament illustrates this truth when Jesus told a rich young man, who asked what he must do to follow Him, that he had to give away all that he had (Luke 18:22). Jesus didn't do this to demonstrate possessions are evil. He did it to illustrate the power the possessions had over this individual's life. If the man was not willing to cast off the controlling power of his possessions, then Jesus could never really be the Lord of his life. After the man left, Jesus said, "How difficult it is for those who have wealth to enter the kingdom of God! For it is easier for a camel to go through the eye of a needle than for a rich person to enter the kingdom of God" (Luke 18:24-25).

Third, simple living allows us to enjoy what we have without wishing we had something someone else has or feeling self-conscious because we have more possessions than the average person. Simple living requires contentment. From the time of the Old Testament Law through all of the teaching in the New Testament, there are mandates for God's followers to not covet or envy what someone else has. (See Exodus 20:17; Romans 1:29; Galatians 5:19-21; 1 Timothy 6:4; Titus 3:3; and 1 Peter 2:1-2.)

Envy shows a dissatisfaction with God and His treatment of us. We will never enjoy what we have, if we are always looking at what someone else has. There will always be somebody who possesses something newer, shinier, and faster than what we possess. But no matter how little we think we have, what we own is newer, shinier, and faster than what somebody else possesses. It really is all a matter of perspective. If people have an envious attitude, they will always feel shortchanged, and they will never think they have enough.

Simple living allows me to be happy with what I have and use it joyfully. If God chooses to give me more, I will receive it. If someone else receives a blessing, I will rejoice with them as well. The apostle Paul taught that we should rejoice with those who rejoice and be sad with those who are sad (Romans 12:15). Most of us do better with being compassionate with those who are hurting, than celebrating with those who get blessings beyond what we personally possess.

Fourth, people who embrace the simple life gain possessions for their usefulness, not for their status. People are inherently insecure. Many people try to cover up their insecurities by purchasing items that shout to others that we have value. Instead of buying a purse from a department store that will withstand the rigors of life at a reasonable price, a person buys a $5000 purse that has a recognizable design that says "I have wealth." What is the difference between a T-shirt that has no logo and a shirt that has a logo of a famous company? About $25, but both shirts provide the same warmth and coverage. And why do many people feel it is important to have a Macintosh computer and name brand shoes?

Please don't get me wrong. Simple living says if you need the applications that are run on a Macintosh computer, in order to accomplish the tasks you need to do, by all means buy the Macintosh computer. But if all you're going to do is send emails and surf the web, then a much less expensive PC should do. The same with the high-priced athletic shoe. If you are an athlete whose feet take a pounding on a regular basis, buy the best shoe possible. But if all you are doing is walking around the campus, simple living says purchase a shoe which will provide your foot support, without making a fashion statement. When you buy items for status, you are saying "Look at me, I am a success." Simple living allows you to use your money wisely, realizing God has already deemed you a success.

Fifth, simple living helps us to appreciate creation. Spending time in nature helps individuals avoid the trappings of consumerism. Life has changed dramatically as income has increased in our nation. There was a day when a kid would pick up a stick and find ways to play with it for hours, as his/ her imagination ran unabated. Today, children are not happy unless they have an iPad in their hands, or they are playing an expensive videogame. You can walk into most homes, which have children living there, and find more toys in the house than the child has opportunity to play with. God's creation has lost its appeal for many children. Buying fewer toys and taking time to go to the park will provide much more fulfillment for children than the most expensive gadget.

Adults have also lost an appreciation for creation. When was the last time you went for a walk simply for the pleasure of looking at the sights and smelling the natural fragrances God provided in His creation? And when was the last time you stood gazing at the stars on a clear evening? Too many of us depend on what technology can provide to bring pleasure to our lives. Instead of having a picnic in the park, we insist on going to an expensive restaurant that brings very little pleasure, compared to the cost. Simple living allows us to take a step back from all the advertising that shouts at us and realize there is so much to be appreciated which has already been provided by God that can be ours at no cost whatsoever.

Sixth, the simple life permits the Christian to enjoy the blessings of God without guilt, but disallows self-centered greed. The life of simplicity need not require the Christian to forgo modern conveniences such as automobiles and computers. Rather, the life of simplicity recognizes that technology has provided tools that aid the Christian in accomplishing the tasks God has called them to undertake.

Conclusion

Jesus has called Christians to abundant living (John 10:10). Being a contented Christian does not mean denial of desires such as clothing, housing, and food. Using money to meet the basic needs of life is not a sign of selfishness. Finding the balance between using money for personal needs and pleasure, and giving money to meet the needs of others, is the key to being good stewards of the resources God places in the Christian's hands.

Study Guide Questions

1. What is materialism?

2. What is the underpinning of materialism?

3. How does materialism impact a person's generosity?

4. Why does God bless Christians with finances?

5. When are acts of generosity actually greed?

6. What does the way people show respect to others reveal about their level of materialism?

7. How does our attitude toward God reveal our level of materialism?

8. What is asceticism?

9. How is asceticism displayed in today's culture?

10. How has asceticism crept into the church?

11. What was Jesus' view of asceticism?

12. What six principles does the author give concerning the simple life?

TWENTY SIX

THE CHRISTIAN AND PERSONAL DEBT

The Bible speaks clearly on the issue of debt. Christians are not to be co-signers (Proverbs 6:1; 17:18; 22:26). A co-signer is a person who secures a loan for someone who cannot secure a loan based on their own credit. This is a dangerous practice because if the person who is taking the loan fails to pay, the co-signer is obligated to pay back the loan. The Bible is also straight forward about taking out personal loans. Paul tells the Roman Christians to not be borrowers, so they can freely do whatever God calls them to do without concern about financial obligations (Romans 13:8). Some theologians believe the debt, referred to in Romans 13, is debt that cannot be repaid. This may be true, but any debt that prevents a Christian from being generous must be rejected, based on the law of love.

A few years ago, the power that debt has to keep an individual from being generous was exposed in my church home. The pastor was promoting a very important need and discovered, even though the congregation members wanted to give, they couldn't because of their level of personal debt. Many of the people were living from paycheck to paycheck. Most were giving a tithe of their income, but they could not stretch themselves beyond their current giving without jeopardizing their family's well-being. Later in this chapter, I will tell you the story of how this church helped people find margins in their finances, so they could become the generous people God desired for them to be.

So why do so many Christians continue to violate Scripture by burying themselves in debt or stretching themselves to the point they cannot be generous? Let's explore this topic and hopefully discover ways to break the stronghold of debt in the lives of so many Christians and churches today.

Understanding Contentment

"Keep your lives free from the love of money and be content with what you have, because God has said, 'Never will I leave you; never will I forsake you'" (Hebrews 13:5).

Hebrews 13:5 used to be my favorite verse. Growing up in a poor family, my view of wealth was limited. By the time I was in my mid-20s, I held my Master's degree, was teaching full-time at a high school, and was pastoring a small church in California. Compared to my parents, I was making outstanding money. Although I was only renting a duplex, I owed no one anything, and I even had a little money in the bank. I remember pulling up in front of our duplex and parking my car. As I sat there, I thought how wonderful it was to be as contented as I was with life. I was married to a beautiful woman. I had two outstanding children. And I loved my work. In addition to this, I was in a financial condition that would be envied by many. I remember sitting there wondering why everyone else could not be as contented as I was.

Fast-forward to the year I turned 30 years-old. I was convinced my time in California was coming to an end, so I resigned my position at the church and did not sign my contract at the high school for the coming year. I packed up my family, and we moved to Missouri. Upon getting there, I went to the admissions office of the seminary I was going to attend. I asked the recruiter where I should rent a home in the city. He took out a map and drew a circle around a section of town I was not familiar with. He indicated it would be a great place to bring up my kids. I took his advice and leased a three bedroom house with a beautiful front yard, and a large fenced backyard for the kids to play. When I signed a one-year lease, I thought little about the cost because, compared to California, I was getting a steal. It didn't take me long to realize I should have done a bit of research before committing myself to this obligation.

Being a rather cocky individual at this point in my life, I thought I would easily find a good job that paid well and had excellent benefits. After a couple of weeks of searching, I got desperate and went to my alma mater to see if there were any jobs I could do there to hold me over until something better was obtained. I took a job that paid minimum wage, with no benefits. One day as I was working, I began to calculate my weekly wage times four and realized if I spent every cent I earned that month to pay the lease, I would still come up short.

Desperation set in. I remember standing in front of the picture window in the living room that overlooked the beautiful front lawn. I began to yell at God, much like the children of Israel yelled at Him in the Wilderness (Numbers 14:2). I asked Him why He had brought my family to Missouri, when we had been doing so well in California. Hebrews 13:5 had lost its appeal for me. I was the epitome of a discontented person.

Just about the time I was done with my rant, I saw a rabbit jumping across the recently mowed grass. God spoke to my heart. He asked me who I thought took care of the rabbit. Somewhat embarrassed, I told Him that He did. God then reminded me He could take care of me and my family, as well. It was at that moment I shifted my focus in regard to Hebrews 13:5. No longer did I pride myself on being content because of the provisions that I possessed. Now I began to recognize my contentment was in the fact Jesus said He would never leave me or forsake me, regardless of my circumstances. A few weeks later, my wife and I both found jobs that paid well and had excellent benefits.

God knew money and possessions would be a challenge for humanity. The Bible is filled with information that provides God's perspective on money. In the Gospels, Jesus spoke more about money than anything else, other than the kingdom of God. All told, there are over 2000 verses in the Bible that address the subject of finances or possessions. Nearly all passages that refer to contentment in Scripture, identify money or possessions as a potential cause of dissatisfaction. (See 1 Timothy 6:7-8; Hebrews 13:5; Philippians 4:11-13; 2 Corinthians 12:9-10; Luke 3:14; and Luke12:15.)

The first narrative in Scripture reveals the contest between seeking God and seeking possessions. Adam and Eve were in a beautiful garden where they had every conceivable need met. They had ongoing conversations with God, plenty of food, and didn't even have to worry about wearing clothes. Much like in the New Heavens and New Earth, the animals got along with each other and evil had no influence.

It is inconceivable what happened when a serpent approached Eve. He told her she may indeed have most everything, but she did not have everything. He pointed to trees that were off-limits to her and her husband. He challenged her to consider the character of God and His goodness in light of this new enlightened discovery. Eve became dissatisfied with the provisions God had given to her. What should have been clearly enough to make anyone content became a source of bitterness in the heart of Eve.

Eve took the bait Satan had dangled before her. See, Satan understood the nature of sin because it was his lack of contentment with his position in heaven that caused his separation from God. Unfortunately, Eve was seduced by the serpent's craftiness and she decided she could no longer trust God with her well-being. She took her welfare into her own hands and ate of the forbidden tree and convinced her husband to join her in this act of defiance. Both Adam and Eve forfeited the best God had to offer because they chose to indulge their desires rather than trust and obey God. (See Genesis 3:1-24.)

The essence of sin is a lack of contentment and trust in God. If we cannot trust God, we will never obey Him. If we do not obey Him, then we don't really view Him as our ultimate superior. The Bible teaches if you love Him, you will obey Him.

Jesus answered him, 'If anyone loves me, he will keep my word, and my Father will love him, and we will come to him and make our home with him. Whoever does not love me does not keep my words. And the word that you hear is not mine but the Father's who sent me" (John 14:23-24).

A person's lack of love for God is rooted in the person's distrust of Him. Each one of us must put our trust in something. We will trust God and be content with what He has given to us, or we will trust possessions and seek them. This is why Jesus said, "No one can serve two masters, for either he will hate the one and love the other, or he will be devoted to the one and despise the other. You cannot serve God and money" (Matthew 6:24).

Avoid Debt

The debt level in the United States reveals the dysfunctional way people use money and possessions. Consider your own situation. You may discover you waste a good portion of the money God provides to you. If a person could simply stop wasting money, they might discover God has already provided all the money they need.

As I mentioned, I have struggled with the love of money in my past. After moving to Missouri, I accumulated a great deal of debt. Then I was confronted with the truth that I'm trying to teach you in this chapter. I never seemed to have enough money, even though I was making a good salary. I begrudged my employer because my raises did not seem significant, but the truth is, no matter how much I would have been given, it still would not have been enough. I had an insatiable desire to impress others and ended up racking up credit card debt in an attempt to quench my thirst.

I began to study the subject of money, as part of one of my doctoral research papers. The author, of one of the books I was reading, suggested we waste 30% of our income. I thought this was unbelievable until I did a quick examination of how my wife and I used our money. I discovered we had been spending around $250-$300 a month eating at restaurants.

We did this for convenience because we both worked, but it really was unnecessary. My wife and I discussed this misuse of resources and chose to make a very hard decision. We limited ourselves to $25 a month to eat out. Immediately, we had given ourselves a raise of $225 a month or nearly $3000 a year, without asking my employer for a dime. We began to look at other areas where we were spending money mindlessly. We reduced waste and were able to use that money to pay off the bills we had accumulated over the years. It took us nearly 10 years of tight control on our finances to pay off all of our debts. If I had learned this lesson of wasteful spending earlier in my life, it would have given my family the freedom to be generous, and to not live under the constant stress financial mismanagement brings.

Accumulating debt reveals a basic dissatisfaction with what God has provided and shows a lack of trust regarding God's care for us. Christians, who use someone else's money to buy something they can't afford, declare that God has not provided what they need so they must put their trust in others to satisfy their desires. When Christians do this, they are denying Jesus' promise to meet all of our needs, if we will seek God's kingdom and His righteousness (Matthew 6:33).

Beware of Credit Cards

The advent of credit cards has changed the way we view God and money. Before the credit card, other than stealing from others, people could not easily gain possessions they could not afford. During those days, in order to get a loan, you had to go to the bank, fill out a lengthy application, and wait on the loan committee to determine if you could get the money you desired. It wasn't like today, when if you want a taco and can't afford it, you can go to the restaurant and pull out a credit card to make the purchase. My mother would never have thought of going to the bank to secure a loan to buy a two dollar fast-food item. People today think nothing of putting fast food on a credit card, until the bill arrives and they discover the balance is more than they can pay off that month. Many people end up paying for their two dollar fast-food item for many months, in addition to the interest that accrues.

If credit cards did not make loans so easy, or if Christians could learn to be satisfied and say "No" to their late-night cravings, much of the debt that entraps Christians could be avoided. My financial woes all began when I couldn't afford a Christmas present for my wife the first year we were married. Instead of limiting my purchases to what I could afford, like my friend next door, I went to a department store and bought a beautiful present for my wife by opening a revolving credit card account. I set an unrealistic expectation, on the part of my wife that year. I taught her we could have nice things, even when we couldn't afford them. She never required these gifts, but I knew if I purchased them, she would enjoy them. I never really let her know the mounting credit card balances were causing me to be anxious about our financial situation. Credit cards were not my friend and, in all likelihood, they will not be your friend either.

Credit cards have had another ill effect on the Christian community. Before credit cards existed, Christians relied on God and fellow believers when they lacked the basic necessities of life. It was not uncommon when a person lacked clothes, food, or money to pay the rent, to begin praying earnestly. More times than not, God would answer their prayer by sending an individual to their home with the items needed. Sometimes there would be a knock on the door and by the time the person answered it, a bag of groceries or clothes or even an envelope with money would appear. Sometimes the generous person would be standing there with the gifts, and at other times they had walked away anonymously. The beauty of these occurrences was that the lack one person experienced refocused their family on their reliance on God and it gave another person the joy of reaching out to a fellow Christian in love. Credit cards have removed the need to pray until the debt load is so heavy that people in the local church don't have the resources or willingness to rescue them.

Early in the chapter, I mentioned a church that had discovered its people were so financially stressed they were not able to be generous to meet the challenge of the pastor. The pastor's wife was not satisfied with this condition. Her heart broke for the people deeply in debt in the congregation. She realized before the church, which she and her husband led, could reach out to the community, they had to figure out a way to reach out to the people within their own congregation. She came up with a plan and called it "Eradicate Poverty." Her plan was relatively simple but considering the magnitude of the problem it seemed impossible. Her plan was to have individuals who were stressed financially to sit down with financial experts in the congregation and learn the principles of budgeting, and the importance of prioritizing their responsibilities to God. During this time, those who needed this assistance would be required to be faithful in their tithing and submit to a tight budget, which was constructed by the financial advisor. In return for the financially strapped individual's effort to become financially responsible, the church promised to provide financial resources to assist them in paying off a significant portion of their debt.

This was a grand idea, but how would the church pay for it. Once again, the pastor's wife had a plan. During the early days of the plan, the congregation was challenged to bring offerings and to lay them on the altar throughout the church service. The envelopes were gathered and the money was used to assist these families who are learning to get control of their finances. After a while, there was little mention of the need for money to be donated, but people continue, to this day, bringing money to the altar to help others.

I have watched many families go to the stage and receive sizable checks to pay off their loans, after successfully completing the required process. But more remarkable were the lives being transformed by learning to use finances in a responsible way, according to God's priorities. Incidentally, the church offerings increased dramatically, as more and more people gained the ability to be generous, which was their desire all along. It is my prayer those reading this chapter will never have to go through a program like this, but if you do, don't be too proud to ask for the assistance.

There are some financial experts who argue Christians should not own a credit card. There is good reason for this opinion. Over 90% of individuals who carry credit cards use them improperly. But credit cards can be an excellent financial tool, if used correctly. If an individual is able to pay the total balance on their credit card statement each month, then the use of a credit card shows a great deal of wisdom. Using someone else's money for a month allows you to enjoy an extra month's interest on your own money and gain the additional benefits that often come with the use of a credit card. But be very sure you can pay off your bill each month because missing just one month will wipe away most of the benefits you have gained through its use, due to the extremely high interest rates associated with most cards.

Learn to Say No

Marketers have two primary responsibilities in a capitalistic society. The first is admirable. The marketer explains how a product can be used to help people to better their lives. The second, in my opinion, is less honorable. This task is to make the consumer feel they cannot live without purchasing the product. To do this, they must convince the consumer to be dissatisfied with what they currently possess. If the marketer cannot convince the consumer to buy the product, then the marketer will be replaced or the company they represent will go out of business. Fortunately, there are Christian marketers who focus their attention on the first task and do it well. But it is very important for Christians to not be seduced by marketing campaigns which attempt to separate them from their money through dissatisfaction. Remember, the key to living a simple life is to be content with what God has given you. The key to financial disaster is to always be on a quest for more.

Those who seek to separate you from your money is not limited to marketers. Some preachers will seduce Christians into believing they should not be content with the size of their bank account. They promise to share secrets that will force God to give them what they want, if they will just give more money to the preacher. Do not be seduced by religious charlatans who play on your financial desperation. When we give to God, from a motivation to receive more based on our investment, this is not generosity; it is greed.

Sometimes you have to say "No" to yourself at the most inconvenient time. I learned how difficult it was to say "No" to myself, just as I had started to take the turn toward financial responsibility. I was teaching a course, at the college, which required me to help my students understand how to use money in an effective fashion. One day, I was explaining to them that it was unwise to go into debt for depreciable items, like automobiles. At the time, my wife and I owned two vehicles. They were both old, but they were both paid off.

After classes that day, I drove home in our Pontiac Bonneville and parked in front of our house. The car had around 229,000 miles on the odometer, so it had served us well. As I pulled the car to a stop, I heard an unfamiliar noise. I got out of the vehicle and orange fluid engulfed my feet. I quickly discovered my engine had rusted from the inside out. There was no need to call a mechanic. Our beloved Bonneville had died. All that was left to do was call the junkyard to come haul it away.

I remember going into the house and telling my wife that she would have to drive me to school the next day. I shared with her my plan to go to a car lot on the weekend to purchase a different car. She agreed to go with me and pick out a vehicle. Almost immediately upon sharing my plan with my wife, I felt the conviction of the Holy Spirit concerning what I had told my students about a Christian and depreciable debt. He asked me if I was willing to trust Him with my vehicle needs, or if I was going to go out and spend money I didn't have. I returned to my wife and told her what I had just heard from the Holy Spirit. I explained to her that if I was going to yield to the Holy Spirit, and be a person of integrity, she would have to take me to work and pick me up until He provided a different vehicle. She agreed to do so.

I wish I could tell you God provided a car the next week, or even the next month. My wife ended up driving me to work and picking me up for over a year. During that time, we saved as much money as we could. After we had accumulated $4500, I suggested it was time for us to begin looking to see what we could buy with that amount of money. I don't know if it was a midlife crisis, or just the fact I had never owned a convertible, but I set my sights on buying an old Mazda Miata. One day I drove by a private car lot and saw the car of my dreams. They were asking a little less than the $4500 we had saved for the car. We were able to pay for car, title, and taxes without incurring debt. I still have the vehicle, nearly a decade later. The car has caused me almost no problems during this time. I wonder sometimes if God gave me a wonderful vehicle, which has stood the test of time, because I was willing to wait and trust Him, even when it would've been easier to go into debt, to satisfy my perceived need in an unwise manner.

Investment vs Debt

The subject of debt has great relevance to young adults in a private university like the one I teach in. They often feel directed by God to attend the university, but do not have the means to pay their bill through personal savings, grants, and scholarships. Some students make poor choices and take out unreasonable amounts of student loans. Others use responsible calculations and take out loans they will be able to pay back once they get a job. But I have often been asked how a Christian University can justify offering loans, if God is against debt.

Some borrowing for school can be considered an investment, if the projected income from a vocation the degree prepares the student for will cover the debt upon leaving school. Most estimates suggest a person with a college degree will earn 25% to 40% more than their high school counterpart. Young adults must use wisdom whenever they apply for school loans. Preparing for a ministry they cannot afford to perform, due to a heavy debt load, will reveal the foolishness of their actions. A student preparing to be a medical doctor or a business person can invest much more through the use of loans than a student preparing to be a missionary or a youth pastor. Wisdom is called for when students request student loans.

There are other times in a person's life that taking a loan is an investment, rather than a debt. I remember when my wife and I purchased our first house for $69,000. My family lived in the house for 12 years. We sold the house for $104,000. After real estate fees, we made about $30,000 which represented a gain of about 5% per year on our investment; plus we got to live in the house virtually free, during that time. We could have decided to wait to buy a house until we had the cash to pay for it, and this would have been okay. But, if we had done so, we would have lost the ability to earn a profit and would still have had to pay for a place to live. Only on rare occasions will real estate not turn a profit, given time. By contrast, unless you buy a collector automobile, every car purchased for personal use will depreciate from the moment you drive it off the lot.

During biblical times, it was not uncommon for a person to borrow "seed money." This money was used to buy the seed necessary to plant their fields. It was a reasonable expectation that the seed would bring a harvest which would be used to pay back the loan, provide for the farmers families' needs, as well as provide seed for the next year. Farmers unwilling to borrow to plant their fields, after a bad yield the previous year, would have shown a lack of wisdom.

If there is a reasonable expectation for a positive return on the money you borrow, it is an investment. The biblical instruction to avoid debt refers to buying today what you can't afford, simply because you can't delay your gratification.

Solving Your Debt Problem

People deeply entrenched in debt often believe if they could win the lottery and pay off all their debt, then everything would be better. Getting out of debt is not the answer to the "debt problem." Many, who have struggled to get out of debt, find themselves back in debt quickly, if they have not dealt with the root problem. Paul teaches the love of money is at the root of the problem (1 Timothy 6:10). Loving the pleasure possessions bring, rather than finding one's satisfaction in Christ, will result in perpetual spending and debt. Money and possessions make promises they cannot fulfill. Instead of using money as God intends, those who love money attempt to embrace it as the source of contentment.

My own life is a testimony of how the love of money can nearly destroy you. Twice in my life, I got completely out of debt. Each time I found myself entrenched again. It was not a desire to own many great things that entrapped me. Rather it was my love of the way I felt when others thought that I had more than I actually had. I also loved the appreciation I received as a result of my generosity. When I went out to eat with my friends, I would pick up the bill for everyone at the table so I could see the smiles on their faces. I have to admit, I also wanted them to know I was doing better than my parents had done financially; even though most of them didn't even know my parents.

When I selected a house for my family to live in, instead of buying or renting an average house in an average neighborhood, I would buy or rent the cheapest house in the most expensive area so my kids could go to the wealthy schools and be perceived as being part of that socioeconomic class. Ironically it backfired because my kids never had the luxuries expected of individuals who lived in those neighborhoods. And I always wanted to see the smiles on the faces of my wife and children on their birthdays and Christmas, so I would use credit to appease my addiction to pleasing others. It got to the point in my life that I actually hated Christmas, not because of the Christ of Christmas, but because of the consumerism of Christmas I had bought into.

Thankfully, I am in the process of being freed from my love of money. But the secret to getting out of debt is not getting out of debt. Just as a person who violates God's principles regarding sex needs to address his/her brokenness, the first step for me was to recognize my brokenness. It was not until I realized I was trying to escape the shame I felt as a child who grew up in poverty that I could begin to find freedom in the arena of finances.

Conclusion

It is my hope you will learn the lessons of contentment much earlier than I did, and you will not suffer the consequences of loving money and putting your trust in it, rather than loving God and putting your trust in Him. It is impossible to serve both God and money. Neither will share its affection. It is my prayer you will join Joshua when he said, "But as for me and my house, we will serve the LORD" (Joshua 24:15). When you do, you will experience freedom in all areas of your life, including in your finances.

Study Guide Questions

1. What does the Bible say about borrowing or becoming a co-signer on a loan?

2. According to the author, what is the secret to living contently?

3. What is the definition of debt?

4. What does debt reveal about a person's understanding of God?

5. What is the difference between a good use of a credit card and a bad use of one?

6. What does the author suggest is the easiest way to get a pay raise?

7. What are two goals of a marketer in our society?

8. How can a Christian stay out of financial trouble?

9. What is the difference between debt and an investment?

10. Why is getting out of debt not the answer to a person's money problems?

TWENTY SEVEN

A BIBLICAL APPRAOACH TO PERSONAL FINANCE

As with all gifts God provides, Christians must be good stewards of the financial resources entrusted to them. Christians must come to grips with four key areas regarding the use of money: (1) debt, (2) accumulation, (3) giving, and (4) spending. I have dedicated an entire chapter to debt, due to the amount of material to cover, so I will use this chapter to address the other three areas.

Christians and Accumulation

The Bible clearly declares Christians must provide for their families (1 Timothy 5:8). But, Jesus taught that accumulation, based on greed, results in personal downfall (Luke 12:16-21). The task of the Christian concerning savings and possessions is to determine the balance between responsible accumulation and greed. Unfortunately, the Bible does not give us a definitive number to help us determine when we have accumulated enough.

Much of what factors into individuals finding a balanced approach to the accumulation of money is their view of the nature of money. Those who believe money is good and a sign of God's blessing will tend to believe a Christian should not limit the amount of money they accumulate, as long as a portion of their money is being used in a generous fashion. Those who feel money is evil believe it is something they need to control, so it does not control them. They would tend to argue Christians should accumulate just enough to get by and then give the rest away. They would say they trust God for their future. It is the people who feel money is neutral that have the real dilemma in determining how much accumulation is appropriate for a believer. People who see money as neutral understand money can be used for good or for evil. They have to search their own heart to determine if they are greedy people, who will use the accumulated wealth inappropriately, or generous people, who will follow God's direction when He tells them to give some of their accumulated wealth away.

There are a number of principles a Christian should consider when thinking about accumulation of wealth. The first is tied to the expectation that Christians will take care of their families. I'm writing from a father's perspective when I say a Christian man must think about the future welfare of his children. He must make financial decisions before an emergency arises, and he is no longer around to care for his family.

In 2017, the average cost of bringing up a child, from birth to age 18 was $233,610. This number will increase each year going forward, but let's use this number for our purposes. If you have two children in preschool, and you were to die unexpectedly, someone would have to pick up the $450,000 it would cost to get those two children through high school. Assuming your wife does not have somebody she plans to marry in the next few days after you pass away, she will need assistance providing resources she had come to count on coming from your income while you were alive.

For our purposes, let's say you made the average salary in America of $50,000 per year. We will remove the portion that would have been set aside for the children, which is roughly $26,000, leaving a gap of $24,000. Your wife is unlikely to get a $24,000 a year raise upon your death, so this gap must be made up. Once again for our purposes, let's assume she spends the next 10 years bringing up the children, as a single mom. Over that 10 years, she would need $240,000 to be able to maintain her lifestyle, without considering inflation.

So how can a man make sure his wife and children are taken care of financially, in the event of his untimely death? He can either pray someone in the church will hand her a check for $700,000, or he can buy life insurance, for at least that amount to cover his responsibilities. If you factor in the cost of higher education, if he thinks he would have assisted his children with their college education if he had been alive, it is not unreasonable for this young man to take out a term life insurance policy for $1 million. In the illustration I just gave, the million dollar life insurance policy can be reduced each year by $25,000 and get the necessary benefit needed to take care of his family, if that is the desire of his wife. If the wife is bringing in a sizable portion of the family income, it would be wise for her to have a term life insurance policy as well. I once heard a person jokingly say he dropped his life insurance because he wanted his death to be a real tragedy. A Christian father, who loves his family, will not want to leave his family to face two tragedies upon his death.

On the other end of life's journey is planning for retirement. Most young adults don't give a great deal of thought to their retirement years. This is really unfortunate. The greatest impact on your retirement future can be made when you are young, due to the principle of compound interest. Let's look at an example of how compound interest works and the power of time.

For our illustration let's put $10,000 one time in the bank at 5% interest. We will let it sit there, without adding to it. If we wait until we are 55 years old to deposit the money, and it sits there until we are at a retirement age of 65, our $10,000 will become $16,470.09 providing us a gain of $6470.09. If we had shown a little more wisdom, and put the $10,000 in the bank when we're 45, at the same interest rate, our $10,000 will become $27,126.40 providing us a gain of $17,126.40 or nearly an extra $11,000. If we are really on top of things, and put our $10,000 in the bank, at the same interest rate when we are 35 years old, at retirement we will have $44,677.44 providing us a gain of $34,677.44 or nearly doubling the result by investing 10 years sooner. Now let's assume that we are extremely wise and we put the $10,000 in the bank when we are 25 years old, at the same interest rate. At retirement our $10,000 will become $73,584.17 or an increase of $63,584.17, once again nearly doubling what we would get if we wait until we are 35 and quadrupling what we would get if we wait until we are 45 and nearly a ten times yield over what we would receive if we waited until we are 55 to put the $10,000 in the bank. It doesn't cost any more to put the money in the bank when you 25 than it does when you 55, but you can see the power time has in determining your future financial situation.

I used 5%, which historically is a low percentage rate on long-term savings accounts. I also used $10,000 that was stagnant, rather than a typical retirement plan where you add more money each month, throughout your life. If you start early in your retirement planning, you can be a very wealthy individual upon retirement using the exact same amount of money as someone who gets a very late start and tries to catch up. It is wise to maximize the money God has placed in your hands, through the use of compound interest.

Jesus' parable of the talents (Matthew 25:15-30) demonstrates His perspective on being a good steward with the resources He has given to you. There can be many interpretations of what Jesus was communicating through this parable, but He used a monetary illustration to show how it was normal practice for individuals to seek to be good stewards of resources. It is likely, no matter what else Jesus may have been referring to, His underlying assumption was God expects people to be good stewards over all the resources He gives to them, including their finances.

The motivation behind one's desire to accumulate wealth determines the morality of his/her decision to accumulate wealth. Christians who see the purpose of money as a vehicle to meet their basic needs, plan for the future, and then to help others demonstrate a positive motive for accumulation. If Christians view the accumulation of wealth as a way to free them from reliance on God, and others within the body of Christ, the motive for accumulation is negative. Accumulation of money should never move a Christian away from dependency on God.

A person may wonder how accumulation of money can move a person away from dependency on God. Consider the characteristics of money and what people perceive money having the ability to do. Many people believe if they have money, they have security. The Scripture teaches us our security must be found in our relationship with God. It is only in Him that we can have confidence (Isaiah 32:17; Ephesians 3:12; Philippians 4:13).

Some people will argue money can provide freedom. To some extent this is true. If we have unlimited financial resources, we can pick up and go where we want to go, do what we want to do, and live in luxury, if we desire to do so. We no longer have to rely on the provisions of God to live abundantly. Often, when we have great wealth, we do not think of God as often as we would if we lived in poverty. The Bible is clear that true freedom can only be found through our relationship with Jesus Christ (John 8:36; 2 Corinthians 3:17; Galatians 5:1, 13) and it is God who provides for our every need (Psalm 81:6; 84:11; Proverbs 10:3; Malachi 3:10; Matthew 6:33; Philippians 4:19).

Others will suggest money is the source of power. People with money tend to be given positions which allow them to make decisions that impact their lives, as well as the life of others. Many wealthy individuals begin to believe the lie that says they deserve to be in positions of power because they have earned it. But the Bible teaches it is God who sets up kings, and God who brings them down (Daniel 2:21; John 19:11; Romans 13:1-2). No amount of money can raise a person to power unless God allows it to take place.

These are just a few examples of the ways accumulation of money creates a danger for Christians to reduce their dependency on God. But money is not the real issue. The real issue is what the Christian believes about the money. Having a great deal of money does not preclude a person from being a dedicated Christian. The Bible portrays Barnabas as an outstanding Christian brother, yet he had possessions which he used to assist the fledgling group of believers in Jerusalem (Acts 4:32-37).

Christians should predetermine how much money they will need to fulfill the ministry God has called them to accomplish, care for their families, and how much money they will need in their retirement years. Christians should not feel they have to cut corners when it comes to their families and their future financial security. There is nothing wrong with enjoying the fruits of one's labor. But it is important to know how much a person will actually need. The person can then set this as a goal. Once the goal is met, the Christian must be willing to give the excess away. It is amazing how God provides for people who are willing to be funnels of His love. Taking time to determine one's accumulation goals, under the guidance of the Holy Spirit, will help a believer avoid falling into the trap of always wanting more.

Christians and Giving

The key to successful Christian stewardship is giving. If a person does not have a generous heart, stewardship will be replaced with an ownership mindset. It must be remembered a steward takes care of someone else's resources. If the owner of those resources chooses to give a portion of those resources away, a steward will be faithful to execute the wishes of the owner. But if Christians believe they own the resources in their possession, they are less likely to listen to God when He instructs them to release finances into the hands of others.

When a Christian gives money away, the power of money loses its grip. Hoarding money reveals a basic fear that when possessions are given away, there will be no more money to take its place. This type of thinking is sometimes called a "poverty mentality." Those who grew up in homes where there was little food or other resources often find it difficult to give things away as adults, no matter how wealthy they become. The fear of returning to a state of poverty causes many people to be greedy.

Giving demonstrates trust in God. Christians who are generous know God will provide for their needs from His limitless supply. Ironically, most Christians will testify, the more they give to others, the more money is available to meet their own needs. This should not be surprising. God is generous and He blesses those who embrace His values.

Those who are stingy may accumulate what they can earn in their own strength, but they will never experience the financial blessings available to them. Malachi explains why the Israelites were not receiving God's blessings. In the Old Testament, it was a requirement for all followers of God to tithe. The tithe was the first 10% of any type of income. The Israelites were choosing to withhold this tithe because they did not see the practical value in giving this money to God. Malachi directly ties their lack of prosperity to their unwillingness to give God the portion of their income that He required. Malachi states, "Will man rob God? Yet you are robbing me. But you say, 'How have we robbed you?' In your tithes and contributions. You are cursed with a curse, for you are robbing me, the whole nation of you" (Malachi 3:8-9).

God goes on to say, He will bless the people of Israel if they will tithe. In case the people did not believe God would fulfill His promise, He tells the Israelites to test Him. Listen to God's words through Malachi:

> Bring the full tithe into the storehouse, that there may be food in my house. And thereby put me to the test, says the LORD of hosts, if I will not open the windows of heaven for you and pour down for you a blessing until there is no more need. I will rebuke the devourer for you, so that it will not destroy the fruits of your soil, and your vine in the field shall not fail to bear, says the LORD of hosts (Malachi 3:10-11).

I hate to admit there have been times in my life when I did not trust God fully with my family's finances. During these times, I gave to God, but not the full tithe. It was remarkable that nearly every time I decided I did not have enough money to give a full 10% to God, something would break down around my house, a child would get sick, or there would be unexpected auto repairs. Almost always, the cost of these unexpected expenses were the same, if not a little more, as what I should've given to make up a full 10% of my income. Equally remarkable is when I faithfully give 10% of my income, there are far fewer unexpected expenditures. I have not gotten wealthy because I have given to God, but the wealth I do have has been protected. My testimony is when I have been faithful to obey God with my finances, God has been faithful to do His part as promised through the prophet Malachi.

Some people argue tithing is an Old Testament concept eliminated with the advent of the New Testament. These individuals will point to the fact the New Testament never specifically commands Christians to give 10% of their income to the church. They would point out there is no longer a priestly class who has to be taken care of which was the primary purpose for the tithe in the Old Testament era.

This concern, regarding the validity of tithing today, is admirable if the individual is arguing that giving should not be limited to a tithe. If Christians walked in the Spirit in regard to giving, there would not be a need to address the tithe. It would be a bare minimum, a starting place, for the Christian who has a cheerful heart. If the argument against a requirement to tithe in the New Testament is an excuse to not be generous, then this attitude is not reflective of the nature of God. Considering the fact very few people give at least 10% of their income to God, or to any other charitable organization, reveals most people don't have a desire to be more generous. The average Christian family today, according to a recent study, gives $817 to the church per year. If the average income of a family in America is roughly $50,000, this represents a mere 1.6% of their annual salary. This doesn't reflect a generous heart by most standards.

So how much should a person give?

Most Christian money experts agree the amount of the gift is irrelevant in giving. The relevant issue, as with all Christian behavior, is our motivation. Most of these same experts assume the tithe as a minimum because no true disciple of Jesus would give less than their Old Testament counterparts. The Christian has been given the most generous gift available. God was not stingy when He gave us His only begotten Son (John 3:16). Our gifts to God, and others, should reflect our appreciation of what He has done for us.

The apostle Paul provides two insights regarding the proper motivation to give. First he points to the Macedonian church as an example of a pure motive to give. He states,

> We want you to know, brothers, about the grace of God that has been given among the churches of Macedonia, for in a severe test of affliction, their abundance of joy and their extreme poverty have overflowed in a wealth of generosity on their part. For they gave according to their means, as I can testify, and beyond their means, of their own accord, begging us earnestly for the favor of taking part in the relief of the saints (2 Corinthians 8:1-4).

The Macedonians were so eager to give, Paul had to put a brake on their generosity.

The second insight Paul provides for us is we should be motivated by a cheerful heart. He tells the Corinthians, "Each one must give as he has decided in his heart, not reluctantly or under compulsion, for God loves a cheerful giver" (2 Corinthians 9:7). God does not hold us hostage in regard to giving. It seems clear, He would rather you give nothing than to give begrudgingly. Christians should give out of a heart of generosity and willingness.

Giving is an act of worship. When you work, you exchange your time for money. If you make $10 an hour you will receive $400 in exchange for 40 hours of your life. When you give 10% of your income, you are actually putting four hours of your life into the offering plate. Giving yourselves to God is the highest form of worship. Giving in the offering is a tangible way to literally giving yourself to God.

We must be very careful not to give God abundant worship through our singing, which costs us very little, yet withhold the more costly form of worship through our finances. In the Old Testament, God required the best, if a person was going to worship Him. He was very clear as to His attitude towards those who attempted to shortchange Him by giving Him less than their very best. God told the Israelites:

> A son honors his father, and a servant his master. If then I am a father, where is my honor? And if I am a master, where is my fear? says the LORD of hosts to you, O priests, who despise my name. But you say, "How have we despised your name?" By offering polluted food upon my altar. But you say, "How have we polluted you?" By saying that the LORD's table may be despised. When you offer blind animals in sacrifice, is that not evil? And when you offer those that are lame or sick, is that not evil? Present that to your governor; will he accept you or show you favor? says the LORD of hosts (Malachi 1:6-8).

Should we expect God's standards have dropped in this era of grace? We must never insult God by giving Him our financial leftovers.

Giving should not produce shame, nor should it produce pride in the giver. Some individuals feel like lesser Christians because they do not have as much to give. Sometimes the church has been guilty of endorsing this mentality by the way they champion those who give a great deal to the church. Church leaders would do well to rehearse Jesus' statement about giving:

> And he sat down opposite the treasury and watched the people putting money into the offering box. Many rich people put in large sums. And a poor widow came and put in two small copper coins, which make a penny. And he called his disciples to him and said to them, "Truly, I say to you, this poor widow has put in more than all those who are contributing to the offering box. For they all contributed out of their abundance, but she out of her poverty has put in everything she had, all she had to live on" (Mark 12:41-44).

All the apostle Paul required, of the Corinthian believers, was they would be consistent givers (See 1 Corinthians 16: 1-4.), and they would give proportionally in accordance to what they had. This proportional giving is the rationale behind the Old Testament tithe. Even though you may believe the New Testament never specifically requires a Christian to tithe, the principle of proportional giving is consistent in both the Old Testament and New Testament. Paul told the Corinthians:

> For if the readiness is there, it is acceptable according to what a person has, not according to what he does not have. For I do not mean that others should be eased

and you burdened, but that as a matter of fairness your abundance at the present time should supply their need, so that their abundance may supply your need, that there may be fairness. As it is written, "Whoever gathered much had nothing left over, and whoever gathered little had no lack." (2 Corinthians 8:12-15).

Christians and Spending

God calls Christians to be stewards over all the money He places in their hands, not just over the portion placed in the offering plate. Many of the debt problems Christians face result from improper use of the portion they believe they control. The way Christians use the portion of money not given away tells a great deal about them. If money is saved in order to make purchases without debt, it shows wisdom and discipline. If they consult God when they consider financial decisions, it reveals their desire to have God involved in every aspect of their life.

Christians must avoid allowing their bank account to be the ultimate decider of the purchases and investments they make. There will be times when God asks the believer to act in generosity beyond what their bank account can justify. If it is God who is making the request, then we can be confident He will make up the difference between what we have and what it cost to do what He requested. I have seen potential students who have felt God told them to come to our university, but they choose to go to a community college because they did not believe they could afford to be where God asked them to be. These individuals often transfer to our university later and say they wish they had listened to God earlier. But there are some students who hear God and come to the university, even though their bank account says paying their tuition is impossible. They step out in faith because they know that God is faithful. Year after year, I have seen God provide for these students in miraculous ways, often at the very last moment.

Christians must also avoid allowing their bank account to be the ultimate decider of their purchases and investments when their bank account is overflowing. Some Christians believe simply because they have ample money, they should be able to spend money at their discretion. This is lazy Christianity. Instead of asking God concerning the wise use of the money He has given to them to steward, they make decisions on their own. Often this prohibits God from accomplishing, through their resources, what He intends. Consulting God in all financial matters demonstrates a life of discipleship.

Since all of a person's money ultimately belongs to God, every purchase or investment is a heavenly decision. As a result, a true disciple makes wise purchases based on the best research possible. Purchasing a subscription to a resource like "Consumer Reports" will pay for itself, if you will avail yourself of the knowledge it provides regarding the quality and workmanship of most all products.

One of the best ways to govern spending is to have a good budget. The advantage of a budget is it will help you determine your priorities and help you to stay within prescribed spending limits. Some people can develop a budget and stick to it with no problem. Others, like myself, put a budget on paper and seldom refer back to it.

My wife and I solved our problem with administrating a budget by using the "envelope system." With this system, you prioritize your expenditures based on your monthly income. After you have determined how much money you are going to spend in each major category of your budget, you sit down with a stack of envelopes and write one of the categories on each of the envelopes. In our case, we write the amount of money to be deposited in the envelope at the top of the envelope, and then we list each of the months of the year with a box beside the month on the envelope that can be checked off. Each month we go to the credit union and withdraw enough cash to fill our envelopes. Once the envelopes are filled, we are free to begin spending.

The beauty of the envelope system is when there is no more money in the envelope, you stop spending. If there is excess money in the envelope at the end of the month, you can either use the money to begin filling the next month's envelopes, or you can build up money to be used in that category in the months to come. Having an emergency fund envelope will help you take care of unexpected expenditures, like purchasing a tire or having to pay for an unexpected dentist visit.

I mentioned in a previous chapter, there was a point in my life where I hated Christmas. I know I sound like Scrooge, and some Christians may wonder how a believer could hate our Savior's birthday. It wasn't the birthday of Jesus I despised, as a matter fact, I usually celebrated Jesus' birthday by singing Christmas carols in July. What I hated was the commercialization of the Christmas season and the fact I felt obligated to spend money I didn't have, in order to buy things I thought would make other people happy.

The envelope system saved Christmas for me. My wife and I sat down and determined we would like to spend about $1000 during the Christmas season on presents. The envelope system allowed us to intentionally put $85 per month into an envelope designated for Christmas gifts. By the time December comes around, we now have $1000 to spend on gifts, without using a credit card. It also provides us an opportunity to buy gifts throughout the year when we see something we think someone would like because the money is already accumulating in the envelope. I now sing Christmas carols in December, but you'll probably still hear me singing them at Walmart in July, if you are checking out behind me.

Conclusion

Finding true contentment, in a materialistic society, requires Christians to learn to trust God and find satisfaction in Him, regardless of their condition. Finding contentment is not really a money issue; it is a heart issue.

The Christian disciple must wrestle with the issues of accumulation, giving, and the use of discretionary income. The Bible provides insights into each of these areas, but ultimately, the decision to obey is up to the individual Christian. Our decisions will not always be correct. Fortunately, God is full of grace and mercy which extends to decisions regarding our finances.

If you find yourself in financial trouble, God has a plan to rescue you even if it takes 10 years, as it did in my case. If you are not currently in financial trouble, praise God and continue to practice godly principles regarding your finances.

The Christian's use of money provides a window into the person's heart. As a person grows in his/her relationship with Jesus, money usage will more closely reflect the priorities of Jesus. Providing for family, giving to others, and living within the means God has provided will be evidence a person is taking steps toward God.

Study Guide Questions

1. What is the task of the Christian concerning savings and possession?

2. Who tends to have the most difficult time deciding a proper level of accumulation?

3. What is the advantage of planning for retirement at an early age?

4. What did Jesus teach regarding investments?

5. What determines the morality of a person's decision to accumulate wealth?

6. What characteristics of God does money attempt to mimic?

7. What is the key to successful Christian stewardship?

8. What promise did God give the Israelites, if they would tithe?

9. What two principles does the apostle Paul give regarding a proper motivation for giving?

10. How should Christians determine how they spend their money?

11. What is the advantage of having a budget?

12. What is the "envelope system" of budgeting?

TWENTY EIGHT

CONCLUDING THOUGHTS

As we arrive at the end of our journey of exploring spiritual formation, I feel a little like the apostle John when he said "Now there are also many other things that Jesus did. Were every one of them to be written, I suppose that the world itself could not contain the books that would be written" (John 21:25).

There is so much more that could be said about spiritual formation. I am aware I have left out important topics such as service, rest, confession, and many more. Fortunately, there are books available to help believers as they seek to draw closer to God through these avenues. I have included a good representation of books that cover various topics we have explored in this book, as well as topics not covered, in the bibliography. I would challenge you to select books from the bibliography and read one or two of them each month. There is no end to learning how to become more intimate with Jesus.

As you are about ready to set this book aside, it is my hope you have moved a little closer to Jesus, even if it was just a few steps. There will be set backs in your Christian walk, but overall, making steady advancement toward spiritual maturity should be your quest.

If you remember anything from this book let it be these things: (1) God created you to be a unique being, with unique abilities, to complete a unique task within His kingdom. Be content to function within your uniqueness and do not allow someone to fit you into their mold; (2) God loves you just the way you are. You do not have to try to earn His love. All God wants from you is your unconditional love in return. When you make decisions in life, filter them through your love for Him with consideration to His desires; (3) God desires that you will see people the way He sees them. As a result, please have compassion on those who have not yet submitted their lives to Jesus. Love those who mistreat you and be quick to forgive. Be light in a dark world and attempt to allow the love of God to flow through you; and (4) Learn to be content. Satan will play on your emotions if you begin to look at what others have and wish for what they have, or even more. Do not envy relationships, finances, positions, or even the spiritual level of others. If you are committed to trust God with your life, you can be confident that what you have today is enough. Remember Jesus' words, "But seek first the kingdom of God and his righteousness, and all these things will be added to you. 'Therefore do not be anxious about tomorrow, for tomorrow will be anxious for itself. Sufficient for the day is its own trouble'" (Matthew 6:33-34).

As we go our separate ways, let me end by offering a prayer that I hope you can agree with:

Heavenly Father,

We know you love us more than we even love ourselves. We thank you for sending your Son to earth to live as an example, to die to pay for our sins, and to be raised from the dead to give us life and hope for the future. Help us to live our lives in the abundance you have made available to us. As we live in victory, help us to tell our stories of redemption to those who need hope, which is only found through salvation. And please help us to live our lives in a way that reflects the transformation which has taken place in our lives. Let this transformation shape us into accurate reflections of Jesus. When we face times of trials, temptations, and suffering, please allow us to hear the clear voice of the Holy Spirit as He encourages, convicts, and comforts. Most of all, thank you for allowing us to live a life with purpose, as we join with you in establishing your kingdom on earth, as it is in heaven. Please give us strength to walk in the Spirit, as He directs our steps toward you.

In the strong name of Jesus, we offer this prayer. Amen.

Selected Bibliography

Alcorn, Randy. *Money, Possessions and Eternity*. Wheaton, IL: Tyndale House, 1989.

_____. "Strategies to Keep from Falling." *Leadership Journal* 9, no. 1 (Winter 1988): 42-47.

Anderson, Ray S. *Living the Spiritually Balanced Life*. Grand Rapids, MI: Baker, 1998.

Arnold, Jeffrey. *The Big Book on Small Groups*. Downers Grove, IL: InterVarsity, 1992.

Bacik, James. *Catholic Spirituality, Its History and Challenge*. New York: Paulist Press, 2002.

Bailey, Derrick. *Sexual Relations in Christian Thought*. New York: Harper and Brothers Publishers, 1959.

Barna, George. *Growing True Disciples*. Colorado Springs, CO: WaterBrook Press, 2001.

Barton, Ruth. *Sacred Rhythms: Arranging Our Lives for Spiritual Transformation*. Downers Grove, IL: Intervarsity Press, 2006.

Blaising, Craig A. "Spiritual Formation in the Early Church." In *The Christian Educator's Handbook on Spiritual Formation*. Edited by Kenneth O. Gangel and James C. Wilhoit. Wheaton, IL: Victor, 1994.

Bloesch, Donald. *Spirituality Old and New*. Downers Grove, IL: InterVarsity, 2007.

Boa, Kenneth. *Conformed to His Image: Biblical and Practical Approaches to Spiritual Formation*. Grand Rapids, MI: Zondervan, 2001.

Bolsinger, Tod. *It Takes A Church To Raise A Christian*. Grand Rapids, MI: Brazos Press, 2004.

Bonhoeffer, Dietrich. *The Cost of Discipleship*. Riverside, NJ: Macmillan, 1967.

————. *Life Together*. New York: Harper and Row, 1956.

Boshers, Bo and Judson Poling. *The Be With Factor: Mentoring Students in Everyday Life.* Grand Rapids, MI: Zondervan, 2006.

Bullough, Vern L. *The Subordinate Sex.* Urbana, IL: University of Illinois, 1973.

Burgess, John P. *After Baptism.* Louisville, KY: Westminister/John Knox Press, 2005.

Calhoun, Adele Ahlberg. *Spiritual Disciplines Handbook: Practices that Transform Us.* Downers Grove, IL: InterVarsity, 2005.

Carson, D.A. *The Gagging of God.* Grand Rapids, MI: Zondervan, 1996.

Clark, Chap and Kara E. Powell. *Deep Ministry in a Shallow World.* Grand Rapids, MI: Zondervan, 2006.

Cloud, Henry. *Changes that Heal: How to Understand Your Past to Ensure a Healthier Future.* Grand Rapids, MI: Zondervan, 1992.

Cloud, Henry and John Townsend. *Boundaries.* Grand Rapids, MI: Zondervan, 1992.

_____. *How People Grow: What the Bible Reveals about Personal Growth.* Grand Rapids, MI: Zondervan, 2001.

Cole, William Graham. *Sex in Christianity and Psychoanalysis.* New York: Oxford University Press, 1955.

Crabb, Larry. *Connecting: Healing for Ourselves & Our Relationships.* Nashville, TN: Word, 1997.

_____. *Inside Out.* Colorado Springs, CO: Navpress, 1991.

Creps, Earl. "Moving Target: Reframing Discipleship for Postmoderns." In *Enrichment Journal* 13, no. 1 (Winter 2008): 68-73.

_____. *Off-Road Disciplines.* San Francisco: Jossey-Bass, 2006.

_____. *Reverse Mentoring.* San Francisco: Jossey-Bass, 2008.

Cunningham, Lawrence S. and Keith J. Egan. *Christian Spirituality: Themes from the Tradition.* Mahwah, NJ: Paulist Press, 1996.

Dayton, Howard. *Your Money Counts.* Gainsville, GA: Crown Financial Ministries, 1996.

De Reuver, Arie. *Sweet Communion.* Grand Rapids, MI: Baker, 2004.

Dobbins, Richard. "Your Church Should Be Into Sex Education." *Enrichment Journal* 13, no. 1 (Winter 2008): 144-146.

Donahue, Bill and Russ Robinson. *Walking the Small Group Tightrope*. Grand Rapids, MI: Zondervan, 2003.

Drummond, Lewis. *Reaching Generation Next*. Grand Rapids, MI: Baker, 2002.

Dunn, Richard R. *Shaping the Spiritual Life of Students*. Downers Grove, IL: InterVarsity, 2001.

Eller, Vernard. *The Simple Life*. Grand Rapids, MI: Wm. B. Eermans Publishing, 1973.

Evans, Pamela. *The Over-Committed Christian: Serving God Without Wearing Out*. Downers Grove, IL: InterVarsity, 2001.

Feldmeier, Peter. *Christianity Looks East*. New York: Paulist Press, 2006.

Feucht, Oscar, E., ed. *Sex and the Church*. St. Louis: Concordia Publishing House, 1961.

Foster, Richard. *Celebration of Discipline*. Rev. ed. New York: HarperSanFransico, 1988.

———. *The Challenge of the Disciplined Life*. New York: HarperSanFransico, 1985.

———. *Prayer: Finding the Heart's True Home*. New York: Harper and Row, 1992.

——— *Streams of Living Water*. New York: HarperSanFrancisco, 1998.

Fowler, James. *Stages of Faith: The Psychology of Human Development and the Quest for Meaning*. San Francisco: Harper and Row, 1981.

Garber, Steven. *The Fabric of Faithfulness*. Downers Grove, IL: InterVarsity, 1996.

Gorman, Julie. *Community that is Christian: A Handbook of Small Groups*, 2nd ed., Grand Rapids, MI: Baker, 2002.

Haman, Mike. *The Second Mile: Because Ordinary Living is Never Enough*. Baton Rouge, LA: Healing Place Productions, 2007.

Hart, Archibald. *Secrets of Eve: Understanding the Mystery of Female Sexuality*. Nashville, TN: Word, 1998.

———.*The Sexual Man*. Dallas: Word, 1994.

Hayford, Jack. *Living the Spirit-Formed Life*. Ventura, CA: Regal Books, 2001.

Howard, Evan B. *A Guide to Christian Spiritual Formation: How Scripture, Spirit, Community, and Mission Shape Our Souls*. Grand Rapids, MI: Baker Academic, 2018.

Huggett, Joyce. *The Joy of Listening to God*. Downers Grove, IL: InterVarsity, 1986.

Hull, Bill. *The Complete Book of Discipleship*. Colorado Springs: NavPress, 2006.

Hybels, Bill. *Honest to God: Becoming an Authentic Christian*. Grand Rapids, MI: Zondervan, 1990.

Irenaeus. *Against Heresies, III, 22, 4* In *Messages of the Fathers of the Church 13 volumes* Edited by Thomas Halton. Wilmington, DE: Michael Glazier, Inc, 1983, Volume 13: *Women of the Early Church* by Elizabeth A. Clark.

James, Edwin Oliver. *Marriage and Society*. New York: Hutchinson's University Library, 1952.

Johnson, Greg. *The World According to God: A Biblical View of Culture, Work, Science, Sex and Everything Else*. Downers Grove, IL: InterVarsity, 2002.

Kelcourse, Felicity, ed. *Human Development and Faith*. St. Louis: Chalice Press, 2004.

Kingma, Daphne. *Finding True Love: The Four Essential Keys to Finding the Love of Your Life*. Berkeley, CA: Conari Press, 1996.

Koessler, John. *True Discipeship: The Art of Following Jesus*. Chicago: Moody, 2003.

Lawrence, Mel. *The Dynamics of Spiritual Formation*. Grand Rapids, MI: Baker, 2000.

Leman, Kevin. *Sex Begins in the Kitchen*. Grand Rapids, MI: Fleming H. Revell, 1999.

Lewis, C.S. *Mere Christianity*. New York: Macmillan, 1943.

Lim, Stephen. "Overcoming Hindrances to Discipleship." In *Enrichment Journal* 13, no. 1 (Winter 2008): 54.

Lim, Stephen, ed. *Your Call to Work and Mission*. Springfield, MO: Assemblies of God Theological Seminary at Evangel University, 2015.

Linder, Ray. *Financial Freedom: Seven Secrets to Reduce Financial Worry*. Chicago: Moody Press, 1999.

Mouw, Richard. *Uncommon Decency: Christian Civility in an Uncivilized World*. Downers Grove, IL: InterVarsity, 1992.

Nouwen, Henri. *Here and Now*. New York: Crossroad Publishing, 1994.

———. *Life of the Beloved*. New York: Crossroad Publishing, 1995.

———. *Lifesigns*. New York: Doubleday, 1986.

————. *Reaching Out: Three Movements of the Spiritual Life*. Garden City, NY: Doubleday, 1975.

Nouwen, Henri and Michael Christensen. *Spiritual Formation: Following the Movements of the Spirit*. New York: HarperCollins Publishers, 2010.

Macchia, Stephen. *Becoming a Healthy Disciple: 10 Traits of a Vital Christian*. Grand Rapids, MI: Baker, 2004.

MacDonald, Gordan. *Restoring Your Spiritual Passion*. Nashville: Oliver Nelson, 1986.

McGee, Robert. *The Search for Significance*. Nashville: Word, 2003.

Matthaei, Sondra. *Making Disciples: Faith Formation in the Wesleyan Tradition*. Nashville, TN: Abingdon Press, 2000.

Mueller, Walt. *Engaging the Soul of Youth Culture*. Downers Grove, IL: InterVarsity, 2006.

Mulholland, Jr. M. Robert. *Invitation to a Journey: A Road Map for Spiritual Formation*. Downers Grove: InterVarsity, 2006.

————. *Shaped By The Word: The Power of Scripture in Spiritual Formation*. Revised Edition. Nashville, TN: Upper Room Books, 2000.

Myers, David. *The Pursuit of Happiness*. New York: Avon Books, 1992.

O'Connell, Timothy E. *Making Disciples*. New York: Crossroad Herder Books, 1998.

Ogden, Greg. *Discipleship Essentials: A Guide to Building Your Life in Christ*. Downers Grove, IL: InterVarsity, 1998.

Ortberg, John. *The Life You've Always Wanted*. Grand Rapids, MI: Zondervan, 1997.

Packer, James. *Growing in Christ*. Wheaton, IL: Crossway Books, 1994.

Pagitt, Doug. *Reimaging Spiritual Formation*. Grand Rapids, MI: Baker, 2000.

Peterson, Eugene. *A Long Obedience in the Same Direction: Discipleship in an Instant Society*. Downers Grove, IL: InterVarsity, 2001.

Rice, Howard L. *Reformed Spirituality*. Louisville, KY: Westminister/John Knox Press, 1991.

Robbins, Maggie and Duffy Robbins. *Enjoy the Silence*. Grand Rapids, MI: Zondervan, 2005.

Roberts, Mark. *After I Believe*. Grand Rapids, MI: Baker, 2002.

Roberts, Ted. *Pure Desire*. Ventura, CA: Regal Books, 1999.Senn, Frank, ed. *Protestant Spiritual Traditions*. New York: Paulist Press, 1986.

Setran, David P. and Chris A. Kiesling. *Spiritual Formation in Emerging Adulthood: A Practical Theology for College and Young Adult Ministry*. Grand Rapids, MI: Baker Academic, 2013.

Short, Ray. *Sex, Love, or Infatuation: How Can I Really Know?* Minneapolis, MN: Augsburg/Fortress, 1990.

Sider, Ronald. *Living Like Jesus: Eleven Essentials for Growing a Genuine Faith*. Grand Rapids, MI: Baker, 1996.

Simon, Arthur. *How Much is Enough?* Grand Rapids, MI: Baker, 2003.

Small, Dwight. *Christian: Celebrate Your Sexuality*. Old Tappan, NJ: Fleming H. Revell Co., 1974.

Smith, Gordon. *Beginning Well: Christian Conversion and Authentic Transformation*. Downers Grove, IL: InterVarsity, 2001.

Smith, Harold Ivan. "What to Say About Sex." *Leadership Journal.Net*. http:/www.christianity today.com/le/2002/spring/7.54.html4/01/2002 (accessed May 13, 2009).

Smith, James Bryan. "Spiritual Formation of Adolescents." In *The Christian Educator's Handbook on Spiritual Formation*. Edited by Kenneth O. Gangel and James C. Wilhoit. Wheaton, IL: Victor, 1994.

Stowell, Joseph. *Following Christ: Experiencing Life the Way it Was Meant to Be*. Grand Rapids, MI: Zondervan, 1996.

Sweet, Leonard. *Learn to Dance the Soul Salsa —17 Surprising Steps for Godly Living in the 21st Century*. Grand Rapids, MI: Zondervan, 2000.

Swindoll, Charles. *Strengthening Your Grip*. Rev. ed. Nashville, TN: Word, 1998.

Temple, William. Nature, Man, and God. Edinburgh: R. & R. Clark, 1934.

Tertullian. On the Dress of Women, I,1,1 In *Messages of the Fathers of the Church 13 volumes* Edited by Thomas Halton. Wilmington, DE: Michael Glazier, Inc, 1983, Volume 13: *Women of the Early Church* by Elizabeth A. Clark.

Tucker, Ruth A. and Walter Liefeld. *Daughters of the Church*. Grand Rapids, MI: Zondervan, 1987.

Vandergrift, Nicki. *Organic Spirituality*. Maryknoll, NY: Orbis Press, 2000.

Veith, Jr., Gene Edward, *God at Work: Your Christian Vocation in All Your Life*. Wheaton, IL: Crossway Books, 2002.

Webb, Heather. *Small Group Leadership as Spiritual Direction*. Grand Rapids, MI: Zondervan, 2005.

White, James. "Regaining a Christian Worldview in the Church." *Enrichment Journal* 13, no. 4 (Fall 2008):26-38.

White, John. *Money Isn't God, So Why is the Church Worshiping It?* Downers Grove, IL: InterVarsity, 1993.

Wilkerson, Bryan. "The Joy of Preaching Sex." *Leadership Journal.Net* http://www.christianity today.com/le/2006/winter/2.44.html?start=5 (accessed May 13, 2009).

Willard, Dallas. *The Divine Conspiracy*. New York: HarperSanFransico, 1997.

————. *The Great Omission*. HarperSan Francisco, 2006.

_____. *Hearing God: Developing a Conversational Relationship with God*. Downers Grove, IL: InterVarsity, 1999.

————. *Renovation of the Heart: Putting on the Character of Christ*. Colorado Springs, CO: Navpress, 2002.

Williams, Rowan. *Christian Spirituality*. Atlanta, John Knox Press, 1980.

Wilson, Earl. *Steering Clear: Avoiding the Slippery Slope to Moral Failure*. Downers Grove, IL: InterVarsity, 2002.

Wilson, Fred. "Adult Development." In *Nurture That is Christian*. Edited by John Wilholt. Wheaton, IL: Victor, 1995.

Wilson, Sandra. *Hurting People Hurt People: Hope and Healing for Yourself and Your Relationships*. Grand Rapids, MI: Discovery House, 2001.

Wright, Walter C. *Relational Leadership: A Biblical Model for Leadership Service*. Waynesboro, GA: Paternoster Press, 2000.

"National Survey of Adolescents and Young Adults: Sexual Health Knowledge, Attitudes and Experiences." Enrichment Online. http://enrichmentjournal.ag.org /200604/200604-2sex%20health%20know.pdf (accessed May 13, 2009).

Made in the USA
Middletown, DE
11 August 2019